A.W.

Pursuit Of God

I Talk Back To The Devil

Who Put Jesus On The Cross?

OM
publishing

WORKS BY A. W. TOZER

The Best of A. W. Tozer
Christ the Eternal Son
The Coming King
The Divine Conquest
Echoes from Eden
Explaining the Deeper Life
Faith Beyond Reason
Five Vows to Spiritual Power
God Tells the Man Who Cares
How to be Filled with the Holy Spirit
I Call it Heresy
I Talk Back to the Devil
Jesus, Our Man in Glory
Jesus, Author of Our Faith
The Knowledge of the Holy
Leaning Into the Wind
Let My People Go
Man, the Dwelling Place of God
Men Who Met God
The Next Chapter After the Last.
Of God and Men
Paths to Power
The Pursuit of God
Renewed Day by Day
The Root of the Righteous
The Set of the Sail
That Incredible Christian
This World: Playground or Battleground?
We Travel an Appointed Way
Whatever Happened to Worship?
Who Put Jesus on the Cross?
Worship, the Missing Jewel of the Evangelical Church

THE PURSUIT OF GOD

A. W. TOZER

OM
publishing

This A.W. Tozer Omnibus edition first published by OM Publishing,
an imprint of Paternoster Publishing.

1–85078–251–2

The Pursuit of God

© Christian Publications, Inc. 1982

Tozer Legacy Edition
First published in the USA by Christian Publications,
3825 Hartzdale Drive, Camp Hill, PA 17011

First STL edition 1984
This Anglicised edition 1987
Reprinted 1989, 1990 (twice), 1993 (twice), 1994, 1996

Biblical quotations are from the Authorised Version
(Crown copyright)

British Library Cataloguing-in-Publication Data.

Tozer, A.W.
The Pursuit of God.
1. Christian life
I. Title
248.4 BV4501.2
ISBN 1 85078 033 1

Cover photo: Tony Stone Associates Ltd.

OM Publishing is an imprint of Paternoster Publishing,
PO Box 300, Carlisle, Cumbria, CA3 0QS, U.K.

Printed in the U.K. by Cox & Wyman Ltd., Reading, Berkshire

Contents

Tozer's Legacy

Quietness of soul, the fruit of truly seeking God, is seldom found in twentieth-century Christians. Far too many have come to accept turbulence of soul as the norm and have ceased to seek God with their whole hearts. Some have fled the cities to cloistered retreats in the hope of finding this quietness, only to discover their hearts still restless.

One unusual American minister who found for his own soul the secret of quietness and articulated his discovery to the Christian community was A. W. Tozer. He came upon this closer walk with God in the bustle and noise of the city of Chicago. Tozer never enjoyed the luxury of a cloistered life. Born in a poor home in the hills of western Pennsylvania, he had known hardship from as long as he could remember. Forced by his home situation to forfeit an education, Tozer entered the ministry without either high school or college training.

A. W. Tozer came to Christ at the age of fifteen, after hearing a lay preacher speaking at a street meeting in Akron, Ohio. He joined the Methodist church and became an active witness for Christ. A dingy corner of the basement of the family home became his private prayer chamber. There, at the very beginning of his Christian life, Tozer established what was to be a lifelong practice of waiting on God.

Having become a lay preacher, Tozer found himself in disfavour with his church and decided to join with The Christian and Missionary Alliance where he found opportunity to use his gifts. His preaching ability soon made a place for him. In 1919 the district superintendent assigned Tozer to pastor the Alliance Church in Nutters Fort, West Virginia. After subsequent pastorates in Toledo and Indianapolis, he accepted a call in 1928 to the Southside Alliance Church in Chicago, Illinois. His ministry in that congregation continued for thirty-one years. Avenue Road Alliance Church in Toronto, Ontario, Canada was the last pastorate he served.

For many of the years he pastored the Chicago congregation, Tozer also preached on the Moody Bible Institute radio station WMBI. Thousands of lay people and pastors listened regularly to his rich exposition of Bible truth given on 'Talks from a Pastor's Study'.

His literary skills were soon recognised by his own denomination and eventually by the whole evangelical church community. In 1950 the General Council elected him editor of *The Alliance Witness*, a position he held until his death.

Aiden W. Tozer educated himself by years of diligent study and a constant prayerful seeking of the mind of God. With Tozer, seeking truth and seeking God were one and the same thing. For example, when he felt he needed an understanding of the great English works of Shakespeare, he read them through on his knees, asking God to help him understand their meaning. This procedure was typical of his method of self-education.

With no teacher but the Holy Spirit and good books, A. W. Tozer became a theologian, a scholar, and a master craftsman in the use of the English language. There are not many quotes in his writings, for he had so assimilated all he had read that he could freely write in simple but attractive language the principles of truth he had discovered across those years of anointed study. The evangelical mystics were his favourite study. The longings of his own heart were satisfied by what he learned from the men and women who kept the light of spiritual reality burning in a time when apostasy and spiritual darkness seemed almost universal.

Much of the strong meat in *The Pursuit of God* came out of the crucible of Tozer's own personal experience. The chapter entitled 'The Blessedness of Possessing Nothing' reflected his desperate struggle to turn his only daughter over to God. The battle was intense and devastating, but when full surrender came a new and glorious release became his. He had learned to know God in the school of practical experience.

Since the first edition of *The Pursuit of God* was published in 1948, hundreds of thousands of copies have been printed and distributed in several languages around the world. While all of Tozer's writings are well received, *The Pursuit of God* continues to be the most popular.

The writing of this book was for A. W. Tozer a deep spiritual experience. Dr David J. Fant, Jr, his biographer, describes the process.

Tozer literally wrote *The Pursuit of God* on his knees. Perhaps that explains its power and the blessing that has rested on it.

Perhaps the continued usefulness of this book can be attributed to the writer's great spiritual discovery that to seek God does not narrow one's life, but brings it, rather, to the level of highest possible fulfilment.

A. W. Tozer was something of a twentieth-century prophet calling the modern church back to the practice of godliness and to that level of spiritual reality enjoyed by serious seekers after God from the days of the apostles. In the legacy of his writings, none speaks more clearly to our deepest heart need than *The Pursuit of God*.

Preface

In this hour of all-but-universal darkness one cheering gleam appears: within the fold of conservative Christianity there are to be found increasing numbers of persons whose religious lives are marked by a growing hunger after God Himself. They are eager for spiritual realities and will not be put off with words, nor will they be content with correct 'interpretations' of truth. They are athirst for God, and they will not be satisfied till they have drunk deep at the fountain of living water.

This is the only real harbinger of revival which I have been able to detect anywhere on the religious horizon. It may be the cloud the size of a man's hand for which a few saints here and there have been looking. It can result in a resurrection of life for many souls and a recapture of that radiant wonder which should accompany faith in Christ, that wonder which has all but fled the church of God in our day.

But this hunger must be recognised by our religious leaders. Current evangelicalism has (to change the figure) laid the altar and divided the sacrifice into parts, but now seems satisfied to count the stones and rearrange the pieces with never a care that there is not a sign of fire upon the top of lofty Carmel. But God be thanked that there are a few who care. They are those who, while they love the altar and delight in the sacrifice, are yet unable to reconcile themselves to the continued absence of fire. They desire God above all. They are athirst to taste for themselves the 'piercing sweetness' of the love of Christ about whom all the holy prophets did write and the psalmists did sing.

There is today no lack of Bible teachers to set forth correctly the principles of the doctrines of Christ, but too many of these seem satisfied to teach the fundamentals of the faith year after year, strangely unaware that there is in their ministry no manifest Presence, nor anything unusual in their personal lives. They minister constantly to believers who feel within their breasts a longing which their teaching simply does not satisfy.

I trust I speak in charity, but the lack in our pulpits is real. Milton's terrible sentence applies to our day as accurately as it did to his: 'The hungry sheep look up, and are not fed.' It is a solemn thing, and no small scandal in the kingdom, to see God's children starving while actually seated at the Father's table. The truth of Wesley's words is established before our eyes: 'Orthodoxy, or right opinion, is, at best, a very slender part of religion. Though right tempers cannot subsist without right opinions, yet right opinions may subsist without right tempers. There may be a right opinion of God without either love or one right temper toward Him. Satan is a proof of this.'

Thanks to our splendid Bible societies and to other effective agencies for the dissemination of the Word, there are today many millions of people who hold 'right opinions', probably more than ever before in the history of the church. Yet I wonder if there was ever a time when true spiritual worship was at a lower ebb. To great sections of the church the art of worship has been lost entirely, and in its place has come that strange and foreign thing called the 'programme'. This word has been borrowed from the stage and applied with sad wisdom to the type of public service which now passes for worship among us.

Sound Bible exposition is an imperative *must* in the church of the living God. Without it no church can be a New Testament church in any strict meaning of that term. But exposition may be carried on in such a way as to leave the hearers devoid of any true spiritual nourishment whatever. For it is not mere words that nourish the soul, but God Himself, and unless and until the hearers find God in personal experience they are not the better for having heard the truth. The Bible is not an end in itself, but a means to bring men to an intimate and satisfying knowledge of God, that they may enter into Him, that they may delight in His presence, may taste and know the inner sweetness of the very God Himself in the core and centre of their hearts.

This book is a modest attempt to aid God's hungry children so to find Him. Nothing here is new except in the sense that it is a discovery which my own heart has made of spiritual realities most delightful and wonderful to me. Others before me have gone much farther into these holy mysteries than I have done, but if my fire is not large it is yet real, and there may be those who can light their candle at its flame.

A. W. Tozer
Chicago, Illinois, 16 June 1948

1

Following Hard after God

Psalm 63:8 *My soul followeth hard after thee: thy right hand upholdeth me.*

Christian theology teaches the doctrine of prevenient grace, which, briefly stated, means that before a man can seek God, God must first have sought the man.

Before a sinful man can think a right thought of God, there must have been a work of enlightenment done within him. Imperfect it may be, but a true work nonetheless, and the secret cause of all desiring and seeking and praying which may follow.

We pursue God because, and only because, He has first put an urge within us that spurs us to the pursuit. 'No man can come to me,' said our Lord, 'except the Father which hath sent me draw him,' and it is by this prevenient *drawing* that God takes from us every vestige of credit for the act of coming. The impulse to pursue God originates with God, but the outworking of that impulse is our following hard after Him. All the time we are pursuing Him we are already in His hand: 'Thy right hand upholdeth me.'

In this divine 'upholding' and human 'following' there is no contradiction. All is of God, for as von Hügel teaches, *God is always previous*. In practice, however, (that is, where God's previous working meets man's present response) man must pursue God. On our part there must be positive reciprocation if this secret drawing of God is to eventuate in identifiable experience of the Divine. In the warm language of personal feeling, this is stated in Psalm 42:1–2: 'As the hart panteth after the water brooks, so panteth my soul after thee, O God. My soul thirsteth for God, for the living God: when shall I come and appear before God?' This is deep calling unto deep, and the longing heart will understand it.

The doctrine of justification by faith—a biblical truth, and a blessed relief from sterile legalism and unavailing self-effort—has in our time fallen into evil company and been interpreted by many in such a manner as actually to bar men from the knowledge of God. The whole transaction of religious conversion has been made mechanical and spiritless. Faith may now be exercised without a jar to the moral life and without embarrassment to the Adamic ego. Christ may be 'received' without creating any special love for Him in the soul of the receiver. The man is 'saved', but he is not hungry nor thirsty after God. In fact, he is specifically taught to be satisfied and is encouraged to be content with little.

The modern scientist has lost God amid the wonders of His world; we Christians are in real danger of losing God amid the wonders of His Word. We have almost forgotten that God is a person and, as such, can be cultivated as any person can. It is inherent in personality to be able to know other personalities, but full knowledge of one personality by another cannot be achieved in one encounter. It is only after long and loving mental intercourse that the full possibilities of both can be explored.

All social intercourse between human beings is a response of personality to personality, grading upward from the most casual brush between man and man to the fullest, most intimate communion of which the human soul is capable. Religion, so far as it is genuine, is in essence the response of created personalities to the creating personality, God. 'This is life eternal, that they might know thee the only true God, and Jesus Christ whom thou hast sent' (Jn 17:3).

God is a person, and in the deep of His mighty nature He thinks, wills, enjoys, feels, loves, desires, and suffers as any other person may. In making Himself known to us He stays by the familiar pattern of personality. He communicates with us through the avenues of our minds, our wills and our emotions. The continuous and unembarrassed interchange of love and thought between God and the soul of the redeemed man is the throbbing heart of New Testament religion.

This intercourse between God and the soul is known to us in conscious personal awareness. It is personal: it does not come through the body of believers, as such, but is known to the individual, and to the body through the individuals which compose it. It is conscious; it does not stay below the threshold of consciousness and work there unknown to the soul (as, for instance, infant baptism is thought by some to do), but comes within the field of awareness where the man can know it as he knows any other fact of experience.

17

You and I are in little (our sins excepted) what God is in large. Being made in His image we have within us the capacity to know Him. In our sins we lack only the power. The moment the Spirit has quickened us to life in regeneration our whole being senses its kinship to God and leaps up in joyous recognition. That is the heavenly birth without which we cannot see the kingdom of God. It is, however, not an end but an inception, for now begins the glorious pursuit, the heart's happy exploration of the infinite riches of the Godhead. That is where we begin, I say, but where we stop no man has yet discovered, for there is in the awful and mysterious depths of the Triune God neither limit nor end.

> Shoreless Ocean, who can sound Thee?
> Thine own eternity is round Thee,
>   Majesty divine!

To have found God and still to pursue Him is the soul's paradox of love, scorned indeed by the too-easily-satisfied religionist, but justified in happy experience by the children of the burning heart. St Bernard stated this holy paradox in a musical quatrain that will be instantly understood by every worshipping soul:

> We taste Thee, O Thou Living Bread,
>   And long to feast upon Thee still:
> We drink of Thee, the Fountainhead
>   And thirst our souls from Thee to fill.

Come near to the holy men and women of the past and you will soon feel the heat of their desire after God.

They mourned for Him, they prayed and wrestled and sought for Him day and night, in season and out, and when they had found Him the finding was all the sweeter for the long seeking. Moses used the fact that he knew God as an argument for knowing Him better. 'Now, therefore, I pray thee, if I have found grace in thy sight, show me now thy way, that I may know thee, that I may find grace in thy sight'; and from there he rose to make the daring request, 'I beseech thee, show me thy glory.' God was frankly pleased by this display of ardour, and the next day called Moses into the mount, and there in solemn procession made all His glory pass before him.

David's life was a torrent of spiritual desire, and his psalms ring with the cry of the seeker and the glad shout of the finder. Paul confessed the mainspring of his life to be his burning desire after Christ. 'That I may know him,' was the goal of his heart, and to this he sacrificed everything. 'Yea doubtless, and I count all things but loss for the excellency of the knowledge of Christ Jesus my Lord: for whom I suffered the loss of all things, and do count them but refuse, that I may win Christ' (Phil 3:8).

Hymnody is sweet with the longing after God, the God whom, while the singer seeks, he knows he has already found. 'His track I see and I'll pursue,' sang our fathers only a short generation ago, but that song is heard no more in the great congregation. How tragic that we in this dark day have had our seeking done for us by our teachers. Everything is made to centre upon the initial act of 'accepting' Christ (a term, incidentally, which is not found in the Bible) and we are not expected thereafter to crave any further revelation of God to our souls. We have been snared in the coils of a spurious logic which insists that if we have found Him, we need no more seek Him. This is set before us as the last word in orthodoxy, and it is taken for granted that no Bible-taught Christian ever believed otherwise. Thus the whole testimony of the worshipping, seeking, singing church on that subject is crisply set aside. The experiential heart-theology of a grand army of fragrant saints is rejected in favour of a smug interpretation of Scripture which would certainly have sounded strange to an Augustine, a Rutherford or a Brainerd.

In the midst of this great chill there are some, I rejoice to acknowledge, who will not be content with shallow logic. They will admit the force of the argument, and then turn away with tears to hunt some lonely place and pray, 'O God, show me Thy glory.' They want to taste, to touch with their hearts, to see with their inner eyes the wonder that is God.

I want deliberately to encourage this mighty longing after God. The lack of it has brought us to our present low estate. The stiff and wooden quality about our religious lives is a result of our lack of holy desire. Complacency is a deadly foe of all spiritual growth. Acute desire must be present or there will be no manifestation of Christ to His people. He waits to be wanted. Too bad that with many of us He waits so long, so very long, in vain.

Every age has its own characteristics. Right now we are in an age of religious complexity. The simplicity which is in Christ is rarely found among us. In its stead are programmes, methods, organisations and a world of nervous activites which occupy time and attention but can never satisfy the longing of the heart. The shallowness of our inner experience, the hollowness of our worship, and that servile imitation of the world which marks our promotional methods all testify that we, in this day, know God only imperfectly, and the peace of God scarcely at all.

If we would find God amid all the religious externals, we must first determine to find Him, and then proceed in the way of simplicity. Now, as always, God discovers Himself to 'babes' and hides Himself in thick darkness from the wise and the prudent. We must simplify our approach to Him. We must strip down to essentials (and they will be found to be blessedly few). We must put away all effort to impress, and come with the guileless candour of childhood. If we do this, without doubt God will quickly respond.

When religion has said its last word, there is little that we need other than God Himself. The evil habit of seeking *God-and* effectively prevents us from finding God in full revelation. In the *and* lies our great woe. If we omit the *and* we shall soon find God, and in Him we shall find that for which we have all our lives been secretly longing.

We need not fear that in seeking God only we may narrow our lives or restrict the motions of our expanding hearts. The opposite is true. We can well afford to make God our all, to concentrate, to sacrifice the many for the one.

The author of the quaint old English classic, *The Cloud of Unknowing*, teaches us how to do this. 'Lift up thine heart unto God with a meek stirring of love; and mean Himself, and none of His goods. And thereto, look thee loath to think on aught but God Himself. So that nought work in thy wit, nor in thy will, but only God Himself. This is the work of the soul that most pleaseth God.'

Again, he recommends that in prayer we practise a further stripping down of everything, even of our theology. 'For it sufficeth enough, a naked intent direct unto God without any other cause than Himself.' Yet underneath all his thinking lies the broad foundation of New Testament truth, for He explains that by 'Himself' he means 'God that made thee, and bought thee, and that graciously called thee to thy degree'. And he is all for simplicity: If we would have religion 'lapped and folden in one word, for that thou shouldst have better hold thereupon, take thee but a little word of one syllable; for so it is better than of two, for even the shorter it is the better it accordeth with the work of the Spirit. And such a word is this word "God" or this word "love".'

When the Lord divided Canaan among the tribes of Israel Levi received no share of the land. God said to him simply, 'I am thy part and thine inheritance,' and by those words made him richer than all his brethren, richer than all the kings and rajas who have ever lived in the world. And there is a spiritual principle here, a principle still valid for every priest of the Most High God.

The man who has God for his treasure has all things in one. Many ordinary treasures may be denied him, or if he is allowed to have them, the enjoyment of them will be so tempered that they will never be necessary to his happiness. Or if he must see them go, one after one, he will scarcely feel a sense of loss, for having the source of all things he has in one all satisfaction, all pleasure, all delight. Whatever he may lose he has actually lost nothing, for he now has it all in one, and he has it purely, legitimately and for ever.

O God, I have tasted Thy goodness, and it has both satisfied me and made me thirsty for more. I am painfully conscious of my need of further grace. I am ashamed of my lack of desire. O God, the Triune God, I want to want Thee; I long to be filled with longing; I thirst to be made more thirsty still. Show me Thy glory, I pray Thee, that so I may know Thee indeed. Begin in mercy a new work of love within me. Say to my soul, 'Rise up, my love, my fair one, and come away.' Then give me grace to rise and follow Thee up from this misty lowland where I have wandered so long. In Jesus' name. Amen.

2

The Blessedness of Possessing Nothing

Matthew 5:3 *Blessed are the poor in spirit: for theirs is the kingdom of heaven.*

Before the Lord God made man upon the earth He first prepared for him a world of useful and pleasant things for his sustenance and delight. In the Genesis account of the creation these are called simply 'things'. They were made for man's use, but they were meant always to be external to the man and subservient to him. In the deep heart of the man was a shrine where none but God was worthy to come. Within him was God; without, a thousand gifts which God had showered upon him.

But sin has introduced complications and has made those very gifts of God a potential source of ruin to the soul.

Our woes began when God was forced out of His central shrine and things were allowed to enter. Within the human heart things have taken over. Men have now by nature no peace within their hearts, for God is crowned there no longer, but there in the moral dusk stubborn and aggressive usurpers fight among themselves for first place on the throne.

This is not a mere metaphor, but an accurate analysis of our real spiritual trouble. There is within the human heart a tough, fibrous root of fallen life whose nature is to possess, always to possess. It covets things with a deep and fierce passion. The pronouns *my* and *mine* look innocent enough in print, but their constant and universal use is significant. They express the real nature of the old Adamic man better than a thousand volumes of theology could do. They are verbal symptoms of our deep disease. The roots of our hearts have grown down into things, and we dare not pull up one rootlet lest we die. Things have become necessary to us, a development never originally intended. God's gifts now take the place of God, and the whole course of nature is upset by the monstrous substitution.

Our Lord referred to this tyranny of things when He said to His disciples, 'If any man will come after me, let him deny himself, and take up his cross, and follow me. For whosoever will save his life shall lose it: and whosoever shall lose his life for my sake shall find it' (Matt. 16:24–25).

Breaking this truth into fragments for our better understanding, it would seem that there is within each of us an enemy which we tolerate at our peril. Jesus called it 'life' and 'self', or as we would say, the *self-life*. Its chief characteristic is its possessiveness: the words *gain* and *profit* suggest this. To allow this enemy to live is, in the end, to lose everything. To repudiate it and give up all for Christ's sake is to lose nothing at last, but to preserve everything unto life eternal. And possibly also a hint is given here as to the only effective way to destroy this foe:

it is by the cross. 'Let him take up his cross and follow me.'

The way to deeper knowledge of God is through the lonely valleys of soul poverty and abnegation of all things. The blessed ones who possess the kingdom are they who have repudiated every external thing and have rooted from their hearts all sense of possessing. These are the 'poor in spirit'. They have reached an inward state paralleling the outward circumstances of the common beggar in the streets of Jerusalem. That is what the word *poor* as Christ used it actually means. These blessed poor are no longer slaves to the tyranny of things. They have broken the yoke of the oppressor; and this they have done not by fighting but by surrendering. Though free from all sense of possessing, they yet possess all things. 'Theirs is the kingdom of heaven.'

Let me exhort you to take this seriously. It is not to be understood as mere Bible teaching to be stored away in the mind along with an inert mass of other doctrines. It is a marker on the road to greener pastures, a path chiseled against the steep sides of the mount of God. We dare not try to bypass it if we would follow on in this holy pursuit. We must ascend a step at a time. If we refuse one step, we bring our progress to an end.

As is frequently true, this New Testament principle of spiritual life finds its best illustration in the Old Testament. In the story of Abraham and Isaac we have a dramatic picture of the surrendered life as well as an excellent commentary on the first beatitude.

Abraham was old when Isaac was born, old enough indeed to have been his grandfather, and the child became at once the delight and idol of his heart. From the moment he first stooped to take the tiny form awkwardly in his arms, he was an eager love-slave of his son. God went out of His way to comment on the strength of this affection. And it is not hard to understand. The baby represented everything sacred to his father's heart: the promises of God, the covenants, the hopes of the years and the long messianic dream. As he watched him grow from babyhood to young manhood, the heart of the old man was knit closer and closer with the life of his son, till at last the relationship bordered upon the perilous. It was then that God stepped in to save both father and son from the consequences of an uncleansed love.

'Take now thy son,' said God to Abraham, 'thine only son Isaac, whom thou lovest, and get thee into the land of Moriah; and offer him there for a burnt-offering upon one of the mountains which I tell thee of' (Gen 22:2). The sacred writer spares us a close-up of the agony that night on the slopes near Beersheba when the aged man had it out with his God, but respectful imagination may view in awe the bent form wrestling convulsively alone under the stars. Possibly not again until one greater than Abraham wrestled in the Garden of Gethsemane did such mortal pain visit a human soul. If only the man himself might have been allowed to die. That would have been a thousand times easier, for he was old now, and to die would have been no great ordeal for one who had walked so long with God. Besides, it would have been a last, sweet pleasure to let his dimming vision rest upon the figure of his stalwart son who would live to carry on the Abrahamic line and fulfill in himself the promises of God made long before in Ur of the Chaldees.

How should he slay the lad! Even if he could get the consent of his wounded and protesting heart, how could he reconcile the act with the promise, 'In Isaac shall thy seed be called'? This was Abraham's trial by fire, and he did not fail in the crucible. While the stars still shone like sharp white points above the tent where the sleeping Isaac lay, and long before the gray dawn had begun to lighten the east, the old saint had made up his mind. He would offer his son as God had directed him to do, and *then trust God to raise him from the dead*. This, says the writer to the Hebrews, was the solution his aching heart found sometime in the dark night, and he rose 'early in the morning' to carry out the plan. It is beautiful to see that, while he erred as to God's method, he had correctly sensed the secret of His great heart. And the solution accords well with the New Testament Scripture, 'Whosoever will lose ... for my sake shall find.'

God let the suffering old man go through with it up to the point where He knew there would be no retreat, and then forbade him to lay a hand upon the boy. To the wondering patriarch He now says in effect, 'It's all right, Abraham. I never intended that you should actually slay the lad. I only wanted to remove him from the temple of your heart that I might reign unchallenged there. I wanted to correct the perversion that existed in your love. Now you may have the boy, sound and well. Take him and go back to your tent. Now I know that thou fearest God, seeing that thou hast not withheld thy son, thine only son, from me.'

Then heaven opened and a voice was heard saying to him, 'By myself have I sworn, saith the Lord, for because thou hast done this thing, and hast not withheld thy son, thine only son: that in blessing I will bless thee, and in multiplying I will multiply thy seed as the stars of the heaven, and as the sand which is upon the sea shore; and thy seed shall possess the gate of his enemies; and in thy seed shall all the nations of the earth be blessed; because thou hast obeyed My voice' (Gen 22:16–18).

The old man of God lifted his head to respond to the voice, and stood there on the mount strong and pure and grand, a man marked out by the Lord for special treatment, a friend and favourite of the Most High. Now he was a man wholly surrendered, a man utterly obedient, a man who possessed nothing. He had concentrated his all in the person of his dear son, and God had taken it from him. God could have begun out on the margin of Abraham's life and worked inward to the centre. He chose rather to cut quickly to the heart and have it over in one sharp act of separation. In dealing thus, He practised an economy of means and time. It hurt cruelly, but it was effective.

I have said that Abraham possessed nothing. Yet was not this poor man rich? Everything he had owned before was his still to enjoy: sheep, camels, herds, and goods of every sort. He had also his wife and his friends, and best of all he had his son Isaac safe by his side. He had everything, *but he possessed nothing*. There is the spiritual secret. There is the sweet theology of the heart which can be learned only in the school of renunciation. The books on systematic theology overlook this, but the wise will understand.

After that bitter and blessed experience I think the words *my* and *mine* never again had the same meaning for Abraham. The sense of possession which they connote was gone from his heart. 'Things' had been cast out for ever. They had now become external to the man. His inner heart was free from them. The world said, 'Abraham is rich,' but the aged patriarch only smiled. He could not explain it, but he knew that he owned nothing, that his real treasures were inward and eternal.

There can be no doubt that this possessive clinging to things is one of the most harmful habits in the life. Because it is so natural, it is rarely recognised for the evil that it is. But its outworkings are tragic.

We are often hindered from giving up our treasures to the Lord out of fear for their safety. This is especially true when those treasures are loved relatives and friends. But we need have no such fears. Our Lord came not to destroy but to save. Everything is safe which we commit to Him, and nothing is really safe which is not so committed.

Our gifts and talents should also be turned over to Him. They should be recognised for what they are, God's loan to us, and should never be considered in any sense our own. We have no more right to claim credit for special abilities than for blue eyes or strong muscles. 'For who maketh thee to differ from another? and what hast thou that thou didst not receive?' (1 Cor 4:7).

The Christian who is alive enough to know himself even slightly will recognise the symptoms of this possession malady, and will grieve to find them in his own heart. If the longing after God is strong enough within him, he will want to do something about the matter. Now, what should he do?

First of all, he should put away all defence and make no attempt to excuse himself either in his own eyes or before the Lord. Whoever defends himself will have himself for his defence, and he will have no other. But let him come defenceless before the Lord and he will have for his defender no less than God Himself. Let the inquiring Christian trample under foot every slippery trick of his deceitful heart and insist upon frank and open relations with the Lord.

Then he should remember that this is holy business. No careless or casual dealings will suffice. Let him come to God fully determined to be heard. Let him insist that God accept his all, that He take things out of his heart and Himself reign there in power. It may be he will need to become specific, to name things and people by their names one by one. If he will become drastic enough, he can shorten the time of his travail from years to minutes and enter the good land long before his slower brethren who coddle their feelings and insist upon caution in their dealings with God.

Let us never forget that a truth such as this cannot be learned by rote as one would learn the facts of physical science. They must be *experienced* before we can really know them. We must, in our hearts, live through Abraham's harsh and bitter experiences if we would know the blessedness which follows them. The ancient curse will not go out painlessly; the tough, old miser within us will not lie down and die in obedience to our command. He must be torn out of our heart like a plant from the soil; he must be extracted in agony and blood like a tooth from the jaw. He must be expelled from our soul by violence, as Christ expelled the money changers from the temple. And we shall need to steel ourselves against his piteous begging, and to recognise it as springing out of self-pity, one of the most reprehensible sins of the human heart.

If we would indeed know God in growing intimacy, we must go this way of renunciation. And if we are set upon the pursuit of God, He will sooner or later bring us to this test. Abraham's testing was, at the time, not known to him as such, yet if he had taken some course other than the one he did, the whole history of the Old Testament would have been different. God would have found His man, no doubt, but the loss to Abraham would have been tragic beyond the telling. So we will be brought one by one to the testing place, and we may never know when we are there. At that testing place there will be no dozen possible choices for us—just one and an alternative—but our whole future will be conditioned by the choice we make.

Father, I want to know Thee, but my cowardly heart fears to give up its toys. I cannot part with them without inward bleeding, and I do not try to hide from Thee the terror of the parting. I come trembling, but I do come. Please root from my heart all those things which I have cherished so long and which have become a very part of my living self, so that Thou mayest enter and dwell there without a rival. Then shalt Thou make the place of Thy feet glorious. Then shall my heart have no need of the sun to shine in it, for Thou wilt be the light of it, and there shall be no night there. In Jesus' name, Amen.

3

Removing the Veil

Hebrews 10:19 *Having therefore, brethren, boldness to enter into the holiest by the blood of Jesus.*

Among the famous sayings of the church fathers, none is better known than Augustine's, 'Thou hast formed us for Thyself, and our hearts are restless till they find rest in Thee.'

The great saint states here in few words the origin and interior history of the human race. God made us for Himself—this is the only explanation that satisfies the heart of a thinking man, whatever his wild reason may say. Should faulty education and perverse reasoning lead a man to conclude otherwise, there is little that any Christian can do for him. For such a man I have no message. My appeal is addressed to those who have been previously taught in secret by the wisdom of God. I speak to thirsty hearts whose longings have been wakened by the touch of God within them, and such as they need no reasoned proof. Their restless hearts furnish all the proof they need.

God formed us for Himself. The *Shorter Catechism*,

'Agreed upon by the Reverend Assembly of Divines at Westminster,' as the old *New-England Primer* has it, asks the ancient questions 'what?' and 'why?' and answers them in one short sentence hardly matched in any uninspired work. '*Question*: What is the chief end of man? *Answer*: Man's chief end is to glorify God and enjoy Him for ever.' With this agree the four and twenty elders who fall on their faces to worship Him that liveth for ever and ever, saying, 'Thou art worthy, O Lord, to receive glory and honour and power: for thou hast created all things, and for thy pleasure they are and were created' (Rev 4:11).

God formed us for His pleasure, and so formed us that we, as well as He, can, in divine communion, enjoy the sweet and mysterious mingling of kindred personalities. He meant us to see Him and live with Him and draw our life from His smile. But we have been guilty of that 'foul revolt' of which Milton speaks when describing the rebellion of Satan and his hosts. We have broken with God. We have ceased to obey Him or love Him, and in guilt and fear have fled as far as possible from His presence.

Yet, who can flee from His presence when the heaven and the heaven of heavens cannot contain Him?—when as the wisdom of Solomon testifies, 'the Spirit of the Lord filleth the world'? The omnipresence of the Lord is one thing, and is a solemn fact necessary to His perfection. The manifest Presence is another thing altogether, and from that Presence we have fled, like Adam, to hide among the trees of the garden, or like Peter, to shrink away crying, 'Depart from me, for I am a sinful man, O Lord.'

So the life of man upon the earth is a life away from the Presence, wrenched loose from that 'blissful centre' which is our right and proper dwelling place, our first estate which we kept not, the loss of which is the cause of our unceasing restlessness.

The whole work of God in redemption is to undo the tragic effects of that foul revolt, and to bring us back again into right and eternal relationship with Himself. This requires that our sins be disposed of satisfactorily, that a full reconciliation be effected and the way opened for us to return again into conscious communion with God and to live again in the Presence as before. Then by His prevenient working within us He moves us to return. This first comes to our notice when our restless hearts feel a yearning for the presence of God and we say within ourselves, 'I will arise and go to my Father.' That is the first step, and as the Chinese sage Lao-tze has said, 'The journey of a thousand miles begins with a first step.'

The interior journey of the soul from the wilds of sin into the enjoyed presence of God is beautifully illustrated in the Old Testament tabernacle. The returning sinner first entered the outer court where he offered a blood sacrifice on the brazen altar and washed himself in the laver that stood near it. Then he passed through a veil into the holy place where no natural light could come, but the golden candlestick which spoke of Jesus, the Light of the world, threw its soft glow over all. There also was the shewbread to tell of Jesus, the Bread of Life, and the altar of incense, a figure of unceasing prayer.

Though the worshipper had enjoyed so much, still he had not yet entered the presence of God. Another veil separated him from the Holy of Holies where above the mercy seat dwelt the very God Himself in awful and glorious manifestation. While the tabernacle stood, only the high priest could enter there, and that but once a year, with blood which he offered for his sins and the sins of the people. It was this last veil which was rent when our Lord gave up the ghost on Calvary, and the sacred writer explains that this rending of the veil opened the way for every worshipper in the world to come by the new and living way straight into the divine presence.

Everything in the New Testament accords with this Old Testament picture. Ransomed men need no longer pause in fear to enter the Holy of Holies. *God wills that we should push on into His presence and live our whole life there*. This is to be known to us in conscious experience. It is more than a doctrine to be held; it is a life to be enjoyed every moment of every day.

This 'flame of the Presence' was the beating heart of the Levitical order. Without it all the appointments of the tabernacle were characters of some unknown language, having no meaning for Israel or for us. The greatest fact of the tabernacle was that *Jehovah was there*; a Presence was waiting within the veil.

Similarly, the presence of God is the central fact of Christianity. At the heart of the Christian message is God Himself waiting for His redeemed children to push in to conscious awareness of His presence. That type of Christianity which happens now to be the vogue knows this Presence only in theory. It fails to stress the Christian's privilege of present realisation. According to its teachings we are in the presence of God positionally, and nothing is said about the need to experience that

Presence actually. The fiery urge that drove men like McCheyne is wholly missing. And the present generation of Christians measures itself by this imperfect rule. Ignoble contentment takes the place of burning zeal. We are satisfied to rest in our judicial possessions and, for the most part, we bother ourselves very little about the absence of personal experience.

Who is this within the veil who dwells in fiery manifestations? It is none other than God Himself, 'One God, the Father Almighty, Maker of heaven and earth, and of all things visible and invisible.' It is 'one Lord Jesus Christ, the only begotten Son of God; begotten of His Father before all worlds, God of God, Light of Light, Very God of Very God; begotten, not made; being of one substance with the Father.' And it is 'the Holy Ghost, the Lord and Giver of life, who proceedeth from the Father and the Son, who with the Father and the Son together is worshipped and glorified.' Yet this holy Trinity is one God, for 'we worship one God in Trinity, and Trinity in Unity; neither confounding the Persons, nor dividing the Substance. For there is one Person of the Father, another of the Son, and another of the Holy Ghost. But the Godhead of the Father, of the Son, and of the Holy Ghost, is all one: the glory equal and the majesty co-eternal.' So in part run the ancient creeds, and so the inspired Word declares.

Behind the veil is God, that God after whom the world, with strange inconsistency, has felt, 'if haply they might find Him.' He has discovered Himself to some extent in nature, but more perfectly in the Incarnation. Now He waits to show Himself in ravishing fullness to the humble of soul and the pure in heart.

The world is perishing for lack of the knowledge of God and the church is famishing for want of His presence. The instant cure of most of our religious ills would be to enter the Presence in spiritual experience, to become suddenly aware that we are in God and that God is in us. This would lift us out of our pitiful narrowness and cause our hearts to be enlarged. This would burn away the impurities from our lives as the bugs and fungi were burned away by the fire that dwelt in the bush.

What a broad world to roam in, what a sea to swim in is this God and Father of our Lord Jesus Christ. He is *eternal*. He antedates time and is wholly independent of it. Time began in Him and will end in Him. To it He pays no tribute and from it He suffers no change.

He is *immutable*. He has never changed and can never change in any smallest measure. To change He would need to go from better to worse or from worse to better. He cannot do either, for being perfect He cannot become more perfect, and if He were to become less perfect He would be less than God.

He is *omniscient*. He knows in one free and effortless act all matter, all spirit, all relationships, all events. He has no past and He has no future. He *is*, and none of the limiting and qualifying terms used of creatures can apply to Him.

Love and *mercy* and *righteousness* are His, and *holiness* so ineffable that no comparisons or figures will avail to express it. Only fire can give even a remote conception of it. In fire He appeared at the burning bush; in the pillar of fire He dwelt through all the long wilderness journey. The fire that glowed between the wings of the cherubim in the holy place was called the

Shekinah, the Presence, through the years of Israel's glory, and when the Old had given place to the New, He came at Pentecost as a fiery flame and rested upon each disciple.

Spinoza wrote of the intellectual love of God, and he had a measure of truth there. But the highest love of God is not intellectual, it is spiritual. God is spirit and only the spirit of man can know Him really. In the deep spirit of a man the fire must glow or his love is not the true love of God. The great of the kingdom have been those who loved God more than others did. We all know who they have been and gladly pay tribute to the depth and sincerity of their devotion. We have but to pause for a moment and their names come trooping past us, smelling of myrrh and aloes and cassia out of the ivory palaces.

Frederick Faber was one whose soul panted after God as the roe pants after the water brook, and the measure in which God revealed Himself to his seeking heart set the good man's whole life afire with a burning adoration rivaling that of the seraphim before the throne. His love for God extended to the three persons of the Godhead equally, yet he seemed to feel for each one a special kind of love reserved for Him alone. Of God the Father he sings:

> Only to sit and think of God,
>   Oh what a joy it is!
> To think the thought, to breathe the name;
>   Earth has no higher bliss.
>
> Father of Jesus, love's reward!
>   What rapture it will be,

Prostrate before Thy throne to lie,
And gaze and gaze on Thee!

His love for the person of Christ was so intense that it
threatened to consume him. It burned within him as a
sweet and holy madness and flowed from his lips like
molten gold. In one of his sermons he says, 'Wherever
we turn in the church of God, there is Jesus. He is the
beginning, middle and end of everything to us.... There
is nothing good, nothing holy, nothing beautiful, nothing joyous which He is not to His servants. No one need
be poor, because, if he chooses, he can have Jesus for his
own property and possession. No one need be downcast,
for Jesus is the joy of heaven, and it is His joy to enter
into sorrowful hearts. We can exaggerate about many
things; but we can never exaggerate our obligation to
Jesus, or the compassionate abundance of the love of
Jesus to us. All our lives long we might talk of Jesus, and
yet we should never come to an end of the sweet things
that might be said of Him. Eternity will not be long
enough to learn all He is, or to praise Him for all He has
done, but then, that matters not; for we shall be always
with Him, and we desire nothing more.'

And addressing our Lord directly he says to Him:

I love Thee so, I know not how
My transports to control;
Thy love is like a burning fire
Within my very soul.

Faber's blazing love extended also to the Holy Spirit.
Not only in his theology did he acknowledge His deity
and full equality with the Father and the Son, but he

celebrated it constantly in his songs and in his prayers. He literally pressed his forehead to the ground in his eager, fervid worship of the third person of the Godhead. In one of his great hymns to the Holy Spirit he sums up his burning devotion thus:

> O Spirit, beautiful and dread!
>   My heart is fit to break
> With love of all Thy tenderness
>   For us poor sinners' sake.

I have risked the tedium of quotation that I might show by pointed example what I have set out to say, viz., that God is so vastly wonderful, so utterly and completely delightful that He can, without anything other than Himself, meet and overflow the deepest demands of our total nature, mysterious and deep as that nature is. Such worship as Faber knew (and he is but one of a great company which no man can number) can never come from a mere doctrinal knowledge of God. Hearts that are 'fit to break' with love for the Godhead are those who have been in the Presence and have looked with opened eye upon the majesty of Diety. Men of the breaking hearts had a quality about them not known to nor understood by common men. They habitually spoke with spiritual authority. They had been in the presence of God and they reported what they saw there.

They were prophets, not scribes, for the scribe tells us what he has read, and the prophet tells what he has seen. The distinction is not an imaginary one. Between the scribe who has read and the prophet who has seen there is a difference as wide as the sea. We are overrun today with orthodox scribes, but the prophets, where are they? The hard voice of the scribe sounds over evangelicalism, but the church waits for the tender voice of the saint who has penetrated the veil and has gazed with inward eye upon the wonder that is God. And yet, thus to penetrate, to push in sensitive living experience into the holy Presence, is a privilege open to every child of God.

With the veil removed by the rending of Jesus' flesh, with nothing on God's side to prevent us from entering, why do we tarry without? Why do we consent to abide all our days just outside the Holy of Holies and never enter at all to look upon God? We hear the Bridegroom say, 'Let me see thy countenance, let me hear thy voice; for sweet is thy voice, and thy countenance is comely' (Song of Sol 2:14). We sense that the call is for us, but still we fail to draw near, and the years pass and we grow old and tired in the outer courts of the tabernacle. What hinders us?

The answer usually given, simply that we are 'cold', will not explain all the facts. There is something more serious than coldness of heart, something that may be behind that coldness and be the cause of its existence. What is it? What but the presence of *a veil in our hearts?*— a veil not taken away as the first veil was, but which remains there still shutting out the light and hiding the face of God from us. It is the veil of our fleshly, fallen nature living on, unjudged within us, uncrucified and unrepudiated. It is the close-woven veil of the self-life which we have never truly acknowledged, of which we have been secretly ashamed, and which for these reasons we have never brought to the judgement of the cross. It is not too mysterious, this opaque veil, nor is it hard to identify. We have but to look into our own hearts and we shall see it there, sewn and patched and repaired it may be, but there nevertheless, an enemy to our lives and an effective block to our spiritual progress.

This veil is not a beautiful thing and it is not a thing about which we commonly care to talk. But I am addressing the thirsting souls who are determined to follow God, and I know they will not turn back because the way leads temporarily through the blackened hills. The urge of God within them will assure their continuing pursuit. They will face the facts, however unpleasant, and endure the cross for the joy set before them. So I am bold to name the threads out of which this inner veil is woven.

It is woven of the fine threads of the self-life, the hyphenated sins of the human spirit. They are not something we *do*, they are something we *are*, and therein lies both their subtlety and their power.

To be specific, the self-sins are self-righteousness, self-pity, self-confidence, self-sufficiency, self-admiration, self-love and a host of others like them. They dwell too deep within us and are too much a part of our natures to come to our attention till the light of God is focused upon them. The grosser manifestations of these sins— egotism, exhibitionism, self-promotion—are strangely tolerated in Christian leaders, even in circles of impeccable orthodoxy. They are so much in evidence as actually, for many people, to become identified with the gospel. I trust it is not a cynical observation to say that they appear these days to be a requisite for popularity in some sections of the church visible. Promoting self under the guise of promoting Christ is currently so common as to excite little notice.

One should suppose that proper instruction in the doctrines of man's depravity and the necessity for justification through the righteousness of Christ alone would deliver us from the power of the self-sins, but it does not work that way. Self can live unrebuked at the very altar. It can watch the bleeding victim die and not be in the least affected by what it sees. It can fight for the faith of the reformers and preach eloquently the creed of salvation by grace, and gain strength by its efforts. To tell the truth, it seems actually to feed upon orthodoxy and is more at home in a Bible conference that in a pub. Our very state of longing after God may afford it an excellent condition under which to thrive and grow.

Self is the opaque veil that hides the face of God from us. It can be removed only in spiritual experience, never by mere instruction. We may as well try to instruct leprosy out of our system. There must be a work of God in destruction before we are free. We must invite the cross to do its deadly work within us. We must bring our self-sins to the cross for judgement. We must prepare ourselves for an ordeal of suffering in some measure like that through which our Saviour passed when He suffered under Pontius Pilate.

Let us remember that when we talk of the rending of the veil we are speaking in a figure, and the thought of it is poetical, almost pleasant, but in actuality there is nothing pleasant about it. In human experience that veil is made of living spiritual tissue; it is composed of the sentient, quivering stuff of which our whole beings consist, and to touch it is to touch us where we feel pain. To tear it away is to injure us, to hurt us and make us bleed. To say otherwise is to make the cross no cross and death no death at all. It is never fun to die. To rip through the dear and tender stuff of which life is made can never be anything but deeply painful. Yet that is what the cross did to Jesus and it is what the cross would do to every man to set him free.

Let us beware of tinkering with our inner life, hoping ourselves to rend the veil. God must do everything for us. Our part is to yield and trust. We must confess, forsake, repudiate the self-life, and then reckon it crucified. But we must be careful to distinguish lazy 'acceptance' from the real work of God. We must insist upon the work being done. We dare not rest content with a neat doctrine of self-crucifixion. That is to imitate Saul and spare the best of the sheep and the oxen.

Insist that the work be done in very truth and it will be done. The cross is rough and it is deadly, but it is effective. It does not keep its victim hanging there for ever. There comes a moment when its work is finished and the suffering victim dies. After that is resurrection glory and power, and the pain is forgotten for joy that the veil is taken away and we have entered in actual spiritual experience the presence of the living God.

Lord, how excellent are Thy ways, and how devious and dark are the ways of man. Show us how to die, that we may rise again to newness of life. Rend the veil of our self-life from the top down as Thou didst rend the veil of the temple. We would draw near in full assurance of faith. We would dwell with Thee in daily experience here on this earth so that we may be accustomed to the glory when we enter Thy heaven to dwell with Thee there. In Jesus' name, Amen.

4

Apprehending God

Psalm 34:8   *O taste and see.*

Canon Holmes, of India, many years ago called attention
to the inferential character of the average man's faith in
God. To most people God is an inference, not a reality.
He is a deduction from evidence which they consider
adequate, but He remains personally unknown to the
individual. 'He *must* be,' they say, 'therefore we believe
He is.' Others do not go even so far as this; they know
of Him only by hearsay. They have never bothered to
think the matter out for themselves, but have heard
about Him from others, and have put belief in Him into
the back of their minds along with various odds and ends
that make up their total creed. To many others, God is
but an ideal, another name for goodness, or beauty, or
truth; or He is law, or life, or the creative impulse behind
the phenomena of existence.

These notions about God are many and varied, but
they who hold them have one thing in common: they do
not know God in personal experience. The possibility of
intimate acquaintance with Him has not entered their

minds. While admitting His existence they do not think of Him as being knowable in the sense that we know things or people.

Christians, to be sure, go further than this, at least in theory. Their creed requires them to believe in the personality of God, and they have been taught to pray, 'Our Father, which art in heaven.' Now personality and fatherhood carry with them the idea of the possibility of personal acquaintance. This is admitted, I say, in theory, but for millions of Christians, nevertheless, God is no more real than He is to the non-Christian. They go through life trying to love an ideal and be loyal to a mere principle.

Over against all this cloudy vagueness stands the clear scriptural doctrine that God can be known in personal experience. A loving personality dominates the Bible, walking among the trees of the garden and breathing fragrance over every scene. Always a living person is present, speaking, pleading, loving, working, and manifesting Himself whenever and wherever His people have the receptivity necessary to receive the manifestation.

The Bible assumes as a self-evident fact that men can know God with at least the same degree of immediacy as they know any other person or thing that comes within the field of their experience. The same terms are used to express the knowledge of God as are used to express knowledge of physical things. 'O *taste* and see that the Lord is good' (Ps 34:8). 'All thy garments *smell* of myrrh, and aloes, and cassia, out of the ivory palaces' (Ps 45:8). 'My sheep *hear* my voice' (Jn 10:27). 'Blessed are the pure in heart: for they shall *see* God' (Mt 5:8). These are but four of countless such passages from the Word of

...nces underlined are
...in Weathershield Smooth
...xtured Masonry Paint.

Dulux
Colour Palette

Available in many finishes
including Vinyl Matt, Silk,
Soft Sheen, Gloss and Satinwood.

...able in many finishes
...uding Vinyl Matt, Silk,
...een, Gloss and Satinwood.

Dulux
Colour Palette

References underlined are
in Weathershield Smooth

inc...

Soft S...

Soft S...

Dulux
Colour Palette

avail...

an...

f...

C...

D...

Dulux 70GG 11/334

Dulux 70GG 16/234

Dulux 70GG 30/197

Dulux 70GG 57/148

 113

God. And more important than any proof text is the fact that the whole import of Scripture is toward this belief.

What can all this mean except that we have in our hearts organs by means of which we can know God as certainly as we know material things through our familiar five senses? We apprehend the physical world by exercising the faculties given us for that purpose, and we possess spiritual faculties by means of which we can know God and the spiritual world if we will obey the Spirit's urge and begin to use them.

That a saving work must first be done in the heart is taken for granted here. The spiritual faculties of the unregenerate man lie asleep in his nature, unused, and for every purpose dead. That is the stroke which has fallen upon us by sin. They may be quickened to active life again by the operation of the Holy Spirit in regeneration. That is one of the immeasurable benefits which come to us through Christ's atoning work on the cross.

But why do the very ransomed children of God themselves know so little of that habitual, conscious communion with God which Scripture offers? The answer is because of our chronic unbelief. Faith enables our spiritual sense to function. Where faith is defective the result will be inward insensibility and numbness toward spiritual things. This is the condition of vast numbers of Christians today. No proof is necessary to support that statement. We have but to converse with the first Christian we meet or enter the first church we find open to acquire all the proof we need.

A spiritual kingdom lies all about us, enclosing us, embracing us, altogether within reach of our inner selves, waiting for us to recognise it. God Himself is here waiting our response to His presence. This eternal world will come alive to us the moment we begin to reckon upon its reality.

I have just now used two words which demand definition. Or if definition is impossible, I must at least make clear what I mean when I use them. They are 'reckon' and 'reality'.

What do I mean by *reality*? I mean that which has existence apart from any idea any mind may have of it, and which would exist if there were no mind anywhere to entertain a thought of it. That which is real has being in itself. It does not depend upon the observer for its validity.

I am aware that there are those who love to poke fun at the plain man's idea of reality. They are the idealists who spin endless proofs that nothing is real outside of the mind. They are the relativists who like to show that there are no fixed points in the universe from which we can measure anything. They smile down upon us from their lofty intellectual peaks and settle us to their own satisfaction by fastening upon us the reproachful term 'absolutist'. The Christian is not put out of countenance by this show of contempt. He can smile right back at them, for he knows that there is only one who is Absolute, that is God. But he knows also that the Absolute one has made this world for man's use, and while there is nothing fixed or real in the last meaning of the words (the meaning as applied to God), *for every purpose of human life we are permitted to act as if there were*. And every man does act thus except the mentally sick. These unfortunates also have trouble with reality, but they are consistent; they insist upon living in accordance with their ideas of things. They are honest, and it is their very honesty which constitutes them a social problem.

The idealists and relativists are not mentally sick. They prove their soundness by living their lives according to the very notions of reality which they in theory repudiate and by counting upon the very fixed points which they prove are not there. They could earn a lot more respect for their notions if they were willing to live by them; but this they are careful not to do. Their ideas are brain-deep, not life-deep. Wherever life touches them they repudiate their theories and live like other men.

The Christian is too sincere to play with ideas for their own sake. He takes no pleasure in the mere spinning of gossamer webs for display. All his beliefs are practical. They are geared into his life. By them he lives or dies, stands or falls for this world and for all time to come. From the insincere man he turns away.

The sincere, plain man knows that the world is real. He finds it here when he wakes to consciousness, and he knows that he did not think it into being. It was here waiting for him when he came, and he knows that when he prepares to leave this earthly scene it will be here still to bid him goodbye as he departs. By the deep wisdom of life he is wiser than a thousand men who doubt. He stands upon the earth and feels the wind and rain in his face, and he knows that they are real. He sees the sun by day and the stars by night. He sees the hot lightning play out of the dark thundercloud. He hears the sounds of nature and the cries of human joy and pain. These he knows are real. He lies down on the cool earth at night and has no fear that it will prove illusory or fail him while he sleeps. In the morning the firm ground will be under him, the blue sky above him, and the rocks and trees around him as when he closed his eyes the night before. So he lives and rejoices in a world of reality.

With his five senses he engages this real world. All things necessary to his physical existence he apprehends by the faculties with which he has been equipped by the God who created him and placed him in such a world as this.

Now by our definition also God is real. He is real in the absolute and final sense that nothing else is. All other reality is contingent upon His. The great Reality is God, the author of that lower and dependent reality which makes up the sum of created things, including ourselves. God has objective existence independent of and apart from any notions which we may have concerning Him. The worshipping heart does not create its object. It finds Him here when it wakes from its moral slumber in the morning of its regeneration.

Another word that must be cleared up is *reckon*. This does not mean to visualise or imagine. Imagination is not faith. The two are not only different from, but stand in sharp opposition to, each other. Imagination projects unreal images out of the mind and seeks to attach reality to them. Faith creates nothing; it simply reckons upon that which is already there.

God and the spiritual world are real. We can reckon upon them with as much assurance as we reckon upon the familiar world around us. Spiritual things are there (or rather we should say here) inviting our attention and challenging our trust.

Our trouble is that we have established bad thought

habits. We habitually think of the visible world as real and doubt the reality of any other. We do not deny the existence of the spiritual world but we doubt that it is real in the accepted meaning of the word.

The world of sense intrudes upon our attention day and night for the whole of our lifetime. It is clamorous, insistent and self-demonstrating. It does not appeal to our faith; it is here, assaulting our five senses, demanding to be accepted as real and final. But sin has so clouded the lenses of our hearts that we cannot see that other reality, the city of God, shining around us. The world of sense triumphs. The visible becomes the enemy of the invisible; the temporal, of the eternal. That is the curse inherited by every member of Adam's tragic race.

At the root of the Christian life lies belief in the invisible. The object of the Christian's faith is unseen reality.

Our uncorrected thinking, influenced by the blindness of our natural hearts and the intrusive ubiquity of visible things, tends to draw a contrast between the spiritual and the real—but actually no such contrast exists. The antithesis lies elsewhere—between the real and the imaginary, between the spiritual and the material, between the temporal and the eternal; but between the spiritual and the real, never. The spiritual is real.

If we would rise into that region of light and power plainly beckoning us through the Scriptures of truth, we must break the evil habit of ignoring the spiritual. We must shift our interest from the seen to the unseen. For the great unseen Reality is God. 'He that cometh to God must believe that he is, and that he is a rewarder of them that diligently seek him' (Heb 11:6). This is basic in the life of faith. From there we can rise to unlimited heights. 'Ye believe in God,' said our Lord Jesus Christ, 'believe also in me' (Jn 14:1). Without the first there can be no second.

If we truly want to follow God, we must seek to be other-worldly. This I say knowing well that word has been used with scorn by the sons of this world and applied to the Christian as a badge of reproach. So be it. Every man must choose his world. If we who follow Christ, with all the facts before us and knowing what we are about, deliberately choose the kingdom of God as our sphere of interest, I see no reason why anyone should object. If we lose by it, the loss is our own; if we gain, we rob no one by so doing. The 'other world', which is the object of this world's disdain and the subject of the drunkard's mocking song, is our carefully chosen goal and the object of our holiest longing.

But we must avoid the common fault of pushing the 'other world' into the future. It is not future, but present. It parallels our familiar physical world, and the doors between the two worlds are open. 'Ye are come,' says the writer to the Hebrews (and the tense is plainly present), 'unto mount Sion, and unto the city of the living God, the heavenly Jerusalem, and to an innumerable company of angels, to the general assembly and church of the firstborn, which are written in heaven, and to God the Judge of all, and to the spirits of just men made perfect, and to Jesus the mediator of the new covenant, and to the blood of sprinkling, that speaketh better things than that of Abel' (Heb 12:22–24). All these things are contrasted with 'the mount that might be touched' and 'the sound of a trumpet and the voice of words' that might be heard'. May we not safely conclude that, as the realities of Mount Sinai were apprehended by the senses, so the realities of Mount Zion are to be grasped by the soul? And this not by any trick of the imagination but in downright actuality. The soul has eyes with which to see and ears with which to hear. Feeble they may be from long disuse, but by the life-giving touch of Christ they are now alive and capable of sharpest sight and most sensitive hearing.

As we begin to focus upon God, the things of the spirit will take shape before our inner eyes. Obedience to the word of Christ will bring an inward revelation of the Godhead (Jn 14:21–23). It will give acute perception enabling us to see God even as is promised to the pure in heart. A new God-consciousness will seize upon us and we shall begin to taste and hear and inwardly feel God, who is our life and our all. There will be seen the constant shining of 'the true Light, which lighteth every man that cometh into the world' (Jn 1:9). More and more, as our faculties grow sharper and more sure, God will become to us all the great All, and His presence the glory and wonder of our lives.

O God, quicken to life every power within me, that I may lay hold on eternal things. Open my eyes that I may see; give me acute spiritual perception; enable me to taste Thee and know that Thou art good. Make heaven more real to me than any earthly thing has ever been. Amen.

5

The Universal Presence

Psalm 139:7 *Whither shall I go from thy spirit? or whither shall I flee from thy presence?*

In all Christian teaching certain basic truths are found, hidden at times, and rather assumed than asserted, but necessary to all truth as the primary colours are found in and necessary to the finished painting. Such a truth is the divine immanence.

God dwells in His creation and is everywhere indivisibly present in all His works. This is boldly taught by prophet and apostle, and is accepted by Christian theology generally. That is, it appears in the books, but for some reason it has not sunk into the average Christian's heart so as to become a part of his believing self. Christian teachers shy away from its full implications and, if they mention it at all, mute it down till it has little meaning. I would guess the reason for this to be the fear of being charged with pantheism. But the doctrine of the divine Presence is definitely not pantheism.

Pantheism's error is too palpable to deceive anyone. It is that God is the sum of all created things. Nature and

59

God are one, so that whoever touches a leaf or a stone touches God. That is, of course, to degrade the glory of the incorruptible Deity and, in an effort to make all things divine, banish all divinity from the world entirely.

The truth is that while God dwells in His world He is separated from it by a gulf for ever impassable. However closely He may be identified with the works of His hands, they are and must eternally be other than He, and He is and must be antecedent to and independent of them. He is transcendent above all His works even while He is immanent within them.

What does the divine immanence mean in direct Christian experience? It means simply that *God is here*. Wherever we are, God is here. There is no place, there can be no place, where He is not. Ten million intelligences standing at as many points in space and separated by incomprehensible distances can each one say with equal truth, God is here. No point is nearer to God than any other point. It is exactly as near to God from any place as it is from any other place. No one is in mere distance any further from or any nearer to God than any other person.

These are truths believed by every instructed Christian. It remains for us to think on them and pray over them until they begin to glow within us. 'In the beginning God...' (Gen 1:1). Not matter, for matter is not self-causing. It requires an antecedent cause, and God is that cause. Not law, for law is but a name for the course which all creation follows. That course had to be planned, and the planner is God. Not mind, for mind also is a created thing and must have a Creator behind it. In the beginning God, the uncaused cause of matter, mind and law. There we must begin.

Adam sinned and, in his panic, frantically tried to do the impossible: he tried to hide from the presence of God. David also must have had wild thoughts of trying to escape from the Presence, for he wrote, 'Whither shall I go from thy spirit? or whither shall I flee from thy presence?' (Ps 139:7). Then he proceeded through one of his most beautiful psalms to celebrate the glory of the divine immanence. 'If I ascend up into heaven, thou art there: if I make my bed in hell, behold, thou art there. If I take the wings of the morning, and dwell in the uttermost parts of the sea; even there shall thy right hand lead me, and thy right hand shall hold me' (Ps 139:8–10). And he knew that God's *being* and God's *seeing* are the same, that the seeing Presence had been with him even before he was born, watching the mystery of unfolding life. Solomon exclaimed, 'But will God indeed dwell on the earth? behold, the heaven and the heaven of heavens cannot contain thee: how much less this house which I have builded' (1 Kings 8:27). Paul assured the Athenians that 'he be not far from every one of us: for in him we live, and move, and have our being' (Acts 17:27–28).

If God is present at every point in space, if we cannot go where He is not, cannot even conceive of a place where He is not, why then has not that Presence become the one universally celebrated fact of the world? The patriarch Jacob, 'in the waste howling wilderness', gave the answer to that question. He saw a vision of God and cried out in wonder, 'Surely the Lord is in this place; and I knew it not' (Gen 28:16). Jacob had never been for one small division of a moment outside the circle of that all-pervading Presence. But he knew it not. That was his trouble, and it is ours. Men do not know that God is here. What a difference it would make if they knew.

The Presence and the manifestation of the Presence are not the same. There can be the one without the other. God is here when we are wholly unaware of it. He is manifest only when and as we are aware of His presence. On our part, there must be surrender to the Spirit of God, for His work is to show us the Father and the Son. If we co-operate with Him in loving obedience, God will manifest Himself to us, and that manifestation will be the difference between a nominal Christian life and a life radiant with the light of His face.

Always, everywhere God is present, and always He seeks to discover Himself to each one. He would reveal not only that He is, but what He is as well. He did not have to be persuaded to reveal Himself to Moses. 'And the Lord descended in the cloud, and stood with him there, and proclaimed the name of the Lord' (Gen 34:5). He not only made a verbal proclamation of His nature but He revealed His very self to Moses so that the skin of Moses' face shone with the supernatural light. It will be a great moment for some of us when we begin to believe that God's promise of self-revelation is literally true, that He promised much, but no more than He intends to fulfill.

Our pursuit of God is successful just because He is for ever seeking to manifest Himself to us. The revelation of God to any man is not God coming from a distance once upon a time to pay a brief and momentous visit to the man's soul. Thus to think of it is to misunderstand it all. The approach of God to the soul or of the soul to God is not to be thought of in spatial terms at all. There is no idea of physical distance involved in the concept. It is not a matter of miles but of experience.

To speak of being near to or far from God is to use language in a sense always understood when applied to our ordinary human relationships. A man may say, 'I feel that my son is coming nearer to me as he gets older,' and yet that son has lived by his father's side since he was born and has never been away from home more than a day or so in his entire life. What then can the father mean? Obviously he is speaking of experience. He means that the boy is coming to know him more intimately and with deeper understanding, that the barriers of thought and feeling between the two are disappearing, that father and son are becoming more closely united in mind and heart.

So when we sing, 'Draw me nearer, nearer, blessed Lord,' we are not thinking of the nearness of place, but of the nearness of relationship. It is for increasing degrees of awareness that we pray, for a more perfect consciousness of the divine Presence. We need never shout across the spaces to an absent God. He is nearer than our own soul, closer than our most secret thoughts.

Why do some persons 'find' God in a way that others do not? Why does God manifest His presence to some and let multitudes of others struggle along in the half-light of imperfect Christian experience? Of course, the will of God is the same for all. He has no favourites within His household. All He has ever done for any of His children He will do for all of His children. The difference lies not with God but with us.

Pick at random a score of great saints whose lives and testimonies are widely known. Let them be Bible characters or well-known Christians of post-biblical times. You will be struck instantly with the fact that the saints were not alike. Sometimes the unlikenesses were so great as to be positively glaring. How different, for example, was Moses from Isaiah; how different was Elijah from David; how unlike each other were John and Paul, St Francis and Luther, Finney and Thomas á Kempis. The differences are as wide as human life itself— differences of race, nationality, education, temperament, habit and personal qualities. Yet they all walked, each in his day, upon a high road of spiritual living far above the common way.

Their differences must have been incidental and in the eyes of God of no significance. In some vital quality they must have been alike. What was it?

I venture to suggest that the one vital quality which they had in common was spiritual receptivity. Something in them was open to heaven, something which urged them Godward. Without attempting anything like a profound analysis, I shall say simply that they had spiritual awareness and that they went on to cultivate it until it became the biggest thing in their lives. They differed from the average person in that when they felt the inward longing they *did something about it*. They acquired the lifelong habit of spiritual response. They were not disobedient to the heavenly vision. As David put it neatly, 'When thou saidst, Seek ye my face; my heart said unto thee, Thy face, Lord, will I seek' (Ps 27:8).

As with everything good in human life, behind this receptivity is God. The sovereignty of God is here, and is felt even by those who have not placed particular stress upon it theologically. The pious Michelangelo confessed this in a sonnet:

> My unassisted heart is barren clay,
> That of its native self can nothing feed:
> Of good and pious works Thou art the seed,
> That quickens only where Thou sayest it may:
> Unless Thou show to us Thine own true way
> No man can find it: Father! Thou must lead.

These words will repay study as the deep and serious testimony of a great Christian.

Important as it is that we recognise God working in us, I would yet warn against a too-great pre-occupation with the thought. It is a sure road to sterile passivity. God will not hold us responsible to understand the mysteries of election, predestination and the divine sovereignty. The best and safest way to deal with these truths is to raise our eyes to God and in deepest reverence say, 'O Lord, Thou knowest.' Those things belong to the deep and mysterious Profound of God's omniscience. Prying into them may make theologians, but it will never make saints.

Receptivity is not a single thing; rather, it is a compound, a blending of several elements within the soul. It is an affinity for, a bent toward, a sympathetic response to, a desire to have. From this it may be gathered that it can be present in degrees, that we may have little or more, depending upon the individual. It may be increased by exercise or destroyed by neglect. It is not a sovereign and irresistible force which comes upon us as a seizure from above. It is a gift of God, indeed, but one which must be recognised and cultivated as any other gift if we are to realise the purpose for which it was given.

Failure to see this is the cause of a very serious breakdown in modern evangelicalism. The idea of cultivation and exercise, so dear to the saints of old, has now no place in our total religious picture. It is too slow, too common. We now demand glamour and fast-flowing dramatic action. A generation of Christians reared among push-buttons and automatic machines is impatient of slower and less direct methods of reaching their goals. We have been trying to apply machine-age methods to our relations with God. We read our chapter, have our short devotions and rush away, hoping to make up for our deep inward bankruptcy by attending another gospel meeting or listening to another thrilling story told by a religious adventurer lately returned from afar.

The tragic results of this spirit are all about us: Shallow lives, hollow religious philosophies, the preponderance of the element of fun in gospel meetings, the glorification of men, trust in religious externalities, quasi-religious fellowships, salesmanship methods, the mistaking of dynamic personality for the power of the Spirit. These and such as these are the symptoms of an evil disease, a deep and serious malady of the soul.

For this great sickness that is upon us no one person is responsible, and no Christian is wholly free from blame. We have all contributed, directly or indirectly, to this sad state of affairs. We have been too blind to see, or too timid to speak out, or too self-satisfied to desire anything better than the poor, average diet with which others appear satisfied. To put it differently, we have accepted one another's notions, copied one another's lives and made one another's experiences the model for our own. And for a generation the trend has been downward. Now we have reached a low place of sand and burnt wire-grass and, worst of all, we have made the Word of Truth conform to our experience and accepted this low plane as the very pasture of the blessed.

It will require a determined heart and more than a little courage to wrench ourselves loose from the grip of our times and return to biblical ways. But it can be done. Every now and then in the past Christians have had to do it. History has recorded several large-scale returns led by such men as St Francis, Martin Luther and George Fox. Unfortunately, there seems to be no Luther or Fox on the horizon at present. Whether or not another such return may be expected before the coming of Christ is a question upon which Christians are not fully agreed, but that is not of too great importance to us now.

What God in His sovereignty may yet do on a world-scale I do not claim to know. But what He will do for the plain man or woman who seeks His face I believe I do know and can tell others. Let any man turn to God in earnest, let him begin to exercise himself unto godliness, let him seek to develop his powers of spiritual receptivity by trust and obedience and humility, and the results will exceed anything he may have hoped in his leaner and weaker days.

Any man who by repentance and a sincere return to God will break himself out of the mould in which he has been held, and will go to the Bible itself for his spiritual standards, will be delighted with what he finds there.

Let us say it again: the universal Presence is a fact. God is here. The whole universe is alive with His life. And He is no strange or foreign God, but the familiar Father of our Lord Jesus Christ whose love has for these thousands of years enfolded the sinful race of men. And always He is trying to get our attention, to reveal Himself to us, to communicate with us. We have within us the ability to know Him if we will but respond to His overtures. (And this we call pursuing God!) We will know Him in increasing degree as our receptivity becomes more perfect by faith and love and practice.

O God and Father, I repent of my sinful pre-occupation with visible things. The world has been too much with me. Thou hast been here and I knew it not. I have been blind to Thy presence. Open my eyes that I may behold Thee in and around me. For Christ's sake, Amen.

6

The Speaking Voice

John 1:1 *In the beginning was the Word, and the Word was with God, and the Word was God.*

An intelligent, plain man, untaught in the truths of Christianity, coming upon this text, would likely conclude that John meant to teach that it is the nature of God to speak, to communicate His thoughts to others. And he would be right. A word is a medium by which thoughts are expressed, and the application of the term to the eternal Son leads us to believe that self-expression is inherent in the Godhead, that God is for ever seeking to speak Himself out to His creation. The whole Bible supports this idea. God is speaking. Not God spoke, but *God is speaking*. He is, by His nature, continuously articulate. He fills the world with His speaking voice.

One of the great realities with which we have to deal is the voice of God in His world. The briefest and only satisfying cosmogony is this: 'He spake and it was done.' The *why* of natural law is the living voice of God immanent in His creation. And this word of God which brought all worlds into being cannot be understood to mean the Bible, for it is not a written or printed word at all, but the expression of the will of God spoken into the structure of all things. This word of God is the breath of God filling the world with living potentiality. The voice of God is the most powerful force in nature, indeed the only force in nature, for all energy is here only because the power-filled word is being spoken.

The Bible is the written Word of God, and because it is written it is confined and limited by the necessities of ink and paper and leather. The voice of God, however, is alive and free as the sovereign God is free. 'The words that I speak unto you, they are spirit, and they are life' (Jn 6:63). The life is in the speaking words. God's word in the Bible can have power only because it corresponds to God's word in the universe. It is the present voice which makes the written Word all-powerful. Otherwise it would lie locked in slumber within the covers of a book.

We take a low and primitive view of things when we conceive of God at the creation coming into physical contact with things, shaping and fitting and building like a carpenter. The Bible teaches otherwise: 'By the word of the Lord were the heavens made; and all the host of them by the breath of his mouth. . . . For he spake, and it was done; he commanded, and it stood fast' (Ps 33:6, 9). 'Through faith we understand that the worlds were framed by the word of God' (Heb 11:3). Again we must remember that God is referring here not to His written Word, but to His speaking voice. His world-filling voice is meant, that voice which antedates the Bible by uncounted centuries, that voice which has not been silent since the dawn of creation, but is sounding still throughout the full far reaches of the universe.

The Word of God is quick and powerful. In the beginning He spoke to nothing, and it became *something*. Chaos heard it and became order; darkness heard it and became light. 'And God said...and it was so' (Gen 1:9). These twin phrases, as cause and effect, occur throughout the Genesis story of creation. The *said* accounts for the *so*. The *so* is the *said* put into the continuous present.

God is here and He is speaking—these truths are behind all other Bible truths; without them there could be no revelation at all. God did not write a book and send it by messenger to be read at a distance by unaided minds. He spoke a book and lives in His spoken words, constantly speaking His words and causing the power of them to persist across the years. God breathed on clay and it became a man; He breathes on men and they become clay. 'Return, ye children of men' (Ps 90:3) was the word spoken at the Fall by which God decreed the death of every man, and no added word has He needed to speak. The sad procession of mankind across the face of the earth from birth to the grave is proof that His original word was enough.

We have not given sufficient attention to that deep utterance in the book of John, 'That was the true Light, which lighteth every man that cometh into the world' (1:9). Shift the punctuation around as we will, the truth is still there: the Word of God affects the hearts of all men as light in the soul. In the hearts of all men the light shines, the Word sounds, and there is no escaping them. Something like this would of necessity be so if God is alive and in His world. And John says that it is so. Even those persons who have never heard of the Bible have still been preached to with sufficient clarity to remove every excuse from their hearts for ever. 'Which show the work of the law written in their hearts, their conscience also bearing witness, and their thoughts the mean while either accusing or else excusing one another' (Rom 2:15). 'For the invisible things of him from the creation of the world are clearly seen, being understood by the things that are made, even his eternal power and Godhead; so that they are without excuse' (Rom 1:20).

This universal voice of God was by the ancient Hebrews ofen called 'wisdom' and was said to be everywhere sounding and searching throughout the earth, seeking some response from the sons of men. The eighth chapter of Proverbs begins, 'Doth not wisdom cry? and understanding put forth her voice?' The writer then pictures wisdom as a beautiful woman standing 'in the top of the high places, by the way in the places of the paths'. She sounds her voice from every quarter so that no one may miss hearing it. 'Unto you, O men, I call, and my voice is to the sons of men' (v.4). Then she pleads for the simple and the foolish to give ear to her words. It is spiritual response for which this wisdom of God is pleading, a response which she has always sought and is but rarely able to secure. The tragedy is that our eternal welfare depends upon our hearing, and we have trained our ears not to hear.

This universal voice has ever sounded, and it has often troubled men even when they did not understand the source of their fears. Could it be that this voice distilling like a living mist upon the hearts of men has been the undiscovered cause of the troubled conscience and the longing for immortality confessed by millions since the dawn of recorded history? We need not fear to face up to this. The speaking voice is a fact. How men have reacted to it is for any observer to note.

When God spoke out of heaven to our Lord, self-centred men who heard it explained it by natural causes, saying, 'It thundered.' This habit of explaining the voice by appeals to natural law is at the very root of modern science. In the living, breathing cosmos there is a mysterious Something, too wonderful, too awful for any mind to understand. The believing man does not claim to understand. He falls to his knees and whispers, 'God.' The man of earth kneels also, but not to worship. He kneels to examine, to search, to find the cause and the how of things. Just now we happen to be living in a secular age. Our thought habits are those of the scientist, not those of the worshipper. We are more likely to explain than to adore. 'It thundered,' we exclaim, and go our earthly way. But still the voice sounds and searches. The order and life of the world depend upon that voice, but men are mostly too busy or too stubborn to give attention.

Every one of us has had experiences which we have not been able to explain—a sudden sense of loneliness, or a feeling of wonder or awe in the face of the universal vastness. Or we have had a fleeting visitation of light like an illumination from some other sun, giving us in a quick flash an assurance that we are from another world, that our origins are divine. What we saw there, or felt, or heard, may have been contrary to all that we had been taught in the schools and at wide variance with all our former beliefs and opinions. We were forced to suspend our acquired doubts while, for a moment, the clouds were rolled back and we saw and heard for ourselves. Explain such things as we will, I think we have not been fair to the facts until we allow at least the possibility that such experiences may arise from the presence of God in the world and His persistent effort to communicate with mankind. Let us not dismiss such an hypothesis too flippantly.

It is my own belief (and here I shall not feel bad if no one follows me) that every good and beautiful thing which man has produced in the world has been the result of his faulty and sin-blocked response to the creative voice sounding over the earth. The moral philosophers who dreamed their high dreams of virtue, the religious thinkers who speculated about God and immortality, the poets and artists who created out of common stuff pure and lasting beauty: how can we explain them? It is not enough to say simply, 'It was genius.'

What then is genius? Could it be that a genius is a man haunted by the speaking voice, labouring and striving like one possessed to achieve ends which he only vaguely understands? That the great man may have missed God in his labours, that he may even have spoken or written against God does not destroy the idea I am advancing. God's redemptive revelation in Scripture is necessary to saving faith and peace with God. Faith in a risen Saviour is necessary if the vague stirrings toward immortality are to bring us to restful and satisfying communion with God. To me this is a plausible explanation of all that is best out of Christ. But you can be a good Christian and not accept my thesis.

The voice of God is a friendly voice. No one need fear

to listen to it unless he has already made up his mind to resist it. The blood of Jesus has covered not only the human race but all creation as well. 'And, having made peace through the blood of his cross, by him to reconcile all things unto himself; by him, I say, whether they be things in earth, or things in heaven' (Col 1:20). We may safely preach a friendly heaven. The heavens as well as the earth are filled with the good will of Him that dwelt in the bush. The perfect blood of atonement secures this for ever.

Whoever will listen will hear the speaking heaven. This is definitely not the hour when men take kindly to an exhortation to listen, for listening is not today a part of popular religion. We are at the opposite end of the pole from there. Religion has accepted the monstrous heresy that noise, size, activity and bluster make a man dear to God. But we may take heart. To a people caught in the tempest of the last great conflict God says, 'Be still, and know that I am God' (Ps 46:10), and still He says it, as if He means to tell us that our strength and safety lie not in noise but in silence.

It is important that we get still to wait on God. And it is best that we get alone, preferably with our Bible outspread before us. Then if we will we may draw near to God and begin to hear Him speak to us in our hearts. I think for the average person the progression will be something like this: First a sound as of a Presence walking in the garden. Then a voice, more intelligible, but still far from clear. Then the happy moment when the Spirit begins to illuminate the Scriptures, and that which had been only a sound, or at best a voice, now becomes an intelligible word, warm and intimate and clear as the word of a dear friend. Then will come life and light, and best of all, ability to see and rest in and embrace Jesus Christ as Saviour and Lord and all.

The Bible will never be a living book to us until we are convinced that God is articulate in His universe. To jump from a dead, impersonal world to a dogmatic Bible is too much for most people. They may admit that they should accept the Bible as the Word of God, and they may try to think of it as such, but they find it impossible to believe that the words there on the page are actually for them. A man may say, 'These words are addressed to me,' and yet in his heart not feel and know that they are. He is the victim of a divided psychology. He tries to think of God as mute everywhere else and vocal only in a book.

I believe that much of our religious unbelief is due to a wrong conception of and a wrong feeling for the Scriptures of truth. A silent God suddenly began to speak in a book and when the book was finished lapsed back into silence again for ever. Now we read the book as the record of what God said when He was for a brief time in a speaking mood. With notions like that in our heads how can we believe? The facts are that God is not silent, has never been silent. It is the nature of God to speak. The second person of the Holy Trinity is called the Word. The Bible is the inevitable outcome of God's continuous speech. It is the infallible declaration of His mind for us put into our familiar human words.

I think a new world will arise out of the religious mists when we approach our Bible with the idea that it is not only a book which was once spoken, but a book which is *now speaking*. The prophets habitually said, 'Thus *saith* thè Lord.' They meant their hearers to understand that God's speaking is in the continuous present. We may use the past tense properly to indicate that at a certain time a certain word of God was spoken, but a word of God once spoken continues to be spoken, as a child once born continues to be alive, or a world once created continues to exist. And those are but imperfect illustrations, for children die and worlds burn out, but the Word of our God endureth for ever.

If you would follow on to know the Lord, come at once to the open Bible expecting it to speak to you. Do not come with the notion that it is a thing which you may push around at your convenience. It is more than a thing, it is a voice, a word, the very Word of the living God.

Lord, teach me to listen. The times are noisy and my ears are weary with the thousand raucous sounds which continuously assault them. Give me the spirit of the boy Samuel when he said to Thee, 'Speak, for thy servant heareth.' Let me hear Thee speaking in my heart. Let me get used to the sound of Thy voice, that its tones may be familiar when the sounds of earth die away and the only sound will be the music of Thy speaking voice. Amen.

7

The Gaze of the Soul

Hebrew 12:2 *Looking unto Jesus the author and finisher of our faith.*

Let us think of our intelligent, plain man mentioned in chapter six coming for the first time to the reading of the Scriptures. He approaches the Bible without any previous knowledge of what it contains. He is wholly without prejudice; he has nothing to prove and nothing to defend.

Such a man will not have read long until his mind begins to observe certain truths standing out from the page. They are the spiritual principles behind the record of God's dealings with men, and woven into the writings of holy men as they 'were moved by the Holy Ghost'. As he reads on he might want to number these truths as they become clear to him and make a brief summary under each number. These summaries will be the tenets of his biblical creed. Further reading will not affect these points except to enlarge and strengthen them. Our man is finding out what the Bible actually teaches.

High up on the list of things which the Bible teaches

will be the doctrine of *faith*. The place of weighty importance which the Bible gives to faith will be too plain for him to miss. He will very likely conclude that faith is all-important in the life of the soul. 'Without faith it is impossible to please God' (Heb 11:6). Faith will get me anything, take me anywhere in the kingdom of God, but without faith there can be no approach to God, no forgiveness, no deliverance, no salvation, no communion, no spiritual life at all.

By the time our friend has reached the eleventh chapter of Hebrews the eloquent encomium which is there pronounced upon faith will not seem strange to him. He will have read Paul's powerful defence of faith in his Roman and Galatian epistles. Later, if he goes on to study church history, he will understand the amazing power in the teachings of the Reformers as they showed the central place of faith in the Christian religion.

Now if faith is so vitally important, if it is an indispensable *must* in our pursuit of God, it is perfectly natural that we should be deeply concerned over whether or not we possess this most precious gift. And our minds being what they are, it is inevitable that sooner or later we should get around to inquiring after the nature of faith. 'What *is* faith?' would lie close to the question, 'Do I *have* faith?' and would demand an answer if it were anywhere to be found.

Almost all who preach or write on the subject of faith have much the same things to say concerning it. They tell us that it is believing a promise, that it is taking God at His word, that it is reckoning the Bible to be true and stepping out upon it. The rest of the book or sermon is usually taken up with stories of persons who have had their prayers answered as a result of their faith. These answers are mostly direct gifts of a practical and temporal nature such as health, money, physical protection or success in business. Or if the teacher is of a philosophic turn of mind he may take another course and lose us in a welter of metaphysics or snow us under with psychological jargon as he defines and redefines, paring the slender hair of faith thinner and thinner till it disappears in gossamer shavings at last. When he is finished we get up disappointed and go out 'by that same door wherein we went'. Surely there must be something better than this.

In Scripture there is practically no effort made to define faith. Outside of a brief fourteen-word definition in Hebrews 11:1, I know of no biblical definition. Even there faith is defined functionally, not philosophically; that is, it is a statement of what faith is *in operation*, *not* what it is *in essence*. It assumes the presence of faith and shows what it results in, rather than what it is. We will be wise to go just that far and attempt to go no further. We are told from whence it comes and by what means: 'Faith is the gift of God' (Eph 2:8) and 'Faith cometh by hearing, and hearing by the word of God' (Rom 10:17). This much is clear, and, to paraphrase Thomas à Kempis, 'I had rather exercise faith than know the definition thereof.'

From here on, when the words 'faith is' or their equivalent occur in this chapter I ask that they be understood to refer to what faith is in operation as exercised by a believing man. Right here we drop the notion of definition and think about faith as it may be experienced in action. The complexion of our thoughts will be practical, not theoretical.

In a dramatic story in the book of Numbers (21:4–9) faith is seen in action. Israel became discouraged and spoke against God, and the Lord sent fiery serpents among them. 'And they bit the people; and much people of Israel died.' Then Moses sought the Lord for them and He heard and gave them a remedy against the bite of the serpents. He commanded Moses to make a serpent of brass and put it upon a pole in sight of all the people, 'and it shall come to pass, that every one that is bitten, when he looketh upon it, shall live.' Moses obeyed, 'and it came to pass, that if a serpent had bitten any man, when he beheld the serpent of brass, he lived.'

In the New Testament this important bit of history is interpreted for us by no less an authority than our Lord Jesus Christ Himself. He is explaining to His hearers how they may be saved. He tells them that it is by believing. Then to make it clear He refers to this incident in the book of Numbers. 'As Moses lifted up the serpent in the wilderness, even so must the Son of man be lifted up: that whosoever believeth in him should not perish, but have eternal life' (Jn 3:14–15).

Our plain man, in reading this, would make an important discovery. He would notice that *look* and *believe* are synonymous terms. 'Looking' on the Old Testament serpent is identical with 'believing' on the New Testament Christ. That is, the *looking* and the *believing* are the same thing. And he would understand that while Israel looked with their external eyes, believing is done with the heart. I think he would conclude that *faith is the gaze of a soul upon a saving God.*

When he had seen this he would remember passages

he had read before, and their meaning would come flooding over him. 'They looked unto him, and were lightened: and their faces were not ashamed' (Ps 34:5). 'Unto thee lift I up mine eyes, O thou that dwellest in the heavens. Behold, as the eyes of servants look unto the hand of their masters, and as the eyes of a maiden unto the hand of her mistress; so our eyes wait upon the Lord our God, until that he have mercy upon us' (Ps 123:1–2). Here the man seeking mercy looks straight at the God of mercy and never takes his eyes away from Him till He grants mercy. And our Lord Himself looked always at God. 'Looking up to heaven, he blessed, and brake, and gave the bread to his disciples' (Mt 14:19). Indeed, Jesus taught that He wrought His works by always keeping His inward eyes upon His Father. His power lay in His continuous look at God (Jn 5:19–21).

In full accord with the few texts we have quoted is the whole tenor of the inspired Word. It is summed up for us in the Hebrew epistle when we are instructed to run life's race 'looking unto Jesus the author and finisher of our faith' (Heb 12:2). From all this we learn that faith is not a once-done act, but a continuous gaze of the heart at the Triune God.

Believing, then, is directing the heart's attention to Jesus. It is lifting the mind to 'behold the Lamb of God', and never ceasing that beholding for the rest of our lives. At first this may be difficult, but it becomes easier as we look steadily at His wondrous person, quietly and without strain. Distractions may hinder, but once the heart is committed to Him, after each brief excursion away from Him, the attention will return again and rest upon Him like a wandering bird coming back to its window.

I would emphasise this one committal, this one great volitional act which establishes the heart's intention to gaze for ever upon Jesus. God takes this intention for our choice and makes what allowances He must for the thousand distractions which beset us in this evil world. He knows that we have set the direction of our hearts toward Jesus, and we can know it too, and comfort ourselves with the knowledge that a habit of soul is forming which will become, after a while, a sort of spiritual reflex requiring no more conscious effort on our part.

Faith is the least self-regarding of the virtues. It is by its very nature scarcely conscious of its own existence. Like the eye which sees everything in front of it and never sees itself, faith is occupied with the Object upon which it rests and pays no attention to itself at all. While we are looking at God we do not see ourselves—blessed riddance. The man who has struggled to purify himself and has had nothing but repeated failures will experience real relief when he stops tinkering with his soul and looks away to the perfect one. While he looks at Christ, the very things he has so long been trying to do will be getting done within him. It will be God working in him to will and to do.

Faith is not in itself a meritorious act; the merit is in the one toward whom it is directed. Faith is a redirecting of our sight, a getting out of the focus of our own vision and getting God into focus. Sin has twisted our vision inward and made it self-regarding. Unbelief has put self where God should be, and is perilously close to the sin of Lucifer who said, 'I will set my throne above the throne of God.' Faith looks *out* instead of *in* and the whole life falls into line.

All this may seem too simple. But we have no apology to make. To those who would seek to climb into heaven after help or descend into hell, God says, 'The word is nigh thee,...even the word of faith' (Rom 10:8). The Word induces us to lift up our eyes unto the Lord and the blessed work of faith begins.

When we lift our inward eyes to gaze upon God we are sure to meet friendly eyes gazing back at us, for it is written that the eyes of the Lord run to and fro throughout all the earth. The sweet language of experience is 'Thou God seest me.' When the eyes of the soul looking out meet the eyes of God looking in, heaven has begun right here on this earth.

Nicholas of Cusa wrote four hundred years ago:

'When all my endeavour is turned toward Thee because all Thy endeavour is turned toward me; when I look unto Thee alone with all my attention, nor ever turn aside the eyes of my mind, because Thou dost enfold me with Thy constant regard; when I direct my love toward Thee alone because Thou, who art Love's self hast turned Thee toward me alone. And what, Lord, is my life, save that embrace wherein Thy delightsome sweetness doth so lovingly enfold me?'[1]

I should like to say more about this old man of God. He is not much known today anywhere among Christian believers, and among current fundamentalists he is known not at all. I feel that we could gain much from a little acquaintance with men of his spiritual flavour and the school of Christian thought which they represent. Christian literature, to be accepted and approved by evangelical leaders of our times, must follow very closely the same train of thought, a kind of 'party line' from which it is scarcely safe to depart. A half-century of this in America has made us smug and content. We imitate each other with slavish devotion. Our most strenuous efforts are put forth to try to say the same thing that everyone around us is saying—and yet to find an excuse for saying it, some little safe variation on the approved theme or, if no more, at least a new illustration.

Nicholas was a true follower of Christ, a lover of the Lord, radiant and shining in his devotion to the person of Jesus. His theology was orthodox but fragrant and sweet as everything about Jesus might properly be expected to be. His conception of eternal life, for instance, is beautiful in itself and, if I mistake not, is nearer in spirit to John 17:3 than that which is current among us today. Life eternal, says Nicholas, is 'nought other than that blessed regard wherewith Thou never ceasest to behold me, yea, even the secret places of my soul. With Thee, to behold is to give life; 'tis unceasingly to impart sweetest love of Thee; 'tis to inflame me to love of Thee by love's imparting, and to feed me by inflaming, and by feeding to kindle my yearning, and by kindling to make me drink of the dew of gladness, and by drinking to infuse in me a fountain of life, and by infusing to make it increase and endure.'[2]

Now, if faith is the gaze of the heart at God, and if this gaze is but the raising of the inward eyes to meet the all-seeing eyes of God, then it follows that it is one of the easiest things possible to do. It would be like God to make the most vital thing easy and place it within the range of possibility for the weakest and poorest of us.

Several conclusions may fairly be drawn from all this.

The simplicity of it, for instance. Since believing is looking, it can be done without special equipment or religious paraphernalia. God has seen to it that the one life-and-death essential can never be subject to the caprice of accident. Equipment can break down or get lost, water can leak away, records can be destroyed by fire, the minister can be delayed or the church can burn down. All these are external to the soul and are subject to accident or mechanical failure. But looking is of the heart and can be done successfully by any man standing up or kneeling down or lying in his last agony a thousand miles from any church.

Since believing is looking it can be done any time. No season is superior to another season for this sweetest of all acts. God never made salvation depend upon new moons or holy days or sabbaths. A man is not nearer to Christ on Easter Sunday than he is, say, on Saturday 3rd August, or Monday 4th October. As long as Christ sits on the mediatorial throne, every day is a good day and all days are days of salvation.

Neither does *place* matter in this blessed work of believing God. Lift your heart and let it rest upon Jesus and you are instantly in a sanctuary though it be a Pullman berth or a factory or a kitchen. You can see God from anywhere if your mind is set to love and obey Him.

Now, someone may ask, 'Is not this of which you speak for special persons such as monks or ministers who have, by the nature of their calling, more time to devote to quiet meditation? I am a busy worker and have little time to spend alone.' I am happy to say that the life I describe is for every one of God's children regardless of calling. It is, in fact, happily practised every day by many hard-working persons and is beyond the reach of none.

Many have found the secret of which I speak and, without giving much thought to what is going on within them, constantly practise this habit of inwardly gazing upon God. They know that something inside their hearts sees God. Even when they are compelled to withdraw their conscious attention in order to engage in earthly affairs, there is within them a secret communion always going on. Let their attention but be released for a moment from necessary business and it flies at once to God again. This has been the testimony of many Christians, so many that even as I state it thus I have a feeling that I am quoting, though from whom or from how many I cannot possibly know.

I do not want to leave the impression that the ordinary means of grace have no value. They most assuredly have. Private prayer should be practised by every Christian. Long periods of Bible meditation will purify our gaze and direct it; church attendance will enlarge our outlook and increase our love for others. Service and work and activity—all are good and should be engaged in by every Christian. But at the bottom of all these things, giving meaning to them, will be the inward habit of beholding God. A new set of eyes (so to speak) will develop within us enabling us to be looking at God while our outward eyes are seeing the scenes of this passing world.

Someone may fear that we are magnifying private religion out of all proportion, that the 'us' of the New Testament is being displaced by a selfish 'I'. Has it ever occurred to you that one hundred pianos all tuned to the same fork are automatically tuned to each other? They are of one accord by being tuned, not to each other, but to another standard to which each one must individually bow. So one hundred worshippers meeting together, each one looking away to Christ, are in heart nearer to each other than they could possibly be were they to become 'unity' conscious and turn their eyes away from God to strive for closer fellowship. Social religion is perfected when private religion is purified. The body becomes stronger as its members become healthier. The whole church of God gains when the members that compose it begin to seek a better and a higher life.

All the foregoing presupposes true repentance and a full committal of the life to God. It is hardly necessary to mention this, for only persons who have made such a committal will have read this far.

When the habit of inwardly gazing Godward becomes fixed within us we shall be ushered onto a new level of spiritual life more in keeping with the promises of God and the mood of the New Testament. The Triune God will be our dwelling place even while our feet walk the low road of simple duty here among men. We will have found life's *summum bonum* indeed. 'There is the source of all delights that can be desired; not only can nought better be thought out by men and angels, but nought better can exist in any mode of being! For it is the absolute maximum of every rational desire, than which a greater cannot be.'[3]

O Lord, I have heard a good word inviting me to look away to Thee and be satisfied. My heart longs to respond, but sin has clouded my vision till I see Thee but dimly. Be pleased to cleanse me in Thine own precious blood, and make me inwardly pure, so that I may with unveiled eyes gaze upon Thee all the days of my earthly pilgrimage. Then shall I be prepared to behold Thee in full splendour in the day when Thou shalt appear to be glorified in Thy saints and admired in all them that believe. Amen.

Notes

1 Nicholas of Cusa, *The Vision of God*, E. P. Dutton & Co., Inc., New York, 1928. This and the following quotation used by kind permission of the publishers.
2 Ibid.
3 Ibid.

8

Restoring the
Creator-Creature Relation

Psalm 57:5 *Be thou exalted, O God, above the heavens;
let thy glory be above all the earth.*

It is true that order in nature depends upon right
relationships; to achieve harmony each thing must be in
its proper position relative to each other thing. In human
life it is not otherwise.

I have hinted before in these chapters that the cause of
all our human miseries is a radical moral dislocation, an
upset in our relation to God and to each other. For
whatever else the Fall may have been, it was certainly a
sharp change in man's relation to his Creator. He
adopted toward God an altered attitude, and by so doing
destroyed the proper Creator-creature relation in which,
unknown to him, his true happiness lay. Essentially,
salvation is the restoration of a right relation between
man and his Creator, a bringing back to normal of the
Creator-creature relation.

A satisfactory spiritual life will begin with a complete
change in relation between God and the sinner; not a
judicial change merely, but a conscious and experienced

change affecting the sinner's whole nature. The atonement in Jesus' blood makes such a change judicially possible and the working of the Holy Spirit makes it emotionally satisfying. The story of the prodigal son perfectly illustrates this latter phase. He had brought a world of trouble upon himself by forsaking the position which he had properly held as son of his father. At bottom of his restoration was nothing more than a re-establishing of the father-son relation which had existed from his birth and had been altered temporarily by his act of sinful rebellion. This story overlooks the legal aspects of redemption, but it makes beautifully clear the experiential aspects of salvation.

In determining relationships we must begin somewhere. There must be somewhere a fixed centre against which everything else is measured, where the law of relativity does not enter and we can say 'IS' and make no allowances. Such a centre is God. When God would make His name known to mankind He could find no better word that 'I AM'. When He speaks in the first person He says, 'I AM;' when we speak *of* Him we say, 'He is;' when we speak *to* Him we say, 'Thou art.' Everyone and everything else measures from that fixed point. 'I am that I am,' says God, 'I change not.'

As the sailor locates his position on the sea by 'shooting' the sun, so we may get our moral bearings by looking at God. We must begin with God. We are right when, and only when, we stand in a right position relative to God, and we are wrong so far and so long as we stand in any other position.

Much of our difficulty as seeking Christians stems from our unwillingness to take God as He is and adjust our lives accordingly. We insist upon trying to modify Him and to bring Him nearer to our own image. The flesh whimpers against the rigour of God's inexorable sentence and begs like Agag for a little mercy, a little indulgence of its carnal ways. It is no use. We can get a right start only by accepting God as He is and learning to love Him for what He is. As we go on to know Him better we shall find it a source of unspeakable joy that God is just what He is. Some of the most rapturous moments we know will be those we spend in reverent admiration of the Godhead. In those holy moments the very thought of change in Him will be too painful to endure.

So let us begin with God. Behind all, above all, before all is God; first in sequential order, above in rank and station, exalted in dignity and honour. As the self-existent one He gave beings to all things, and all things exist out of Him and for Him. 'Thou art worthy, O Lord, to receive glory and honour and power: for thou hast created all things, and for thy pleasure they are and were created' (Rev 4:11).

Every soul belongs to God and exists by His pleasure. God being who and what He is, and we being who and what we are, the only thinkable relation between us is one of full lordship on His part and complete submission on ours. We owe Him every honour that is in our power to give Him. Our everlasting grief lies in giving Him anything less.

The pursuit of God will embrace the labour of bringing our total personality into conformity to His. And this not judicially, but actually. I do not here refer to the act of justification by faith in Christ. I speak of a voluntary

93

exalting of God to His proper station over us and a willing surrender of our whole being to the place of worshipful submission which the Creator-creature circumstance makes proper.

The moment we make up our minds that we are going on with this determination to exalt God over all, we step out of the world's parade. We shall find ourselves out of adjustment to the ways of the world, and increasingly so as we make progress in the holy way. We shall acquire a new viewpoint; a new and different psychology will be formed within us; a new power will begin to surprise us by its upsurgings and its outgoings.

Our break with the world will be the direct outcome of our changed relation to God. For the world of fallen men does not honour God. Millions call themselves by His name, it is true, and pay some token respect to Him, but a simple test will show how little He is really honoured among them. Let the average man be put to the proof on the question of who or what is *above*, and his true position will be exposed. Let him be forced into making a choice betwen God and money, between God and men, between God and personal ambition, God and self, God and human love, and God will take second place every time. Those other things will be exalted above. However the man may protest, the proof is in the choices he makes day after day throughout his life.

'Be thou exalted' is the language of victorious spiritual experience. It is a little key to unlock the door to great treasures of grace. It is central in the life of God in the soul. Let the seeking man reach a place where life and lips join to say continually, 'Be thou exalted,' and a thousand minor problems will be solved at once. His

Christian life ceases to be the complicated thing it had been before and becomes the very essence of simplicity. By the exercise of his will he has set his course, and on that course he will stay as if guided by an automatic pilot. If blown off course for a moment by some adverse wind, he will surely return again as by a secret bent of the soul. The hidden motions of the Spirit are working in his favour, and 'the stars in their courses' fight for him. He has met his life problem at its centre, and everything else must follow along.

Let no one imagine that he will lose anything of human dignity by this voluntary sell-out of his all to his God. He does not by this degrade himself as a man; rather he finds his right place of high honour as one made in the image of his Creator. His deep disgrace lay in his moral derangement, his unnatural usurpation of the place of God. His honour will be proved by restoring again that stolen throne. In exalting God over all he finds his own highest honour upheld.

Anyone who might feel reluctant to surrender his will to the will of another should remember Jesus' words, 'Whosoever committeth sin is the servant of sin' (Jn 8:34). We must of necessity be servant to someone, either to God or to sin. The sinner prides himself on his independence, completely overlooking the fact that he is the weak slave of the sins that rule his members. The man who surrenders to Christ exchanges a cruel slave driver for a kind and gentle Master whose yoke is easy and whose burden is light.

Made as we were in the image of God we scarcely find it strange to take again our God as our all. God was our original habitat and our hearts cannot but feel at home when they enter again that ancient and beautiful abode.

I hope it is clear that there is a logic behind God's claim to preeminence. That place is His by every right in earth or heaven. While we take to ourselves the place that is His the whole course of our lives is out of joint. Nothing will or can restore order till our hearts make the great decision: God shall be exalted above.

'Them that honour me I will honour,' said God once to a priest of Israel, and that ancient law of the kingdom stands today unchanged by the passing of time or the changes of dispensation. The whole Bible and every page of history proclaim the perpetuation of that law. 'If any man serve me, him will my Father honour,' said our Lord Jesus, tying in the old with the new and revealing the essential unity of His ways with men.

Sometimes the best way to see a thing is to look at its opposite. Eli and his sons are placed in the priesthood with the stipulation that they honour God in their lives and ministrations. This they fail to do, and God sends Samuel to announce the consequences. Unknown to Eli this law of reciprocal honour has been all the while secretly working, and now the time has come for judgement to fall. Hophni and Phineas, the degenerate priests, fall in battle; the wife of Hophni dies in childbirth; Israel flees before her enemies; the ark of God is captured by the Philistines, and the old man Eli falls backward and dies of a broken neck. Thus stark, utter tragedy followed upon Eli's failure to honour God.

Now over against this set almost any Bible character who honestly tried to glorify God in his earthly walk. See how God winked at weakness and overlooked failures as He poured upon His servants grace and blessing untold.

Let it be Abraham, Jacob, David, Daniel, Elijah or whom you will; honour followed honour as harvest the seed. The man of God set his heart to exalt God above all; God accepted his intention as fact and acted accordingly. Not perfection, but holy intention made the difference.

In our Lord Jesus Christ this law was seen in simple perfection. In His lowly manhood He humbled Himself and gladly gave all glory to His Father in heaven. He sought not His own honour, but the honour of God who sent Him. 'If I honour myself,' He said on one occasion, 'my honour is nothing; it is my Father that honoureth me' (Jn 8:54). So far had the proud Pharisees departed from this law that they could not understand one who honoured God at his own expense. 'I honour my Father,' said Jesus to them, 'and ye do dishonour me' (Jn 8:49).

Another saying of Jesus, and a most disturbing one, was put in the form of a question, 'How can ye believe, which receive honour one of another, and seek not the honour that cometh from God only?' (Jn 5:44). If I understand this correctly, Christ taught here the alarming doctrine that the desire for honour among men made belief impossible. Is this sin at the root of religious unbelief? Could it be that those 'intellectual difficulties' which men blame for their inability to believe are but smoke screens to conceal the real cause that lies behind them? Was it this greedy desire for honour from man that made men into Pharisees and Pharisees into deicides? Is this the secret behind religious self-righteousness and empty worship? I believe it may be. The whole course of the life is upset by failure to put

God where He belongs. We exalt ourselves instead of God and the curse follows.

In our desire after God let us keep always in mind that God also has desire, and His desire is toward the sons of men, and more particularly toward those sons of men who will make the once-for-all decision to exalt Him over all. Such as these are precious to God above all treasures of earth or sea. In them God finds a theatre where He can display His exceeding kindess toward us in Christ Jesus. With them God can walk unhindered; toward them He can act like the God He is.

In speaking thus I have one fear: that I may convince the mind before God can win the heart. For this God-above-all position is one not easy to take. The mind may approve it while not having the consent of the will to put it into effect. While the imagination races ahead to honour God, the will may lag behind and the man never guess how divided his heart is. The whole man must make the decision before the heart can know any real satisfaction. God wants the whole person, and He will not rest till He gets us in entirety. No part of the man will do.

Let us pray over this in detail, throwing ourselves at God's feet and meaning everything we say. No one who prays thus in sincerity need wait long for tokens of divine acceptance. God will unveil His glory before His servant's eyes, and He will place all His treasures at the disposal of such a one, for He knows that His honour is safe in such consecrated hands.

O God, be Thou exalted over my possessions. Nothing of earth's treasures shall seem dear unto me if only Thou art glorified in my life. *Be Thou exalted over my friendships. I am determined that Thou shalt be above all, though I must stand deserted and alone in the midst of the earth. Be Thou exalted above my comforts. Though it mean the loss of bodily comforts and the carrying of heavy crosses, I shall keep my vow made this day before Thee. Be Thou exalted over my reputation. Make me ambitious to please Thee even if as a result I must sink into obscurity and my name be forgotten as a dream. Rise, O Lord, into Thy proper place of honour, above my ambitions, above my likes and dislikes, above my family, my health and even my life itself. Let me decrease that Thou mayest increase; let me sink that Thou mayest rise above. Ride forth upon me as Thou didst ride into Jerusalem mounted upon the humble little beast, a colt, the foal of an ass, and let me hear the children cry to Thee, 'Hosanna in the highest.'*

9

Meekness and Rest

Matthew 5:5   *Blessed are the meek: for they shall inherit the earth.*

A fairly accurate description of the human race might be furnished to one unacquainted with it by taking the Beatitudes, turning them wrong side out and saying, 'Here is your human race.' For the exact opposite of the virtues in the Beatitudes are the very qualities which distinguish human life and conduct.

In the world of men we find nothing approaching the virtues of which Jesus spoke in the opening words of the famous Sermon on the Mount. Instead of poverty of spirit we find the rankest kind of pride; instead of mourners we find pleasure-seekers; instead of meekness, arrogance; instead of hunger after righteousness we hear men saying, 'I am rich and increased with goods and have need of nothing'; instead of mercy we find cruelty; instead of purity of heart, corrupt imaginings; instead of peacemakers we find men quarrelsome and resentful; instead of rejoicing in mistreatment we find them fighting back with every weapon at their command.

Of this kind of moral stuff civilised society is composed. The atmosphere is charged with it; we breathe it with every breath, and drink it with our mother's milk. Culture and education refine these things slightly but leave them basically untouched. A whole world of literature has been created to justify this kind of life as the only normal one. And this is the more to be wondered at seeing that these are the evils which make life the bitter struggle it is for all of us. All our heartaches and a great many of our physical ills spring directly out of our sins. Pride, arrogance, resentfulness, evil imaginings, malice, greed are the sources of more human pain than all the diseases that ever afflicted mortal flesh.

Into a world like this the sound of Jesus' words comes wonderful and strange, a visitation from above. It is well that He spoke, for no one else could have done it as well; and it is good that we listen. His words are the essence of truth. He is not offering an opinion; Jesus never uttered opinions. He never guessed; He knew, and He knows. His words are not as Solomon's were, the sum of sound wisdom or the results of keen observation. He spoke out of the fullness of His Godhead, and His words are very truth itself. He is the only one who could say 'blessed' with complete authority, for He is the Blessed One come from the world above to confer blessedness upon mankind. And His words were supported by deeds mightier than any performed on this earth by any other man. It is wisdom for us to listen.

As was often so with Jesus, He used this word *meek* in a brief crisp sentence, and not till sometime later did He go on to explain it. In the same book of Matthew He tells us more about it and applies it to our lives. 'Come unto

me, all ye that labour and are heavy laden, and I will give
you rest. Take my yoke upon you, and learn of me; for I
am meek and lowly in heart: and ye shall find rest unto
your souls. For my yoke is easy, and my burden is light'
(Mt 11:28–30). Here we have two things standing in
contrast to each other, a burden and a rest. The burden
is not a local one, peculiar to those first hearers, but one
which is borne by the whole human race. It consists not
of political oppression or poverty or hard work. It is far
deeper than that. It is felt by the rich as well as the poor,
for it is something from which wealth and idleness can
never deliver us.

The burden borne by mankind is a heavy and a crushing
thing. The word Jesus used means 'a load carried or toil
borne to the point of exhaustion.' Rest is simply release
from that burden. It is not something we do; it is what
comes to us when we cease to do. His own meekness,
that is the rest.

Let us examine our burden. It is altogether an interior
one. It attacks the heart and the mind and reaches the
body only from within. First, there is the burden of
pride. The labour of self-love is a heavy one indeed.
Think for yourself whether much of your sorrow has not
arisen from someone speaking slightingly of you. As
long as you set yourself up as a little god to which you
must be loyal there will be those who will delight to offer
affront to your idol. How then can you hope to have
inward peace? The heart's fierce effort to protect itself
from every slight, to shield its touchy honour from the
bad opinion of friend and enemy, will never let the mind
have rest. Continue this fight through the years and the
burden will become intolerable. Yet the sons of earth

are carrying this burden continually, challenging every word spoken against them, cringing under every criticism, smarting under each fancied slight, tossing sleeplessly if another is preferred before them.

Such a burden as this is not necessary to bear. Jesus calls us to His rest, and meekness is His method. The meek man cares not at all who is greater than he, for he has long ago decided that the esteem of the world is not worth the effort. He develops toward himself a kindly sense of humour and learns to say, 'Oh, so you have been overlooked? They have placed someone else before you? They have whispered that you are pretty small stuff after all? And now you feel hurt because the world is saying about you the very things you have been saying about yourself? Only yesterday you were telling God that you were nothing, a mere worm of the dust. Where is your consistency? Come on, humble yourself, and cease to care what men think.'

The meek man is not a human mouse afflicted with a sense of his own inferiority. Rather, he may be in his moral life as bold as a lion and as strong as Samson; but he has stopped being fooled about himself. He has accepted God's estimate of his own life. He knows he is as weak and helpless as God has declared him to be, but paradoxically, he knows at the same time that he is, in the sight of God, more important than angels. In himself, nothing; in God, everything. That is his motto. He knows well that the world will never see him as God sees him and he has stopped caring. He rests perfectly content to allow God to place His own values. He will be patient to wait for the day when everything will get its own price tag and real worth will come into its own.

Then the righteous shall shine forth in the kingdom of their Father. He is willing to wait for that day.

In the meantime, he will have attained a place of soul rest. As he walks on in meekness he will be happy to let God defend him. The old struggle to defend himself is over. He has found the peace which meekness brings.

Then also he will get deliverance from the burden of *pretence*. By this I mean not hypocrisy, but the common human desire to put the best foot forward and hide from the world our real inward poverty. For sin has played many evil tricks upon us, and one has been the infusing into us of a false sense of shame. There is hardly a man or woman who dares to be just what he or she is without doctoring up the impression. The fear of being found out gnaws like rodents within their hearts. The man of culture is haunted by the fear that he will someday come upon a man more cultured than himself. The learned man fears to meet a man more learned than he. The rich man sweats under the fear that his clothes or his car or his house will sometime be made to look cheap by comparison with those of another rich man. So-called 'society' runs by a motivation not higher than this, and the poorer classes on their level are little better.

Let no one smile this off. These burdens are real, and little by little they kill the victims of this evil and unnatural way of life. And the psychology created by years of this kind of thing makes true meekness seem as unreal as a dream, as aloof as a star. To all the victims of the gnawing disease Jesus says, 'Ye must become as little children.' For little children do not compare; they receive direct enjoyment from what they have without relating it to something else or someone else. Only as

105

they get older and sin begins to stir within their hearts do jealousy and envy appear. Then they are unable to enjoy what they have if someone else has something larger or better. At that early age does the galling burden come down upon their tender souls, and it never leaves them till Jesus sets them free.

Another source of burden is *artificiality*. I am sure that most people live in secret fear that some day they will be careless and by chance an enemy or friend will be allowed to peep into their poor, empty souls. So they are never relaxed. Bright people are tense and alert in fear that they may be trapped into saying something common or stupid. Travelled people are afraid that they may meet some Marco Polo who is able to describe some remote place where they have never been.

This unnatural condition is part of our sad heritage of sin, but in our day it is aggravated by our whole way of life. Advertising is largely based upon this habit of pretence. 'Courses' are offered in this or that field of human learning frankly appealing to the victim's desire to shine at a party. Books are sold, clothes and cosmetics are peddled by playing continually upon this desire to appear what we are not. Artificiality is one curse that will drop away the moment we kneel at Jesus' feet and surrender ourselves to His meekness. Then we will not care what people think of us so long as God is pleased. Then *what we are* will be everything; what we appear will take its place far down the scale of interest for us. Apart from sin we have nothing of which to be ashamed. Only an evil desire to shine makes us want to appear other than we are.

The heart of the world is breaking under this load of

pride and pretence. There is no release from our burden apart from the meekness of Christ. Good, keen reasoning may help slightly, but so strong is this vice that if we push it down one place, it will come up somewhere else. To men and women everywhere Jesus says, 'Come unto me, and I will give you rest.' The rest He offers is the rest of meekness, the blessed relief which comes when we accept ourselves for what we are and cease to pretend. It will take some courage at first, but the needed grace will come as we learn that we are sharing this new and easy yoke with the strong Son of God Himself. He calls it 'my yoke', and He walks at one end while we walk at the other.

Lord, make me childlike. Deliver me from the urge to compete with another for place or prestige or position. I would be simple and artless as a little child. Deliver me from pose and pretence. Forgive me for thinking of myself. Help me to forget myself and find my true peace in beholding Thee. That Thou mayest answer this prayer I humble myself before Thee. Lay upon me Thy easy yoke of self-forgetfulness that through it I may find rest. Amen.

10

The Sacrament of Living

1 Corinthians 10:31 *Whether therefore ye eat, or drink, or whatsoever ye do, do all to the glory of God.*

One of the greatest hindrances to internal peace which the Christian encounters is the common habit of dividing our lives into two areas—the sacred and the secular. As these areas are conceived to exist apart from each other and to be morally and spiritually incompatible, and as we are compelled by the necessities of living to be always crossing back and forth from the one to the other, our inner lives tend to break up so that we live a divided instead of a unified life.

Our trouble springs from the fact that we who follow Christ inhabit at once two worlds—the spiritual and the natural. As children of Adam we live our lives on earth subject to the limitations of the flesh and the weaknesses and ills to which human nature is heir. Merely to live among men requires of us years of hard toil and much care and attention to the things of this world. In sharp contrast to this is our life in the Spirit. There we enjoy another and higher kind of life—we are children of God;

we possess heavenly status and enjoy intimate fellowship with Christ.

This tends to divide our total life into two departments. We come unconsciously to recognise two sets of actions. The first are performed with a feeling of satisfaction and a firm assurance that they are pleasing to God. These are the sacred acts and they are usually thought to be prayer, Bible reading, hymn singing, church attendance and such other acts as spring directly from faith. They may be known by the fact that they have no direct relation to this world, and would have no meaning whatever except as faith shows us another world, 'an house not made with hands, eternal in the heavens' (2 Cor 5:1).

Over against these sacred acts are the secular ones. They include all of the ordinary activities of life which we share with the sons and daughters of Adam: eating, sleeping, working, looking after the needs of the body and performing our dull and prosaic duties here on earth. These we often do reluctantly and with many misgivings, often apologising to God for what we consider a waste of time and strength. The upshot of this is that we are uneasy most of the time. We go about our common tasks with a feeling of deep frustration, telling ourselves pensively that there's a better day coming when we shall slough off this earthly shell and be bothered no more with the affairs of this world.

This the old sacred–secular antithesis. Most Christians are caught in its trap. They cannot get a satisfactory adjustment between the claims of the two worlds. They try to walk the tightrope between two kingdoms and they find no peace in either. Their strength is reduced, their outlook confused and their joy taken from them.

I believe this state of affairs to be wholly unnecessary. We have got ourselves on the horns of a dilemma, true enough, but the dilemma is not real. It is a creature of misunderstanding. The sacred–secular antithesis has no foundation in the New Testament. Without doubt, a more perfect understanding of Christian truth will deliver us from it.

The Lord Jesus Christ Himself is our perfect example, and He knew no divided life. In the presence of His Father He lived on earth without strain from babyhood to His death on the cross. God accepted the offering of His total life, and made no distinction between act and act. 'I do always the things that please him,' was His brief summary of His own life as it related to the Father (Jn 8:29). As He moved among men He was poised and restful. What pressure and suffering He endured grew out of His position as the world's sin-bearer; they were never the result of moral uncertainty or spiritual maladjustment.

Paul's exhortation to 'do all to the glory of God' is more than pious idealism. It is an integral part of the sacred revelation and is to be accepted as the very word of truth. It opens before us the possibility of making every act of our lives contribute to the glory of God. Lest we should be too timid to include everything, Paul mentions specifically eating and drinking. This humble privilege we share with the beasts that perish. If these lowly animal acts can be so performed as to honour God, then it becomes difficult to conceive of one that cannot.

That monkish hatred of the body which figures so prominently in the works of certain early devotional writers is wholly without support in the Word of God. Common modesty is found in the sacred Scriptures, it is true, but never prudery or a false sense of shame. The New Testament accepts as a matter of course that in His incarnation our Lord took upon Him a real human body, and no effort is made to steer around the downright implications of such a fact. He lived in that body here among men and never once performed a non-sacred act. His presence in human flesh sweeps away for ever the evil notion that there is about the human body something innately offensive to the Deity. God created our bodies, and we do not offend Him by placing the responsibility where it belongs. He is not ashamed of the work of His own hands.

Perversion, misuse and abuse of our human powers should give us cause enough to be ashamed. Bodily acts done in sin and contrary to nature can never honour God. Wherever the human will introduces moral evil we have no longer our innocent and harmless powers as God made them; we have instead an abused and twisted thing which can never bring glory to its Creator.

Let us, however, assume that perversion and abuse are not present. Let us think of a Christian believer in whose life the twin wonders of repentance and the new birth have been wrought. He is now living according to the will of God as he understands it from the written Word. Of such a one it may be said that every act of his life is or can be as truly sacred as prayer or baptism or the Lord's Supper. To say this is not to bring all acts down to one dead level; it is rather to lift every act up into a living kingdom and turn the whole life into a sacrament.

If a sacrament is an external expression of an inward

grace, then we need not hesitate to accept the above thesis. By one act of consecration of our total selves to God we can make every subsequent act express that consecration. We need no more be ashamed of our body—the fleshly servant that carries us through life— than Jesus was of the humble beast upon which He rode into Jerusalem. 'The Lord hath need of him' may well apply to our mortal bodies. If Christ dwells in us, we may bear about the Lord of glory as the little beast did of old and give occasion to the multitudes to cry, 'Hosanna in the highest.'

That we *see* this truth is not enough. If we would escape from the toils of the sacred–secular dilemma, the truth must 'run in our blood' and condition the complexion of our thoughts. We must practice living to the glory of God, actually and determinedly. By meditation upon this truth, by talking it over with God often in our prayers, by recalling it to our minds frequently as we move about among men, a sense of its wondrous meaning will take hold of us. The old painful duality will go down before a restful unity of life. The knowledge that we are all God's, that He has received all and rejected nothing, will unify our inner lives and make everything sacred to us.

This is not quite all. Long-held habits do not die easily. It will take intelligent thought and a great deal of reverent prayer to escape completely from the sacred– secular psychology. For instance, it may be difficult for the average Christian to get hold of the idea that his daily labours can be performed as acts of worship acceptable to God by Jesus Christ. The old antithesis will crop up in the back of his head sometimes to disturb his peace of mind. Nor will that old serpent, the devil, take all this lying down. He wll be there in the cab or at the desk or in the field to remind the Christian that he is giving the better part of his day to the things of this world and allotting to his religious duties only a trifling portion of his time. And unless great care is taken, this will create confusion and bring discouragement and heaviness of heart.

We can meet this successfully only by the exercise of an aggressive faith. We must offer all our acts to God and believe that He accepts them. Then hold firmly to that position and keep insisting that every act of every hour of the day and night be included in the transaction. Keep reminding God in our times of private prayer that we mean every act for His glory; then supplement those times by a thousand thought-prayers as we go about the job of living. Let us practice the fine art of making every work a priestly ministration. Let us believe that God is in all our simple deeds and learn to find Him there.

A concomitant of the error which we have been discussing is the sacred–secular antithesis as applied to places. It is little short of astonishing that we can read the New Testament and still believe in the inherent sacredness of some places as distinguished from other places. This error is so widespread that one feels all alone when he tries to combat it. It has acted as a kind of dye to colour the thinking of religious persons and has coloured the eyes as well so that it is all but impossible to detect its fallacy. In the face of every New Testament teaching to the contrary, it has been said and sung throughout the centuries and accepted as a part of the Christian message, the which it most surely is not. Only the

Quakers, so far as my knowledge goes, have had the perception to see the error and the courage to expose it.

Here are the facts as I see them. For four hundred years Israel had dwelt in Egypt, surrounded by the crassest idolatry. By the hand of Moses they were brought out at last and started toward the land of promise. The very idea of holiness had been lost to them. To correct this, God began at the bottom. He localised Himself in the cloud and fire, and later when the tabernacle had been built He dwelt in fiery manifestation in the Holy of Holies. By innumerable distinctions God taught Israel the difference between holy and unholy. There were holy days, holy vessels, holy garments. There were washings, sacrifices, offerings of many kinds. By these means, Israel learned that *God is holy*. It was this that He was teaching them, not the holiness of things or places. The holiness of Jehovah was the lesson they must learn.

Then came the great day when Christ appeared. Immediately He began to say, 'Ye have heard that it was said of them of old time—but I say unto you' (Mt 5:21–22). The Old Testament schooling was over. When Christ died on the cross the veil of the temple was rent from top to bottom. The Holy of Holies was opened to everyone who would enter in faith. Christ's words were remembered, 'The hour cometh, when ye shall neither in this mountain, nor yet at Jerusalem, worship the Father.... But the hour cometh, and now is, when the true worshippers shall worship the Father in spirit and in truth: for the Father seeketh such to worship him. God is a Spirit: and they that worship him must worship him in spirit and in truth' (Jn 4:21, 23).

Shortly after, Paul took up the cry of liberty and declared all meats clean, every day holy, all places sacred and every act acceptable to God. The sacredness of times and places, a half-light necessary to the education of the race, passed away before the full sun of spiritual worship.

The essential spirituality of worship remained the possession of the church until it was slowly lost with the passing of the years. Then the natural *legality* of the fallen hearts of men began to introduce the old distinctions. The church came to observe again days and seasons and times. Certain places were chosen and marked out as holy in a special sense. Differences were observed between one and another day or place or person. 'The sacraments' were first two, then three, then four, until with the triumph of Romanism they were fixed at seven.

In all charity, and with no desire to reflect unkindly upon any Christian, however misled, I would point out that the Roman Catholic church represents today the sacred–secular heresy carried to its logical conclusion. Its deadliest effect is the complete cleavage it introduces between religion and life. Its teachers attempt to avoid this snare by many footnotes and multitudinous explanations, but the mind's instinct for logic is too strong. In practical living the cleavage is a fact.

From this bondage reformers and puritans and mystics have laboured to free us. Today, the trend in conservative circles is back toward that bondage again. It is said that a horse, after it has been led out of a burning building, will sometimes, by a strange obstinacy, break loose from its rescuer and dash back into the building again to perish in the flame. By some such stubborn tendency toward error, fundamentalism in our day is moving back toward spiritual slavery. The observation of days and times is becoming more and more prominent among us. 'Lent' and 'holy week' and 'good' Friday are words heard more and more frequently upon the lips of gospel Christians. We do not know when we are well off.

In order that I may be understood and not be misunderstood I would throw into relief the practical implications of the teaching for which I have been arguing, i.e., the sacramental quality of everyday living. Over against its positive meanings, I should like to point out a few things it does not mean.

It does not mean, for instance, that everything we do is of equal importance with everything else we do or may do. One act of a good man's life may differ widely from another in importance. Paul's sewing of tents was not equal to his writing of an Epistle to the Romans, but both were accepted of God and both were true acts of worship. Certainly it is more important to lead a soul to Christ than to plant a garden, but the planting of the garden *can* be as holy an act as the winning of a soul.

Again, it does not mean that every man is as useful as every other man. Gifts differ in the body of Christ. A Billy Bray is not to be compared with a Luther or a Wesley for sheer usefulness to the church and to the world; but the service of the less gifted brother is as pure as that of the more gifted, and God accepts both with equal pleasure.

The 'layman' need never think of his humbler task as being inferior to that of his minister. Let every man abide in the calling wherein he is called and his work will be as sacred as the work of the ministry. It is not what a man does that determines whether his work is sacred or secular, it is why he does it. The motive is everything. Let a man sanctify the Lord God in his heart and he can thereafter do no common act. All he does is good and acceptable to God through Jesus Christ. For such a man, living itself will be sacramental and the whole world a sanctuary. His entire life will be a priestly ministration. As he performs his never-so-simple task, he will hear the voice of the seraphim saying, 'Holy, Holy, Holy, is the Lord of hosts: the whole earth is full of his glory.'

Lord, I would trust Thee completely; I would be altogether Thine; I would exalt Thee above all. I desire that I may feel no sense of possessing anything outside of Thee. I want constantly to be aware of Thine overshadowing presence and to hear Thy speaking voice. I long to live in restful sincerity of heart. I want to live so fully in the Spirit that all my thoughts may be as sweet incense ascending to Thee and every act of my life may be an act of worship. Therefore I pray in the words of Thy great servant of old, 'I beseech Thee so for to cleanse the intent of mine heart with the unspeakable gift of Thy grace, that I may perfectly love Thee and worthily praise Thee.' And all this I confidently believe Thou wilt grant me through the merits of Jesus Christ Thy Son. Amen.

I TALK BACK TO THE DEVIL

A. W. TOZER

OM
publishing

Copyright © Christian Publications

First published in the USA by Christian Publications,
3825 Hartzdale Drive, Camp Hill, PA 17011

This edition 1994
Reprinted 1996

Unless otherwise stated, Scripture quotations in this
publication are from the Holy Bible, New International Version.
Copyright © 1973, 1978, 1984 International Bible Society.
Published by Zondervan and Hodder and Stoughton.

British Library Cataloguing-in-Publication Data
A Catalogue record for this book
is available from the British Library

ISBN 1-85078-148-6

OM Publishing is an imprint of Paternoster Publishing,
PO Box 300, Carlisle, Cumbria, CA3 0QS, U.K.

Printed in the U.K. by
Cox & Wyman Ltd., Reading, Berkshire

CONTENTS

IN HIS LIFETIME, DR. A. W. TOZER was quick to admit that he could take no delight in preaching on spiritual perfection themes, because of the reality of meeting Satan's opposition head-on.

When preaching the 12 sermons which are published here, Pastor Tozer told his Chicago congregation:

"I have never given more time and more pain and more prayer to any other series of sermons in my ministry.

"Because of their importance, I have literally felt Satan attempting to thwart the purpose of God. I have felt I was in raw contact with hell.

"There are so many in the Church who are spiritually blind that I tell God that I want to be able to see—I want to be a lower-case 'seer.' I want to penetrate and understand and have discernment concerning the whole plan of God. I want to appraise the situation and see it as God sees it—to know the role of God in this day of religious confusion.

"Now, that doesn't make a man easy to live with. It doesn't make him popular and it doesn't create any problem for police taking care of the crowd.

"This course has forced me frequently to follow the trail of opposition and temptation straight to the foe! But I would rather have it this way than to have to admit—as some will have to admit—to having spent a lifetime preaching the Word of God

1

and yet never having met the devil once in open combat!

"In my preparation, there have been struggles and combat, moans and pains. I think this is the conflict of Jesus being re-lived in His people. And some of you have felt it, too. Some of you have come out into a newer, more blessed and happier experience in God, which is only beginning for you!

"I have received mail concerning these sermons. The courageous ones signed. The cowards wrote without signing their names. Their suggestion seems to be that I am a 'show-off' to preach about perfection, and that I am trying to get a reputation for being 'saintly.'

"But, I will tell you something—it is a delightful thing when you know that you are close enough to the adversary that you can hear him roar! Too many Christians never get into 'lion country' at all!"

Most of you who will now go on to read Dr. Tozer's straight-forward appeals for Christ-like living did not hear the sermons as they were preached. So, it is our hope—as it was Dr. Tozer's for his hearers—that you will resist the temptations to become a "run-of-the-mill" Christian and that you will press on into blessed victory in "lion country"!

I Talk Back to the Devil!

"The devil makes it his business to keep Christians in bondage, bound and gagged, actually imprisoned in their own grave clothes!"

WHY DOESN'T THE OLD DEVIL, SATAN, give up and bow out of the picture when a person becomes a believing Christian?

Although he is a dark and sinister foe dedicated to the damnation of humans, I think he knows that it is no use trying to damn a forgiven and justified child of God who is in the Lord's hands.

So, it becomes the devil's business to keep the Christian's spirit imprisoned. He knows that the believing and justified Christian has been raised up out of the grave of his sins and trespasses. From that point on, Satan works that much harder to keep us bound and gagged, actually imprisoned in our own grave clothes.

He knows that if we continue in this kind of bondage, we will never be able to claim our rightful spiritual heritage. He knows also that while we continue bound in this kind of enslavement we are not much better off than when we were spiritually dead.

This is one reason why the Christians in today's churches are behaving like a flock of frightened sheep—so intimidated by the devil that we can't even say "Amen"!

I admit that occasionally you find a few who are just childishly happy about everything, but that is not what I mean. Often these are just like children playing in the market places, having never been seriously engaged in the conflict on the spiritual battlefield.

Show me an individual or a congregation committed to spiritual progress with the Lord, interested in what the Bible teaches about spiritual perfection and victory, and I will show you where there is strong and immediate defiance by the devil!

Satan loves to intimidate

Satan has been in this business of intimidating and silencing and oppressing the people of God for a long, long time.

The armies of Israel experienced this kind of fright in the valley of Elah when Goliath and the Philistines were camped on the opposite mountain. King Saul was leading Israel, but he was sour, fearful, intimidated because of Goliath, that giant of a man who daily shouted his taunts, "This day I defy the ranks of Israel!" (1 Samuel 17:10). So the army cowered in fear.

But a little fellow by the name of David came along, and he was in right fellowship with the Lord. We are told that the spirit of the Lord came upon David, who said to the Israelites, "Let no one lose heart on account of this Philistine; your servant will go and fight with him!" (1 Samuel 17:32).

This was the first word of encouragement to come to these ranks of soldiers who had been able only to gaze in fascinated fear at that great giant who taunted them daily. David was confident and serene because he knew and trusted the Source of all strength. The recorded result was one of the great, miraculous "turn-arounds" of history, David and his sling disposing of Goliath in a way that brought glory to the God of Israel as well as victory to the armies of Israel.

I am sure that it is not glorifying to our God that Christians should be so intimidated and silenced in our day. It was Jesus Christ, the Lord of glory, who came down and took our human body for Himself. He was a man, born of a woman, a man wearing our own nature—but He was also God!

He went to the cross and they sacrificed Him there. The Father, God Almighty, accepted His sacrifice as the one, last, final fulfillment and consumation of all the sacrifices ever made on Jewish altars. After He had been dead three days, He came forth—raised from the dead and out of the grave. After a few days He ascended as Victor over all the forces of death and hell and sat down amid the acclamations of the heavenly hosts!

There He sits at God's right hand—a living man, our representative and advocate and great high priest. Believing this, we ought to be the most fearless, the most relaxed, the happiest and most God-assured people in the whole world!

But Satan is an old dragon who defies us to this hour. He is saying to Christians, "I defy you—what can you do about it?"

We must get free!

I think we had better get free! We must face up to

the issues and attitudes and doubts which constitute our fears, that keep us from being happy and
victorious Christians with the true liberty of the
children of God. We seem to quake about many
things.

In the first place, are you still afraid of your past
sins? God knows that sin is a terrible thing—and
the devil knows it, too. So he follows us around
and as long as we will permit it, he will taunt us
about our past sins.

As for myself, I have learned to talk back to him
on this score. I say, "Yes, Devil, sin is terrible—but I
remind you that I got it from you! And I remind
you, Devil, that everything good—forgiveness and
cleansing and blessing—everything that is good I
have freely received from Jesus Christ!"

Everything that is bad and that is against me I got
from the devil—so why should he have the effron-
tery and the brass to argue with me about it? Yet he
will do it because he is the devil, and he is committed to keeping God's children shut up in a little
cage, their wings clipped so that they can never fly!

In our churches we often sing, "Arise, my soul,
arise; shake off thy guilty fears." But nothing happens and we keep our fears. Why do we claim on
one hand that our sins are gone and on the other
act just as though they are not gone?

Brethren, we have been declared "Not Guilty!"
by the highest court in all the universe. Still there
are honest Christians, earnestly seeking the face of
God, who cannot seem to break loose and find real
freedom. The grave clothes trip them up every time
they try to move on a little faster. Satan uses their
past sins to terrify them.

Now, on the basis of grace as taught in the Word of God, when God forgives a man, He trusts him as though he had never sinned. God did not have mental reservations about any of us when we became His children by faith. When God forgives a man, He doesn't think, "I will have to watch this fellow because he has a bad record." No, He starts with him again as though he had just been created and as if there had been no past at all! That is the basis of our Christian assurance—and God wants us to be happy in it.

Satan magnifies memories

Next, are you allowing Satan to magnify the memories of your spiritual failures? He will always keep them before you unless you take your stand and move up in faith.

The devil will whisper, "You didn't get very far along toward the deeper life, did you?"

He will say, "You made a big 'to-do' about wanting to be filled with the Spirit and you really flopped, didn't you?"

He will taunt you with the fact that you may have stumbled in the faith—and perhaps more than once! The devil wants you to live in a state of discouraged chagrin and remorse.

Remember, the Bible does not teach that if a man falls down, he can never rise again. The fact that he falls is not the most important thing—but rather that he is forgiven and allows God to lift him up!

Perhaps you have read of the saintly Fletcher, whose holy life became so recognized that he was called "the seraphic Fletcher." His testimony reveals that he stumbled and miserably failed God seven times. But after the seventh failure he went to a room and did not come out until he was able to rest his case completely in the strength of God's hands. He came out of the room saying, "Dear Lord, I believe that I am delivered from the bondage of my sin. If you will keep me and help me I will never cease telling the world what you can do for a man!" For the rest of his life Fletcher exhibited to the world God's power to bless and to keep His transformed children on earth.

If our failures are going to hinder us forever, we might just as well never have taken the first step. But God knew all about us and He still loved us and desired His eternal best for us.

God knows humans

The Bible tells us often that God knows humans better than they know themselves—He doesn't have to wait for the information to come from the accuser, the devil. God has said,

> Well do I know how treacherous you are;
>   you were called a rebel from birth.
> For my own name's sake I delay my wrath;
>   for the sake of my praise I hold it back from
>   you,
>   so as not to cut you off.
> See, I have refined you, though not as silver;
>   I have tested you in the furnace of affliction.
> For my own sake, for my own sake, I do this.
>   (Isaiah 48:8b–11a)

God does have a stake in each of us—and it is for His own sake that He will lift us up. He is not going to bless us for our own sake—He is going to bless us for Jesus' sake and for the sake of His own name!

If you think that there is anyone in the world so good that God could do something for that person's sake, you don't know sin; and if you think there is anything that God will not do for you for His sake and for His name, you don't know God!

If you have failed, remember that you are not responsible to men in this regard. You stand responsible before your heavenly Father and Jesus Christ at the right hand of God. Let us be encouraged by this good news!

In the third place, some are fearful that they will lose their reputation as sober and conservative and traditional Christians. In other words, they have never been willing to be a fool for Jesus' sake!

It is amazing that genuine Christians are not willing to stand up wherever they are and give a good word for the Lord. There are great political ideologies sweeping the world now whose members will make double-eyed, long-eared donkeys of themselves for the sake of the party and the cause. There are religious sects whose witnesses are willing to go to jail, to be pushed around, to be lampooned for the sake of a miserable, twisted doctrine! But in our Christian ranks, we prefer to be respectable and smooth, and we have a reputation for being very solemn Christian believers.

I can only conclude from my experience that many solemn, professing Christians will never make any spiritual progress and will never really be happy in the Lord until God finds some way to shake them out of their deadly respectability!

Charles G. Finney, the great American evangelist, knew this experience of becoming God's man and God's mouthpiece in such a way and with such unusual blessing and results that many just stood as critics and tried to frown him down.

Have to lose reputations

So it has been with all of God's saints who have pleased Him and praised Him through the centuries. At some time in their witness and expression of the living Christ they have had to lose their reputations among those who have been traditionally pious and somber, dogmatic and cautious.

This is still happening in our day, and with glorious results.

A young man who is director of one of our American Bible conferences has given me his testimony of great and radical things which the Lord has done for him in recent months.

I realize now that in my service for God I was one of the most self-assured, conceited and horrid young fellows you could ever meet," he told me frankly. "I could raise money, I could put on a great program, and I figured I was a great success in the Lord's work.

But recently on a trip to Wales, I had the opportunity of talking to some older folks who remembered Evan Roberts and the great Welsh revival. They told me about the true working of the Holy Spirit in Christian renewal and revival—and I didn't really know what they were talking about.

Somehow, and they did not realize it, it was just as though they were burying me under a great load of crushing bricks, and God spoke to me about my own great spiritual lack.

He told me that he made his way to the little cottage where he was staying and got down on his knees and began to sweat it out before God.

Do you know what this was? It was the act of dying! It was the end of self. That man died to reputation, ability, presumption, success, conceit, personality—all of that stuff!

He said to me, "Mr. Tozer, I was filled with the Holy Spirit and my whole life has been transformed. Now I only want this cheated and betrayed generation to see the glory of God once more!"

I said to him then, "Brother, do you realize that if you carry through with this message and this blessing that you will lose some of your best fundamentalist friends? You will be described as having gone off your rocker."

"I am not worried any more about my reputation," he replied. "I am perfectly willing because I am going to let the Lord have His way in the whole operation."

The interesting thing is that he hasn't had to switch or change his doctrines around at all—he just found out that he needed the fire of God on his doctrine, and he got it!

Fear of fanaticism

Also related to reputation is the fear of many Christians that they will be considered fanatical or extreme for their Christian faith. I think it is ironic that the devil gives the world all of its extremists in every realm—entertainment, politics, society, education, anarchy, intrigue—you name it! Yet it is the same devil that frightens believers about the great danger of becoming "extreme."

I passed an auditorium recently where one of the young crowd of singing stars was appearing. Police were having great trouble with the crowds and in the erotic fury of that concert, girls began to tear off their clothes; many were weeping and screaming. Those who had fainted were being carried out.

It is the same devil, but he uses different tactics in dealing with Christians. Should a Christian get blessed and say, "Amen," the devil quickly intervenes and whispers, "Don't be a fanatic—you ought to stay quiet and stable in the faith!"

Oh, what a devil the devil is! He frightens us first and then sells us a bill of goods about caution, caution, caution in the church.

Some Christians also are greatly awed by the fear of ostracism. The devil says to them, "Be careful about religion—you will be lonely. You will have to go it alone!"

I have heard one of our preachers tell about the experience he had years ago in coming to a decision concerning the claims of Christ on his life. It was at the close of a service, and he was standing with the rest of the congregation while an invitation was being given to come forward in submission to the will of God. There was a struggle going on in his own soul, and he knew that the Spirit of God was pressing him to make the decision to sell out completely and to become a real Christian in commitment to the Lord.

But the devil knows how to join in these arguments, and he whispered, "Charlie, you must be careful at this point. You know how easy it would be to break up your marriage and break up your home. You know how staid and strait-laced and conservative your wife is about religion. Don't do anything that would break up your home, Charlie!"

But the Spirit of God persisted, and Charlie found himself answering the call. He went forward and knelt at the altar for heart-searching and prayer.

Suddenly he thought he heard someone weeping at his side. Then he was sure that it sounded like his wife. Turning, he found that it was his wife, for she had been just a few feet behind him when he made his way to the altar. Together they made their commitment to Christ and to His service.

For a long time, you see, Satan had been telling Charlie that his wife would never be willing to yield to joyful Christian dedication. But the devil is a liar and the father of lies! He never tells the truth unless he can use it to whip you and embarrass you — unless he can use it in his attempts to ruin you and destroy you!

Fear of holy enthusiasm

There also seems to be a chilling fear of holy enthusiasm among the people of God. We try to tell how happy we are — but we remain so well-controlled that there are very few waves of glory experienced in our midst.

Some of you go to the ball game and you come back whispering because you are hoarse from shouting and cheering. But no one in our day ever goes home from church with a voice hoarse from shouts brought about by a manifestation of the glory of God among us.

Actually our apathy about praise in worship is like an inward chill in our beings. We are under a shadow and we are still wearing the grave clothes. You can sense this in much of our singing in the contemporary church. Perhaps you will agree that in most cases it is a kind of plodding along, without the inward life of blessing and victory and resurrection joy and overcoming in Jesus' name.

Why is this? It is largely because we are looking at what we are, rather than responding to who Jesus Christ is! We have often failed and have not been overcomers because our trying and striving have been in our own strength. That leaves us very little to sing about!

Dr. A.B. Simpson wrote:

> Fainting soldier of the Lord,
> Hear His sweet, inspiring word;
> "I have conquered all thy foes,
> I have suffered all thy woes.
> Struggling soldier, trust in Me,
> I have overcome for thee!"

This has to be the secret of our praise and enthusiasm—Jesus Christ is our Overcomer! In our own strength we cannot overcome anyone or anything.

> Fear not though thy foes be strong,
> Fear not though the strife be long;
> Trust thy glorious Captain's power,
> Watch with Him one little hour.
> Hear Him calling, "Follow Me,
> I have overcome for thee!"

Brethren, human activity and human sweat and tears work not the victory of Christ! It took the sweat and tears and blood of the Lord Jesus Christ. It took the painful dying and the victorious resurrection and ascension to bring us the victory!

We must trust

It is for us to trust, to trust wholly in the Lord Jesus. This is the only way in which we can conquer fear and live in blessed victory.

I have had times in my life and ministry when the burdens and the pressures seemed to be too much. Sometimes physical weariness adds to our problems and our temptation to give in to discouragement and doubt. At these times it seems that even in prayer it is impossible to rise above the load. More than once, by faith that seemed to have been imparted directly from heaven, the Lord has enabled me to claim all that I needed for body, soul and spirit. On my knees I have been given freedom and strength to pray, "Now, Lord, I have had enough of this—I refuse to take any more of this heaviness and oppression! This does not come from God—this comes from my enemy, the devil! Lord, in Jesus' name, I will not take it any longer—through Jesus Christ I am victor!" At these times, great burdens have just melted and rolled away—all at once!

Brethren, God never meant for us to be kicked around like a football. He wants us to be humble and let Him do the chastening when necessary. But when the devil starts tampering with you, dare to resist him!

I stand for believing in God and defying the

devil—and our God loves that kind of courage among His people.

If you are still wrapped in grave clothes and great fears lie upon you, it is time for you to dare to rise and in sweet faith in the risen Jesus Christ declare: "I will not take this any longer. I am a child of God—why should I go mourning all the day?"

Will God answer?

"All right, My child," He will answer as the burden rolls away, "I have waited long to hear you say that. Jesus is Victor and in Him you overcome!"

Christianity—
Fun and Games?

"Certainly, not all of the mystery of the Godhead can be known by man. But, just as certainly, all that man can know of God in this life is revealed in Jesus Christ!"

SOME CHRISTIAN BELIEVERS SEEMINGLY ARE committed to endless dialogue about the deeper life just as though it were some new kind of fun and games.

I almost shrink from hearing the expression, "the deeper life," because so many people want to talk about it as a topic—but no one seems to want to know and love God for Himself!

God is the deeper life! Jesus Christ Himself is the deeper life, and as I plunge on into the knowledge of the triune God, my heart moves on into the blessedness of His fellowship. This means that there is less of me and more of God—thus my spiritual life deepens, and I am strengthened in the knowledge of His will.

I think this is what Paul meant when he penned that great desire, "That I may know Him!" He was expressing more than the desire for acquaintance—he was yearning to be drawn into the full knowledge of fellowship with God which has been provided in the plan of redemption.

God originally created man in His own image so that man could know companionship with God in a unique sense and to a degree which is impossible for any other creature to experience.

Because of his sin, man lost this knowledge, this daily partnership with God. In the first chapter of Romans, Paul gives us a vivid picture of men and women whom God gave over to a reprobate mind because they did not wish to retain God in their knowledge, their foolish hearts being darkened.

This is the Bible portrait of man. He has that great potential of knowing God as no other creature can, but he is lost; and without God in his knowledge, his conduct is unworthy of his high origin and his being despairs in its encompassing emptiness.

Man's great problem

This despair, this emptiness and lostness, reflects man's great problem because he is an intelligent, moral creature who has left his proper sphere and estate of environment. How can he know anything but endless defeat and pain, because as a sinner he is not fulfilling the great end for which he was created?

We believe that God created all living creatures, each with its own peculiar kind of life. God adjusted that life in each case to its own environment. Therefore, as long as each living creature remains in its own environment and lives the kind of life for which it was created, it fulfills the purpose for which it was made. Thus, the highest that can be said of any creature is that it fulfilled the purpose for which God made it.

According to the scriptures, only man was created in God's own image. I can find no reference in the Bible to indicate that God made the seraphim or cherubim, angels or archangels in His own image.

I know that I take a chance of being misunderstood and perhaps of being misjudged when I state that man was more like God than any other creature ever created. Because of the nature of man's creation, there is nothing in the universe so much like God as the human soul. Even in the face of man's sin and lost condition, there is still that basic potential in the soul and nature of man that through grace can become more like God than anything in the universe.

There is no question about man's sin—therefore, there is no question about his being lost. A man is lost if he is not converted—overwhelmed in the vast darkness of emptiness. He was created to know God, but he chose the gutter. That is why he is like a bird shut away in a cage or like a fish taken from the water. That is the explanation of man's disgraceful acts—war and hate, murder and greed, brother against brother!

Once the smart men told us that science and philosophy and psychiatry and sociology would soon make the world a better place in which to live. As time passes, however, men are at one another's throats as never before and there is the greatest volume of hate, suspicion, anarchy, treachery, espionage, murder and criminal acts of all kinds in the history of the world.

A good word

Is there still a good word for man in his lost condition? Is there an answer for man in whom there is
that instinctive groping and craving for the lost
image and the knowledge of the Eternal Being?

Yes, there is a positive answer found in the Word
of God, and it teaches the sinner-man that it is still
possible for him to know God. The Bible teaches us
that God has not abandoned the human race as He
abandoned the angels who sinned and gave up
their first estate.

Studying the Word of God, we must come to the
conclusion that God abandoned the sinning angels
because they had not been created in the image of
God. They were moral creatures, capable of moral
and spiritual perception, but they were not made in
God's image.

And why has God given sinful man another opportunity in salvation through the merits of a Redeemer? Only because he was made in the image
of God, and God has expressed His own everlasting love for man through the giving of His Son.

Now, the Bible has a great deal to say about the
manner in which sinful man may come into the
fellowship and the presence of God, and it all has
to do with forgiveness and grace and regeneration
and justification in Jesus Christ! It all boils down to
the teaching that Jesus Christ is everything that the
Godhead is! The image of the invisible God, the
brightness of His glory, the express image of His
person—all of these we find in and through Jesus
Christ!

We believe with rejoicing that Jesus Christ was

the begotten of the Father, before all ages, that He is God of God, Light of light, very God of very God, begotten and not made, of one substance with the Father, and it is by Him that all things were made!

Look beyond modern terms

I advise you not to listen to those who spend their time demeaning the person of Christ. I advise you to look beyond the cloudiness of modern terms used by those who themselves are not sure who Jesus Christ was, in reality.

You cannot trust the man who can only say, "I believe that God revealed Himself through Christ." Find out what he really believes about the person of the incarnate Son of God!

You cannot trust the man who will only say that Christ reflected more of God than other men do. Neither can you trust those who teach that Jesus Christ was the supreme religious genius, having the ability to catch and reflect more of God than any other man.

All of these approaches are insults to the person of Jesus Christ. He was and is and can never cease to be God, and when we find Him and know Him, we are back at the ancient fountain again! Christ is all that the Godhead is!

This is the wonder, the great miracle—that by one swift, decisive, considered act of faith and prayer, our souls go back to the ancient fountain of our being, and we start over again! This means back beyond the angels, back beyond the beginning of the world, back beyond where Adam started—back to the glorious, flowing fountain we call the being of God, the Triune God!

It is in Jesus Christ Himself that we find our source, our satisfaction. I think this is what John Newton perceived in the miracle of the new birth, causing him to sing, "Now rest my long-divided heart, fixed on this blissful center—rest!"

Can there be any explanation for the fact that we seem to know so little of Jesus Christ even after He has made Himself and His blessings so readily available to His believing children?

Part of the answer may be found in our own human reasoning which becomes so easily discouraged in the face of God's infinity and God's character.

Can never know all

Brethren, it is well for us to remember that as human beings we can never know all of the Godhead. If we were capable of knowing all of the Godhead perfectly, we would be equal to the Godhead. For illustration, we know that we cannot pour an entire quart of water into a vessel which has a capacity of less than a quart. So, you could never pour all of the Godhead into the experience of any being who is less than God Himself.

A similar kind of illustration was used long ago by ancient fathers in the church as they argued for the trinity in the Godhead. They pointed out that God the eternal Father is an infinite God, and He is love. The very nature of love is to give itself but the Father could not give His love fully to anyone not fully equal to Himself. Thus we have the revelation of the Son Who is equal to the Father and of the eternal Father pouring out His love into the Son, who could contain it, because the Son is equal with the Father. Further, these ancient wise men reasoned, if the Father were to pour out His love on the Son, a medium of communication equal both to the Father and to the Son would be required, and this was the Holy Ghost. So we have their concept of the Trinity—the ancient Father in the fullness of His love pouring Himself through the Holy Ghost, who is in being equal to Him, into the Son who is in being equal to the Spirit and to the Father.

Certainly not all of the mystery of the Godhead can be known by man, but just as certainly, all that man can know of God in this life is revealed in Jesus Christ. When the Apostle Paul said with yearning, "That I may know Him," he was not speaking of intellectual knowledge, that which can be learned and memorized, but Paul was speaking of the reality of an experience, that of knowing God personally and consciously, spirit touching spirit and heart touching heart.

There are many in the churches of our day who talk some of the Christian language but who know God only by hearsay. Most of them have read some book about God. They have seen some reflection of the light of God. They may have heard some faint echo of the voice of God, but their own personal knowledge of God is very slight.

Religious props

Many Christians are staking their reputations on church attendance, religious activity, social fellowship, sessions of singing—because in all of these things they are able to lean on one another. They spend a lot of time serving as religious props for one another in Christian circles.

When Jesus was here upon the earth, the record shows that He had work to do and He also knew the necessity for activity as He preached and healed, taught and answered questions and blessed the people. He also knew the fellowship of His brethren, those who followed Him and loved Him. But these were the incidental things in Jesus' life compared to His fellowship with and personal knowledge of the Father. When Jesus went into the mountain to pray and wait on God all night, He was not alone, for He knew the conscious presence of the Father with Him.

In our modern Christian service we are constantly pressed to do this and to do that, and to go here and go there. How often we miss completely the conscious presence of God with the result that we know God only by hearsay!

Again, part of the answer we are looking for is the fact that so many professing Christians just want to get things from God. Anyone can write a book now that will sell—just give it a title like, *Seventeen Ways to Get Things from God!* You will have immediate sales. Or, write to book called, *Fourteen Ways to Have Peace of Mind*—and away they go by the ton. Many people seem to be interested in knowing God for what they can get out of Him.

They do not seem to know that God wants to give Himself. He wants to impart Himself with His gifts. Any gift that He would give us would be incomplete if it were separate from the knowledge of God Himself.

Seek God Himself

If I should pray for all of the spiritual gifts listed

in Paul's epistles and the Spirit of God should see fit to give me all 17, it would be extremely dangerous for me if, in the giving, God did not give Himself, as well.

We have mentioned creation and the fact that God has created an environment for all of His creatures. Because God made man in His image and redeemed him by the blood of the Lamb, the heart of God Himself is the true environment for the Christian. If there is grief in heaven, I think it must come from the fact that we want God's gifts, but we don't want God Himself as our environment.

I can only say that if God gives you a rose without giving Himself, He is giving you a thorn. If God gives you a garden without giving Himself, He is giving you a garden with a serpent. If He gives you wine without the knowledge of God Himself, He is giving you that with which you may destroy yourself.

I feel that we must repudiate this great, modern wave of seeking God for His benefits. The sovereign God wants to be loved for Himself and honored for Himself, but that is only part of what He wants. The other part is that He wants us to know that when we have Him, we have everything—we have all the rest. Jesus made that plain when He said, "But seek first his kingdom and his righteousness, and all these things will be given to you as well" (Matthew 6:33).

It seems that Christian believers have been going through a process of indoctrination and brainwashing, so it has become easy for us to adopt a kind of creed that makes God to be our servant instead of our being God's servant.

Why should a man write and distribute a tract instructing us on "How to Pray So God Will Send You the Money You Need"? Any of us who have experienced a life and ministry of faith can tell how the Lord has met our needs. My wife and I would probably have starved in those early years of ministry if we couldn't have trusted God completely for food and everything else. Of course, we believe that God can send money to His believing children—but it becomes a pretty cheap thing to get excited about the money and fail to give the glory to Him who is the Giver!

So many are busy "using" God. Use God to get a job. Use God to give us safety. Use God to give us peace of mind. Use God to obtain success in business. Use God to provide heaven at last.

We ought to learn

Brethren, we ought to learn—and learn it very soon—that it is much better to have God first and have God Himself even if we have only a thin dime than to have all the riches and all the influence in the world and not have God with it!

John Wesley believed that men ought to seek God alone because God is love, and he advised people in his day: "If anyone comes preaching and tells you to seek anything more than love, do not listen, do not listen!" I think in our day we are in need of such an admonition as, "Seek more of God—and seek Him for Himself alone!" If we become serious-minded about this, we would soon discover that all of the gifts of God come along with the knowledge and the presence of God Himself.

Actually, anything or anyone that keeps me from

knowing God in this vital and personal way is my enemy. If it is a friend that stands in my way, the friend is an enemy. If it is a gift that stands between us, that gift is an enemy. It may be an ambition, it may be a victory in the past, it may even be a defeat which still overwhelms me—any of these allowed to stand between the Lord and myself becomes an enemy and may keep me from further knowledge of God.

Have you had any part in this cheapening of the gospel by making God your servant? Have you allowed leanness to come to your soul because you have been expecting that God would come around with a basket giving away presents?

Perhaps some of us have a tendency to think of God standing around and tossing dimes to the children as John D. Rockefeller used to do. Can it be true that Christian believers are engaged in scrambling for those shiny, new dimes and then write a tract about it, such as "I Found a Shiny Dime and It Had the Image of God on It!"

Brethren, let's not try to compare anything like that with the deep and satisfying knowledge of God Himself. Know Him! Go on to know Him! Then, if anyone comes to quote scriptures and argue that your experience is all wrong, you can reply, "You are a good expositor—but I happen to know my Lord, and I love Him just for Himself!"

This is all that the Lord desires for us—and it is in this that we fulfill the purpose for which He created us!

Always Slamming
on the Brakes

*"The average, modern Christian is not Christ-like.
He is quick to defend his flaws, his weaknesses and
defeats in fiery, red-faced indignation!"*

IT SEEMS THAT WE HAVE REACHED A TIME in the
Christian church when it has become embarrassing to ask plainly and in so many words: "Is there
anyone for spiritual perfection?"

It is apparent that many people become nervous
and uncomfortable, even in our evangelical Christian circles, when we seek to bring forward this
theme of spiritual perfection. I am amazed that
Christians can continue to read the strong appeals
of the Lord Jesus Christ and the apostles throughout the New Testament for more earnest spiritual
desire—and still want to put on the brakes!

What is their concept of Christianity? Do they
think it is partly religion and partly play and social
fun? Do they reject a true concept of Christianity—
that our spiritual life is really a battlefield, a preparation for a greater life to come? If the cross of Jesus
Christ means what it should to us and we know
that we must carry it and die on it and then rise and
live above it, we will have a constant desire to ad-

vance and gain spiritual ground!

The nervous people who want to put on the brakes, who feel the necessity for restraint in matters of spiritual desire and yearning for perfection, often use the expression, "Let's not get fanatical about this!"

Is it fanaticism?

I can only ask: Is it fanaticism to want to go on until you can perfectly love God and perfectly praise Him?

Is it fanatical to find divine joy leaping up within your heart? Is it fanatical to find the willingness within your being to say, "Yes, Lord! Yes, Lord!" and thus live daily in the will of God so that you are living in heaven while you are living on earth?

If this is fanaticism, then it is the fanaticism of the Old Testament patriarchs and the Law; it is the fanaticism of the psalmist and of the prophets and the New Testament writers as well.

This would have to be the fanaticism that gave us Methodism, that gave us the Salvation Army, the fanaticism that gave birth to Moravianism and the entire Reformation. It is the fanaticism that gave us all the friends of God who held close to the truth, the fanaticism that ultimately brought our own Christian and Missionary Alliance into being.

Throughout the ages, there have been the plain saints, the simple saints, the holy people who would not surrender themselves to the common ways of the world. Unappreciated, often unknown, they were found in many places.

History tells us how they salted down the nations, even in the darkest of times. They set them-

selves to live by a spiritual perfection, or at least the
beginning of spiritual perfection day by day. So it
was that when the time of the Reformation came,
there was a fertile soil into which to put the seed.
Luther, even with his bull neck, could never have
done what he did if there had not been a preparation by John Tawler and others like him, going up
and down the land preaching this kind of spiritual
desire and attainment.

You who study the Word of God know full well
that a hunger for God's will is the mood and temper of the Law and of the Psalms and of the
prophets and of the New Testament writers.

Those of you who have gone on to read the great
books of devotion within the Christian faith know,
too, that this yearning for perfection was the temper of all of the superior souls who have ever lived.
They have written our great works of faith and love
and devotion and they have composed our loftiest
hymns. It is to our shame that we as unworthy
spiritual descendants of those great fathers so often
use their hymns without any spiritual awareness of
what we are singing!

Nibbling at the truth

This is one of the marks of our modern time—
that many are guilty of merely "nibbling" at the
truth of the Christian gospel.

I wonder if you realize that in many ways the
preaching of the Word of God is being pulled down
to the level of the ignorant and spiritually obtuse;
that we must tell stories and jokes and entertain
and amuse in order to have a few people in the
audience? We do these things that we may have

some reputation and that there may be money in the treasury to meet the church bills.

I believe in being honest about it—let's admit that we have to pull down the application of the gospel not to the standard of the one who is really thirsting after God, but to the one who is the most carnal, the cheapest saintling hanging on by the teeth anywhere in the kingdom of God!

In many churches Christianity has been watered down until the solution is so weak that if it were poison it would not hurt anyone, and if it were medicine it would not cure anyone!

Now I want to bring you to my postulate that most present-day Christians live sub-Christian lives.

I repeat: Most modern Christians live sub-Christian lives!

Most Christians are not joyful persons because they are not holy persons, and they are not holy persons because they are not filled with the Holy Spirit, and they are not filled with the Holy Spirit because they are not separated persons.

The Spirit cannot fill whom He cannot separate, and whom He cannot fill, He cannot make holy, and whom He cannot make holy, He cannot make happy!

There you have it—my postulate that the modern Christian, even though he has accepted Christ and has been born again, is not a joyful person because he is not a holy person.

Not Christ-like

My postulate further insists that the average

modern Christian is not Christ-like. The proof of this is apparent in the disposition that we find among the children of God. If I did not have some sense of prophetic vision to see down the years, and like the prophets to be willing to fall asleep not having seen the fulfillment of the promises, I would be deeply despondent to know that I have preached for years to some people who still have bad dispositional flaws. In addition, they have moral weaknesses and suffer frequent defeats. They have a dulled understanding and often live far below the standard of the Scriptures and thus outside the will of God.

The worst of it is that many in this condition will defend their flaws, their weaknesses and defeats in fiery, red-faced indignation!

We should not be too surprised by this substandard spiritual condition, for it is often described in the Bible. You will remember a warning which was spoken concerning Israel, God's people, first in the Old Testament and repeated in the New: though the children of Israel should be as the sand by the seashore in number, only a remnant should be saved.

Our Lord Himself said in the gospel record that the love of many would wax cold. In the letters to the seven churches in the Revelation, we have descriptions of churches that function as churches but have lost their first love and are cold and have very much wrong with them spiritually.

Read in the New Testament and you will find that there were persons who refused completely the teachings of Jesus, even though He lived and served in their midst.

Four stages

The point I am making here is that there are at least four different and distinct stages of Christian experience and maturity which we consistently find among the professing children of God. Lest there be misunderstanding and misinterpretation, I must make it plain that these are four very evident stages of spiritual life and disposition to be found among us every day—but not four works of grace!

I can just hear someone saying, "I have heard about two works of grace, and I have even heard of some who teach that there are three, but now Tozer is teaching four!"

No, not four works of grace!

I will refer to one of God's great souls of the past and his book, *The Cloud of Unknowing*. We do not know the name of the devoted saint who more than 600 years ago wrote in his pre-Elizabethan English for the purpose, as he declares it, "that God's children might go on to be 'oned' with God."

At the beginning of his book, he breathed a brief prayer of longing and devotion, and I come back to it often for the good of my own spirit.

He said, "Oh God, under whom all hearts be open, and unto whom all will speaketh, and unto whom no privy thing is hid, I beseech Thee, so for to cleanse the intent of my heart with the unspeakable gift of Thy grace, that I may perfectly love Thee and worthily praise Thee!"

In this prayer he first acknowledges that in God's sight all hearts are open and fully known. God can see in. Even if you close your heart, lock it and throw away the key, God still sees into your heart.

"And unto whom all will speaketh"—this is one of the doctrines of the Bible and strongly emphasized in his book, that the will of a man's heart is prayer. Centuries later Montgomery expressed it: "Prayer is the soul's sincere desire unuttered or expressed." In other words, what you will in your heart is eloquent, and God is always listening to what you are willing, what you are determining to do, and what you plan.

"And unto whom no privy thing is hid"—nothing can be held as a secret from the living God.

Then, "I beseech Thee, so for to cleanse the intent of my heart with the unspeakable gift of Thy grace, that I may perfectly love Thee and worthily praise Thee."

No fault or error

I can discern no trace of theological fault or error in this prayer of devotion and desire breathed long ago by this saint of God.

"Oh God, fix my heart so I may perfectly love Thee and worthily praise Thee!" Nothing extreme and fanatical there. The true child of God will say "Amen" to this desire within the being to perfectly love God and worthily praise Him.

He points out, "I find four degrees and forms of Christian men's living." He names them: "common," "special," "singular" and "perfect."

He was frank in telling how Christians lived six centuries ago. I think this old saint would have been an outstanding and effective evangelist. If he had come around 600 years later, how we could have used him in our camps and conferences!

He knew the categories among Christians then, and I believe we can see them today.

There are "common" Christians and God knows what a mob we are!

There is also the "special" Christian. He has moved on a little.

Then there is the "singular" Christian, and he is unusual.

But now, this man who is our teacher for the time continues: "These first three stages, common, special and singular, may be begun and ended in this life. But the fourth, the perfect Christian may by the grace of God begin here but shall ever last on without end in the bliss of heaven."

So you see now that neither he nor I are "perfectionists" to the point that we would walk about with a benign St. Francis smile as if to say, "I am perfect; don't bother me!" We will always find that there is ground yet to be taken even though we have entered into the beginning of spiritual perfection.

There is an interesting admonition by the author of *The Cloud of Unknowing* in which he asks that only those who are serious about going on to perfection should read or consider his writings.

He wrote: "Now, I charge thee and I beseech thee, in the name of the Father and of the Son and of the Holy Ghost, that thou neither read this book nor write it nor speak it nor suffer it to be read, except it be such an one as hath by a true will and by a whole intent, purposed him to be a perfect follower of Christ."

He is saying, in other words, "This is such a serious and weighty matter, that no one should fool around with it, or be merely curious or casual about it — only those who have made up their minds and have a true will and a whole intent to be a perfect follower of Jesus Christ."

Curiosity not enough

The old saint then says: "For my intent was never to write such things unto them, therefore, I would that they meddle not herewith, neither they nor any of these curious persons, either lettered or unlettered."

So if the only interest you have in the deeper spiritual life is based on curiosity, it is not enough regardless of your education or scholarship!

In our day we have seen a great revival of interest in mysticism, supposedly a great interest in the deeper life. But I find that much of this interest is academic and based on curiosity. We become interested in aspects of the deeper Christian life much as we become interested in mastering the yo-yo or folk songs or dabbling in Korean architecture or anything else that intrigues us. You can go anywhere now and buy a book about the deeper life because there are curious persons who are swelling the market.

But this saint of old said, "I never want any curious, merely curious person to even bother about this for he will never get anything out of it."

I think I hear him saying to me as well, "Tozer, by the grace of God in the power of the Trinity, I beseech you do not preach this unless people are determined in their hearts to be perfect followers of Christ."

But it is Jesus' blood that makes the difference

and because of this hope that by the blood of Jesus we may be worthy to listen, I differ with the old saint in this point.

Brethren, I am not willing to withhold the open secrets of spiritual power from those who can receive them just because there are others who cannot. I am not going to withhold the open secret of the victorious life from those who can understand it and desire it because of those who are merely curious and without desire. We must leave the sorting out to God. The testing in the matters of spiritual life is by the Spirit of God, not by pastors and preachers.

Tested unconsciously

We have many examples of men and women being tested unconsciously in the Scriptures, for the Holy Spirit rarely tells a person that he is about to be tested.

When you go to a doctor for an examination or take a scheduled examination in the classroom, the testing is conscious and purposeful. Consciously and knowingly you are taking a test to find out where you stand or whether you can fulfill the requirements.

But in the scriptures the testing times were very rarely known to those being tested, and that is a sobering thought.

Abraham was being tested when he was asked to leave Ur of the Chaldees, but he did not know it. And when the Lord asked Abraham to take his only son up into the mountain, he thought he was being ordered. He did not know that he was being tested.

Peter was unconsciously tested. Paul was tested. There comes a time when we have heard enough truth and had sufficient opportunity and the Holy Spirit says, "Today this man is going to have his test!"

The people of Israel in their time of testing came to Kadesh-barnea and instead of crossing into the land, they said, "We will not go over." They were unconscious of the testing, and they went back. They did not realize that they were sentencing themselves to 40 years of aimless, useless wandering in the desert sands. The Lord had not said to them, "Now stand up, everyone. Breathe deeply! This is going to be a test!" He simply let them make their own test and they flunked it.

It is a solemn and frightening thing in this world of sin and flesh and devils, to realize that about 80 or 90 percent of the people whom God is testing will flunk the test!

The Lord will do His own sorting out, and all of us should be aware that we are in a time when every day is a day of testing. Some come to their Kadesh-barnea and turn back. Some simply stand and look across the river. They are only curious.

Is there anyone for spiritual perfection—anyone with an honest desire to be Christlike—to be more like Jesus Christ every day?

You Can't Be a Baby All Your Life!

"God is not honored by our arrested development. The New Testament teaches that we should go on to full maturity, that mediocrity is not the highest that Jesus offers!"

I HAVE LONG RESISTED AND ARGUED against the assumption that all Christians are alike and that there are no distinctions that can be made between them.

"All Christians are saints in God's eyes and that is the end of the matter!" I have been told.

I am acquainted with all of the arguments, but they do not satisfy me in the light of the words of Jesus and the teachings of the apostles. I still think that we must preach and instruct and urge men and women who are toiling along in average and common Christian ways to move forward and claim spiritual victory which they have not yet known.

If all Christians are alike in standing and state, why did Jesus Christ talk about three distinctions in the Christian life: "some thirty, some sixty and some a hundred fold"? Why did He say that some will be qualified to rule over many cities and others over few cities? Why did He teach that some should have higher positions than others in the kingdom of God?

If we are all alike and have arrived at the same place and state, why did the Apostle Paul tell the Philippian Christians: "I have lost all things. I consider them rubbish, that I may gain Christ and be found in him . . . I want to know Christ and the power of his resurrection . . . becoming like him in death, and so, somehow, to attain to the resurrection from the dead" (3:8b–11)?

Ponder the full meaning

Have you ever pondered the full meaning of the much-quoted verse in the Old Testament, Proverbs 4:18: "The path of the righteous is like the first gleam of dawn, shining ever brighter till the first light of day"?

I have compared this verse in a number of translations. Goodspeed says, "The path of the righteous is like the light of the dawn that shines ever more brightly until the day is full." Rotherham says, "The path of the righteous is like the light of the dawn going on and brightening unto a more radiant day."

This is an inspired utterance concerning a true relationship with God. Through it, the writer is saying to us that when a person becomes a Christian the sun comes up. Then, his experience along the path should be like the appearing of the dawn and the glowing of the light which shineth more and more unto the perfect day.

Christians are very fond of this verse. They memorize it. They quote it—but they don't believe it! If they really believed it they would enter into this experience—"shining ever brighter till the first light of day!"

I am of the opinion that we cannot experience that which we have not believed. This is the reason why many Christians remain about where they are—day after day, week after week, year after year. Time moves along and special revival speakers come and go. As a result, we have little spells in which we hope to do better. But if we are honest, we must admit that most Christians stay mired down right where they are.

The sad thing is that there are many in our churches who do not have a long time to live. They have grown old and yet they are not one inch farther up the mountain than they were on that day when the sun first arose on them in conversion. In fact, some are not even as far advanced along the way with God as they were a few years ago! It is a sad truth that they have already known a day in the past when their faith was keener, their love warmer, the tears nearer the surface, their love of prayer greater, purity and separation brighter, and the principle within more marked than it is now.

If these things are true, I can only conclude that these are "common" Christians, men and women who do not hear the Lord speaking to them as they should.

Read, study and obey

God will speak to us if we read and study and obey the Word of God. But when He does speak, we should speak back to Him in prayer and devotion. That which we speak to Him is important, as we can see in the book of Psalms. Here is a man—an inspired man—speaking back to God!

In a similar way, that is why the great devotional literature is so helpful to us. God has spoken to His saints and they have spoken back to Him, and in His wisdom He has preserved many of these examples for us.

We are taking some suggestions from a 600-year-old volume, *The Cloud of Unknowing*, written by an anonymous saint of God. It was his premise that many among us are common Christians, while others press on into "special" and "singular" and "perfect" stages of Christian life and experience.

"The first three of these may be begun and ended in this life," he wrote. "You can enter into perfection but you cannot enter in fully because the fourth may by grace be begun here but it shall last without end in the bliss of heaven."

I believe that is a perfect response to Paul's expression that "I count not myself to have apprehended, neither were already perfect; but let us therefore as many as be perfect be thus minded." (Paraphrase from Philippians 3:12–15). Here is the blessed contradiction—we have entered into perfection, but we have not yet gone all the way!

The Apostle Paul was stretching forth in that light and radiance which shines more and more unto the perfect day. He said that all will be raised from the dead but he pressed forward because of God's promise of a better resurrection out from among the dead.

"Not that I have already obtained all this, or have already been made perfect, but I press on . . . forgetting what is behind" (Philippians 3:12–13), the apostle said.

In the light of Paul's commitment and desire, what shall we say about the shameful mediocrity of the average or common Christian in daily life and experience? What are his reasons for not moving forward in the plan and will of God for his life?

Consider the definition

First, consider the definition of the word "common." It means just plain ordinary—of common rank or quality or ability.

A common Christian is one who is of ordinary quality and ability. He is not distinguished by superiority of any kind. He has begun. He does believe. Perhaps he carries a Bible. But he is not distinguished for spiritual attainment.

I must leave it to each of you whether this is a description of your own kind of spirituality as a Christian. Perhaps you are of just common quality, not distinguished in your Christian life in any way. As a result no one will ever want to consult you for guidance or help. No one will ever want to quote you about the things of God.

Mediocre—most Christians are mediocre!

Actually, I hate the word—mediocre! I get no pleasure out of using it, but I think I am telling the truth when I say that it describes many Christians.

The word mediocre comes from two Latin words and literally means "halfway to the peak." This makes it an apt description of the progress of many Christians. They are halfway up to the peak. They are not halfway to heaven but halfway up to where they ought to be, halfway between the valley and the peak. They are morally above the hardened sinner but they are spiritually beneath the shining saint.

Many have settled down right there, and the tragedy is that years ago some of you said, "I am not going to fail God. I am going to push my way up the mountain until I am at the top of the peak, at the highest possible point of experience with God in this mortal life!"

But you have done nothing about it. If anything, you have lost spiritual ground since that day. You are now a halfway Christian! You are lukewarm, neither hot nor cold. You are halfway up to the peak, halfway to where you could have been if you had pressed on.

Do we really think that this halfway Christian life is the best that Christ offers—the best that we can know? In the face of what Christ offers us, how can we settle for so little? Think of all that He offers us by His blood and by His Spirit, by His sacrificial death on the cross, by His resurrection from the dead, by His ascension to the right hand of the Father, by His sending forth of the Holy Ghost!

Settling for far less

I know that many are settling for far less than God is waiting to give. They try to stay happy by adding something to their religion that tickles their carnality from the outside. They introduce converted cowboys and half-converted movie actors, and I think they would even stoop to talking horses and gospel dogs to be able to join in saying, "We had a wonderful time!" They will pay a big price to feature some "90-day wonder" so they can get the people to crowd in.

Such as these are mediocre Christians. They have not gained the heights where they can feel the warmth of the sun and yet they are not far enough down to be frozen in the valley.

Certainly God is not honored by our arrested development—our permanent halfway spiritual condition. We honor and please Him by going on to full maturity in Christ. We all know that this is what the Bible teaches. Read your New Testament again and you will agree that mediocrity in the Christian life is not the highest that Jesus offers.

Why, then, are we such common Christians? Why have we settled for such shallow pleasures, those little joys that tickle the saintlets and charm the fancy of the carnal?

It is because we once heard a call to take up the cross, and instead of following toward the heights, we bargained with the Lord like a Maxwell Street huckster. We started asking selfish questions and laying down our own conditions.

We had seen the finger of God beckoning. We had been stirred by His Spirit, and all aglow with desire we considered going up to the mountain. We felt an urge to be spent for Christ, to live as near to spiritual perfection as it is possible in this life.

However, instead of going on we started asking questions. We began to bicker and bargain with God about His standards for spiritual attainment.

This is plain truth, not about unbelieving "liberals," but about those who have been born again. We have His life—and yet when He calls us to the heights, we begin to quibble and bargain.

"Lord, what will it cost me?" we ask. "I want to go on but I want to know what it will cost me!"

I am convinced that anyone who brings up the question of consequences in the Christian life is only a mediocre and common Christian. He seems to have completely forgotten that the cross is involved at this point. Jesus himself plainly said, "Take up [your] cross daily and follow me" (Luke 9:23b), and "Whoever serves me must follow me; and where I am, my servant also will be. My Father will honor the one who serves me" (John 12:26). Jesus said that!

So, the devoted and committed person who takes the cross and follows the Lord does not ask what the consequences will be, neither does he argue about God's plan and God's wisdom.

I have known some who were interested in the deeper life, but hesitated for fear of what such a decision would cost in time, in money, in effort or perhaps in the matter of friendships. These are some of the areas that hinder us.

Now, I do not mean to put down the value and meaning of dear friendships. Human friendships can have a beautiful character that will carry over into the world to come. But the point is that if we ask questions about losing friends when the Lord is dealing with us about spiritual blessing and victory, we are not worthy to be among the saints.

Will it be safe?

Another question that people ask of the Lord when He calls them to move forward is: "Will it be safe?"

This question comes out of our constant bleating

about "security" and our everlasting desire for safety above all else.

We ought to be prepared to the fact that faith has a disturbing element within it. In the days of Luther, when it cost something to be a Christian, the old Lutherans said: "Faith is a perturbing thing."

Dare we face the fact that the Word of God more often than not puts us in a place of peril rather than settling us down easily in a place of security? But most Christians in our day want to dictate to God— they will not accept a place of peril. They do not want to trust.

Some of us have had a delightful experience with a Christian brother from England. He had formerly made money in business and never went anywhere without taking large sums with him. But the Holy Spirit began dealing with him about God's provision and God's resources. Sharing his experience with us, he said: "My wife and I have committed everything to God. We don't even own a house. We have no regular income. I do the work of an evangelist and we are just out doing God's will.

"It is not at all unusual now for us to get in our car and travel several hundred miles with only 10 dollars for expenses and not knowing what the next step will be," he told us. "God is spending us. He will not let us down but He is holding us to it so that we will never be able to get our earthly roots in again."

This is the language of the confident Christian who is going on with God. That question, "Is it safe?" is an ignoble question. What is the difference whether it is safe or not as long as He is our Lord?"

Will it be convenient?

A third question that we want Him to answer for us is, "Will it be convenient?"

What must our Lord think of us if His work and His witness depend upon the convenience of His people? The truth is that every advance that we make for God and for His cause must be made at our inconvenience. If it does not inconvenience us at all, there is no cross in it! If we have been able to reduce spirituality to a smooth pattern and it costs us nothing—no disturbance, no bother and no element of sacrifice in it—we are not getting anywhere with God. We have stopped and pitched our unworthy tent halfway between the swamp and the peak.

We are mediocre Christians!

Was there ever a cross that was convenient? Was there ever a convenient way to die? I have never heard of any, and judgment is not going to be a matter of convenience, either! Yet we look around for convenience, thinking we can reach the mountain peak conveniently and without trouble or danger to ourselves.

Actually, mountain climbers are always in peril and they are always advancing at their inconvenience.

Will it be fun?

Still another of those huckster questions that we ask when we hear the voice of Jesus calling us onward is this: "Will it be fun?"

I am sure you know my reaction to this one. No

one who asks this question about spiritual advance will ever be anything but a common Christian. He will be mediocre until he dies. He will never be recognized in any way for significant spiritual qualities and he will never be outstanding for any gifts of the Holy Ghost.

It is because there are so many of these ignoble saintlets, these miniature editions of the Christian way, demanding that Christianity must be fun, that distinct organizations have been launched to give it to them. Yes, there are organizations that exist for the sole purpose of mixing religion and fun for our Christian young people.

In answer to this, I happen to know that young people can be just as responsible before God as older people. The youth who meets Jesus and is converted is just as ready and responsible for inconvenience and cost to himself as is the man of 70. Jesus Christ never offered amusement or entertainment for His disciples, but in our day we have to offer both if we are going to get the people—because they are common Christians.

Because fun and popularity seem to go hand-in-hand, some of the indecisive ask, "Oh Lord, will I still be popular if I follow all the way?"

Ah, the weaklings, the weaklings! They must have the approval and support of the group because they are afraid of standing alone. They want to be able to fit in, seeking a guarantee of solidarity in order to bolster one another in the face of sagging courage. Some just cannot stand alone and when they ask, "Is it popular?", they are avoiding the path of standing alone for God.

Tough to stand alone

I was converted by the grace of God when I was 17 years old and there was no other Christian in my home. It was in the city of Akron and my family took in boarders. We had a house full of people at all times and yet, in the matter of my faith, I was completely alone. I must not leave the impression that I stood as nobly as Stephen in the book of Acts, but I did stand—and it was tough to stand alone. No one else wanted to go to church. No one wanted to pray at the table. No one wanted to read the Bible, but by the good grace of God, I stood alone and I have always been able to thank God for the results.

My mother and father were both converted, as well as two of my sisters. A brother-in-law was converted before he died and several others came to know the Savior.

What if I had argued: "Lord, is it popular? What will it cost me?" Those persons would never have met the Lord. God stands willing to give us His help by His grace and mercy.

Many who are God's children have probably hesitated at times and tried to bargain with God. They have known Him in conversion. They know that the change came—and yet they bear the marks of mediocrity. But the important thing is this—they are not at the end of God's love!

It is one of the devil's oldest tricks to discourage the saints by causing them to look back at what they were. No one will make progress with God until he lifts up his eyes and stops looking at himself. We are not to spend our time looking back and looking in—we are told to look forward!

Our Lord is more than able to take care of our past. He pardons instantly and forgives completely. His blood makes us worthy—all we are and all we have is by the forgiving love of God!

The goodness of God is infinitely more wonderful than we will ever be able to comprehend. If the root of the matter is in you and you are born again, God is prepared to start with you where you are, and He will not belittle you for your years of common Christianity!

Stopped Dead
in Your Tracks?

"God says, 'I stand ready to pour a little liquid fire into your being.' We respond, 'No, Lord, that sounds like fanaticism.' Yet we want all the benefits of His cross!"

I BLAME FAULTY EXPOSITION of the New Testament for stopping many Christians dead in their tracks, causing them to shrug off any suggestion that there is still spiritual advance and progress beckoning them on.

The position of some would-be teachers which insists that when you come into the kingdom of God by faith you immediately have all there is in the kingdom of God is as deadly as cyanide. It kills all hope of spiritual advance and causes many to adopt what I call "the creed of contentment."

Why should a Christian settle down as soon as he has come to know the Lord?

I would have to reply that he must have received faulty counsel and bad exposition of New Testament truth. There is always real joy in the heart of the person who has become a child of God, and proper and sound teaching of the Word of God will awake desire within him to move forward in spiritual adventure with Christ.

But the would-be teacher may tell the new Christian, "You are now complete in Him. The Bible says that and it means that you should just be glad that you are complete and there is nothing more you will ever need!" From that time on any effort to forge ahead for God is put down as some sort of fanaticism. This kind of exposition has brought many Christians into a place of false contentment — satisfied to stay right where they are.

But not so with the Apostle Paul who amazes and humbles us as we read in the third chapter of Philippians of his earnest desire to press forward and to become a special kind of Christian.

With great desire, he wrote: "That I may gain Christ" — and yet he already had Christ!

With obvious longing he said, "That I may 'be found in Him'" — and yet he was already in Him. We go to Paul more than to any other writer in the Bible to learn the doctrine of being in Christ and yet Paul humbly and intensely breathed this great desire, "I want to know Christ," when he already knew Him!

It was this same Paul who gladly testified, "I have been crucified with Christ and I no longer live, but Christ lives in me. The life I live in the body, I live by faith in the Son of God, who loved me and gave himself for me" (Galatians 2:20).

Yet, because he could never be standing still, he further testified, "but I press on to take hold of that for which Christ Jesus took hold of me" (Philippians 3:12b).

How utterly foreign that is to the spirit of modern

orthodoxy! How foreign to the bland assurances that because we can quote the text of Scripture we must have the experience. This strange textualism that assumes that because we can quote chapter and verse we possess the content and experience is a grave hindrance to spiritual progress. I think it is one of the deadliest, most chilling breezes that ever blew across the church of God!

Too many of us are complete strangers to the desire and the spirit which drove the Apostle Paul forward day by day. "That I may gain—that I may know—that I may be found in Him"—these were the words that drove Paul. But now, we are often told that we "have" everything, and that we should just be thankful and "go on to cultivate." I say that the two attitudes are foreign to one another. They do not belong together.

We are told to study the biblical passages in the Greek. We find out what they mean in English. Then we say, "Well, isn't that fine—isn't that fine!" And that is all we do about it. But Paul said, "I press on toward the goal to win the prize for which God has called me heavenward in Christ Jesus" (3:14).

Some have even turned that desire of Paul into a pink cloud. They believe that Paul was talking about a pink cloud which he was going to get when Christ returned. In my opinion, there isn't anything about the return of Christ in that expression of Paul. He was talking about the present, and he was expressing his desire to continue on with Christ. He was talking about experiencing all of that for which Christ had apprehended him.

A deaf ear

Why do Christian people in our day purposely turn a deaf ear to the clear appeals in the Word of God concerning spiritual desire and victory?

In some cases it is because they have heard truth which they are not willing to obey. Our Lord is not going to compromise with anyone over the issue of disobedience to truth which He reveals. As a result those who knowingly refuse to obey will be brought to a distinct halt in their spiritual life. If there is something that they will not do for Him, some confession they will not make, something they refuse to straighten out, some act of obedience they will not perform—they will come to a stop and just sit. It is a dead halt—like the breaking of an axle on a truck or car.

People are sitting all around in the church of Christ, just as though the axle had broken, and they have not made any progress for years and years. They are completely stopped by non-obedience.

In other cases, Christians have been side-tracked and rendered useless by their acceptance of a state of chronic discouragement. As a result, they have come to a place of contented rationalization that their condition is normal for all Christians.

These are people who are believers, but they are not believers for themselves. They say they believe in this progressive, victorious Christian life but that it is for others, not for themselves. They have been to every altar, they have been to all of the Bible conferences, but the blessings are for someone else.

Now that attitude on the part of believers is neither modesty nor meekness. It is discouragement resulting from unbelief. It is rather like those who have been sick so long that they no longer believe they can get well. They have lived with the illness so long that it has become a pet and they don't want to lose it because they would no longer have a subject for conversation. They would say that they want to get well, but in fact, they do not.

Jesus is still saying, as He said to the man lying by the gate at the pool, "Do you want to get well?" Jesus made that man whole and raised him up because he wanted to be healed and delivered. If Jesus had found in him that which He finds in so many Christians today—a chronic state of discouragement—He would have passed him by!

The cult of respectability

A third reason why many make no progress with God is the fact that they have seen fit to join the cult of respectability. They have learned the art of "becoming adjusted." They have chosen to be cool and proper, poised, self-possessed and well-rounded. They would never want anyone to think that they have taken an extreme position, particularly in religious matters.

We are getting so well-rounded and so broadly symmetrical that we forget that every superior soul that has done exploits for God was considered extreme and in many cases even deranged. We talk about the saintly John Wesley, a learned Oxford man and founder of the Methodists, but we forget that he was such a fiery apostle that they used to throw eggs and rocks at him. His clothes looked fine when he went out but when he came back he needed a tailor. Wesley never put poise and adjustment and respectability above that urgency within his soul to make Christ known with all of His saving and keeping power!

Well, thank God for the Wesleys and all the great souls who have not been afraid of being different! Thank God that there are always a few, and the Bible talks about their being worthy. I know that in Revelation 3:4 it says, "They will walk with me, dressed in white, for they are worthy." I am not going to try to persuade you that I know the full meaning, but I know that even in times of backsliding and general coldness of heart there have always been some of God's people who were different. I think there was enough difference in their love and desire and adoration that there would be no question about their walking with Him in white!

Now I wonder if any of you think that I am just trying to whip up spiritual desire in your hearts?

No, I am not trying to whip up desire for the simple reason that I know better. I can agitate you nervously but I cannot put spiritual desire in your being.

The old saint who wrote *The Cloud of Unknowing* expressed it like this: "Our Lord hath of his great mercy called thee and led thee unto him by the desire of thine heart." I have reminded you before that God is always previous, God is always there first, and if you have any desire for God and for the things of God, it is God Himself who put it there.

That old writer continued: "Through the everlasting love of his Godhead, he made thee and wrought thee when thou were not." God was already there—you didn't call up because you were not. And then, "He bought thee with the price of his precious blood when you were lost in Adam." Again, God preceded you—God was previous once more. I believe in prevenient grace, and I don't believe that any person can ever be nudged or pushed or jostled into the kingdom of God or into the deeper life except the Holy Ghost does it. He does it out of the everlasting love of His Godhead, the old saint told us, "so tenderly, he would not suffer thee to be so far from him."

Oh my brothers and sisters! Are we not stirred by the expanse of this great sea of glory in which we Christians find ourselves? "He would not suffer thee to be so far from him." He just wouldn't allow it. He just couldn't stand it. This same God who made us when we were nothing and redeemed us when we were sinners "kindled desire so graciously."

Does it describe us?

How many of us does that describe? Have any of you ever had a gracious, sudden kindling of desire, when everyone else seemed contented with panel discussions and the usual routine of the church which has to do with externals? How many of us go to church regularly and never feel an extra heartbeat, never any kindling of godly desire? We live like that!

So this kind of desire is not something that can be whipped up—God Himself must put it there. We could never have created ourselves and we could never have redeemed ourselves. We cannot talk ourselves into getting a longing for God. It has to come from God.

When I was a young fellow I spent a little time working as "butcher boy" on the train—riding the old Vicksburg and Pacific and selling peanuts, popcorn, chewing gum and candy, as well as books. I really had to quit because I didn't sell enough—I would often sit and read the books from Vicksburg to the end of the line! But I remember that we did try to stir up some desire for peanuts and popcorn among those passengers. We would go through the coaches and give each person just four or five salted peanuts. No one wanted any when we went through but when we came back, nearly everyone was ready to buy. They had gotten a taste and now they had a desire for peanuts. It was a common trick on the trains.

But we cannot do that for you in spiritual matters. It is not possible! If you have accepted a common state of spiritual living and you have no deep desire for Him, no man can give it to you. Unless you are willing for God to move in and have His way, you are never going to have spiritual adventures like those who have been explorers in the kingdom of God.

Seeking a better land

We don't think often enough about all those who have been the prospectors among the hills of God—the spiritual adventurers, the explorers of the kingdom. God wrote in the Bible about them because they were seeking a better land.

Why did Abraham leave Ur of the Chaldees? God promised him spiritual adventures, and he moved out at God's bidding, but it didn't make him a hero at that point.

Think of what the contented people must have said.

"Look at that fool," they said. "What's the matter with him? Everyone else is satisfied to go to the temple once a week and make an offering, but Abraham talks about hearing a voice that said 'get thee into the land which I will show thee.'"

They said, "Abraham, you are a fool!"

But Abraham said, "I heard the Voice, plain and clear. I'm moving out!"

At that point Abraham was no hero. They thought he had lost his mind, that he was at least semi-demented. But you know the rest of the story.

Then there was Moses who could have lived on in the house of his supposed mother in Egypt and perhaps could have become the emperor. But he refused to do it. He got up and left. You know the story and the great list of his spiritual adventures and his favor with God.

Think of the apostles and all of the great souls who have been adventurers. They were not the heroes of the crowd, but they have entered into God's great hall of fame. But something had to happen within each one, an internal fire before it became external. This desire to prospect the hills of God for new lodes of gold had to be inward before it could be outward. These adventurers for God knew the happening on the inside before there was any evidence on the outside.

God expects inward change

Far too many people still believe that changes on

the outside will take care of the whole matter. How many there are who still think that making outward changes in life and character and habits is all that God expects. Many men have made decisions to enter the ministry or to go to work on some foreign field because of advice and pressures from the outside. That can happen to the outside of a man and never really touch his heart at all.

It can happen. It is entirely in the realm of possibility that a missionary could go to the field and spend a lifetime there and yet never have moved beyond the little patch of ground in his own spiritual life. It is not enough just to go in body, moved by something on the outside. This is a journey for the soul—not just for the feet!

This is why God wants to do something within His people. The great problem of the church today is how we may go on to experience and draw upon that which we have in Christ. But we are not doing much about the problem!

One of my preacher friends wrote me that he had been asked to help in a missionary convention in one of our churches. He was to preach on missions. He said that when he arrived, he found there had been no more spiritual preparation for those meetings than there had been for the first game of the world series. The first night there were about 25 people in attendance but the pastor announced that a good, lively quartet would sing on the following night. My friend wrote that the church was packed. The members of the quartet exchanged jibes, lampooned one another and captured the crowd with their clowning. After singing a song which said, "Let's help God some more," and figuring, I suppose, that they had rescued God from what otherwise would have been a boring evening, they took their guitars and rushed out to another engagement to help God some more.

How will anyone grow in grace around a place like that, I ask you? It makes no difference whether it is one of our churches or some other group, or the largest cathedral in the world, no one could grow in grace in such a situation unless he had a private source. We have the Word of God to which we can go. God has not only called us by His love but has promised a place of pasture for our spiritual good.

But some of God's dear children don't have that longing for His best pastures because in spiritual things they have not found the delight of experiencing within themselves all that Christ has provided.

I used to read from the various religions of the East and I recall a passage in the Hindu writings which said, "You who are busy learning texts and not living them are like the man counting other people's cattle without having a single heifer of his own." I thought that was pretty good for an old Hindu, and I could translate that over into my own version and say, "A lot of professing Christians are busy counting other people's cattle—studying theology and archaeology, anthropology and eschatology—but they don't have one little heifer of their own." They have very little from God which is their very own. They only have that which really belongs to someone else. They might write a small tract on what God has done for them, but they could write a huge volume if they would on all that God wants to do for them if they would consent.

God stands ready

God is saying, "I stand ready to pour a little liquid fire into your heart, into your spiritual being!"

We respond: "No, Lord, please excuse me. That sounds like fanaticism—and I would have to give up some things!" So we refuse His desire, even though we want all the benefits of His cross.

There is this thoughtful phrase in *The Cloud of Unknowing*: "He wills thou do but look on Him and let Him alone." Let God alone. In other words, let Him work! Don't stop Him. Don't prevent Him from kindling your heart, from blessing you and leading you out of a common state into that of special longing after Him. You don't have to coax God. He is not like a reluctant father waiting for his child to beg. The blessings are His to give and He waits for us to let Him work.

This is a very hard thing for Americans to do because we are naturally-born "do-it-yourself" artists! We don't just hire a plumber and let him do his work—we stand by and tell him how it should be done. It is amazing really that any American ever lies down and allows the doctor to perform the operation. We always want to get our finger in, and that is the way most Christians behave. We think God does the really hard jobs, but that He is glad to have us along to help out.

"Look on Him—and let Him work, let Him alone." Get your hands down to your side and stop trying to tell God where to cut. Stop trying to make the diagnosis for God. Stop trying to tell God what to give you. He is the Physician! You are the patient.

This is good doctrine, brethren. Dr. A.B. Simpson shocked and blessed and helped dear people in all Christian groups as he taught his truth down through the years—"let God work! Let Him alone! Take your hands off! It is God that worketh in you!"

Let Him work and your spiritual life will begin to blaze like the rising sun.

Denominations Can Backslide, Too!

"Oh, that we would have a naked intent to know Jesus Christ! It means putting the world and things and people beneath our feet, opening our hearts to only one lover.—the Son of God Himself!"

OUR PROBLEMS OF SPIRITUAL COLDNESS and apathy in the churches would quickly disappear if Christian believers generally would confess their great need for rediscovering the loveliness of Jesus Christ, their Savior.

I have good scriptural ground for constantly emphasizing my deep concern that Christians should again begin to love our Lord Jesus with an intensity of love and desire such as our fathers knew.

What is basically wrong with us when we start to backslide as individuals or as churches and denominations?

Jesus Himself gave us a plain answer when He said, "You have forsaken your first love" (Revelation 2:4). He was not speaking of first love as first in consecutive order, but of the degree of our first love for Him.

These words of Jesus reflect one of our great weaknesses in the Christian churches of our day.

The fact that we are not going on to know Christ in rich intimacy of acquaintance and fellowship is apparent—but why are we not even willing to talk about it? We are not hearing anything about spiritual desire and yearning and the loveliness of our Savior which would break down all barriers if we would move into communion with Him. This appeal is not getting into our books. You don't hear it in radio messages. It is not being preached in our churches.

Can it be that we do not believe that Jesus Christ is capable of a growing and increasing intimacy of fellowship with those who are His own? To become acquainted with God is one thing, but to go on in commitment and to experience God in intensity and richness of acquaintance is something more. The Apostle Paul knew this in his yearning as he said, "I want to know Him in that depth and rich intensity of experience (paraphrase of Philippians 3:10)!" Of the many compelling reasons why we ought to know our Savior better than we do certainly the first is that He is a person, Jesus Christ. We all agree that He is a person, that He is the Eternal Son, but have we gone on to adore Him because He is the source and fountain of everything that you and I are created to enjoy?

He is truth itself

He is the fountain of all truth, but He is more—He is truth itself. He is the source and strength of all beauty, but He is more—He is beauty itself. He is the fountain of all wisdom, but He is more—He is wisdom itself. In Him are all the treasures of wisdom and knowledge hidden away!

Jesus Christ our Savior is the fountain of all grace. He is the fountain and source of all life, but He is more than that. He could say, "I *AM* the life!" He is the fountain of love, but again, He is far more than that—He is love!

He is resurrection and He is immortality and as one of the adoring song writers said, He is the "brightness of the Father's glory, sunshine of the Father's face."

In another hymn, "Fairest Lord Jesus," there are at least two verses that are not always included, which tell us in candor and realism that when everything else has perished and vanished, we will find it is Jesus alone who abides for aye. One verse says, "Earth's fairest beauty, heaven's brightest splendor, in Jesus Christ unfolded see; all that here shineth quickly declineth before His spotless purity."

There is excitement in true love, and I think that we Christians who love our Savior ought to be more excited about *who* He is and *what* He is!

A friend of mine has been quite irked because I cannot get excited and steamed up about earthly things. I just cannot stand and strike an attitude of awe when a friend drives up with one of the classy new automobiles. I hear people describing the magnificent new houses that they are building, and they have excitement in their voices. But the Word of God forces me to remember that when you have seen the house or the city that hath foundations and whose builder and maker is God, you cannot really ever get excited again about any house ever built by any man in this world.

It has been said that Abraham could never build a

permanent house for himself after he had seen the city whose builder and maker was God. I know I have made up my mind about that city—and I would be willing to live in a tent here because I have some idea about my future home up there. I am convinced that it will be beautiful and satisfying beyond anything I can know down here. It is a tragedy if we forget that "earth's fairest beauty and heaven's brightest splendor are all unfolded in Jesus Christ, and all that here shineth quickly declineth before His spotless purity."

Special kind of Christians

The man who wrote those words, breathed them from his soul, must have been one of God's special kind of Christians. He must have known Jesus Christ intimately day by day. He probably knew all about the cost of knowing the Savior in this way.

But people are not willing to pay that price, and that is why so many Christians must be described as "common." Most Christians talk piously about the cost of Christianity in terms of the unclean, injurious and grossly sinful things they have "surrendered." But if they never get beyond that they are still common Christians. They talk about having given up the bad things, but the Apostle Paul said that for Christ's sake he surrendered the good things as well as the bad.

"Whatever was to my profit I now consider loss" (Philippians 3:7a), he said. He meant things to which he still had a legal and moral right, things about which he could have said, "These are mine and Christianity is not going to take them from me!"

"I yield them all, I give them all because I have found That which is so much better," he implied in Philippians. He had found "That" which was with the Father, Jesus Christ, the fountain from Whom flows all wisdom and beauty and truth and immortality!

Paul knew something that many Christians still have not learned—that the human heart is idolatrous and will worship anything it can possess. Therein lies the danger of the "good" things. We have surrendered evil things, bad things, but we hold on to the good things and these we are prone to worship. Whatever we refuse to surrender and count but loss we will ultimately worship. It may be something good, but it gets between you and God—whether it be property or family or reputation or security or your life itself.

Jesus warned us about our selfishness in grasping and hanging on to our own lives. He taught that if we make our life on earth so important and so all-possessing that we cannot surrender it gladly to Him, we will lose it at last. He taught that plainly, and He also warned us about trusting earthly security rather than putting our complete confidence in God.

We all want a guarantee of security, but we didn't get that idea from the Apostle Paul. He was hardly ever secure as far as the things of this life were concerned. He said he died daily. He was always in difficulty, whether with the governments of this world or with the stormy elements on the sea.

We want security

Brethren, we want security in this life and eternal

security in the world above! I think that is a kind of definition of our modern-day Christian fundamentalism. But Paul said, "I have been captured by Jesus Christ so I disavow and disown everything."

Now there were certain things that God let Paul have. He let him have a book or two. He let him have a garment, a cloak. In one instance, He let him have his own hired house for two years. But the example Paul gave us was the fact that any "things" which God allowed him to have never touched him at heart, at the point of possession.

Any of our external treasures which really bind us at heart will become a curse. Paul said, "I give them up that I might know Him." He never allowed things to become important enough to mar his relationship with God.

The example and admonitions of Paul cause me to call into question some of the teachings in our current Christian circles that Christ is something "added on"—that by ourselves we can have a rather jolly earthly life, but we also need Jesus to save us from hell and to get us into the mansions on the other side!

Now, that is not New Testament teaching and certainly not the way in which Paul looked at things in this world. Paul said that he found Jesus Christ so infinitely attractive that he was forced to throw out every set of values established on earth.

Paul was a learned man, an intellectual educated at the feet of Gamaliel. We would have honored him as a Ph.D. But Paul said, "That is all dross." His expression actually meant: "It is a kind of garbage."

Paul spoke of his birth and of his register and

standing among the fathers of his religious heritage and then testified that "for the sake of Jesus Christ, I count it nothing at all—I put it under my feet."

That ought to say something to us who have so many things about which we are proud. Some of us boast about our national and cultural forebears until we actually become carnal about it. We are proud of things and proud of what we can do. But Paul said, "Everything about which I could be proud as a man I count but loss for the sake of Jesus Christ."

So Paul gives us the proper motives for loving and following the Savior and for giving up the things that would hold us back. Modern Christianity has a lot to learn from Paul in this area of motives. Because of the nature of our times, some are insisting: "America, you had better turn to God or that final bomb will get you!" Another voice of alarm warns: "America, you had better stop drinking and gambling or you will go down like Rome!"

Our old teacher-friend, *The Cloud of Unknowing*, gives us some light on proper motives in relationship to the nature of God Himself. "God is a jealous lover and He suffereth no rival," this saint wrote more than 600 years ago. "God cannot work in our wills unless He can possess our wills for Himself."

One of our faults

Now brethren, this is one of our greatest faults in our Christian lives. We are allowing too many rivals of God. We actually have too many gods. We have too many irons in the fire. We have too much theology that we don't understand. We have too much churchly institutionalism. We have too much religion. Actually, I guess we just have too much of too much!

God is not in our beings by Himself! He cannot do His will in us and through us because we refuse to put away the rivals. When Jesus Christ has cleansed everything from the temple and dwells there alone, He will work!

God wants to do His work hidden and unseen within the human breast. Have you ever been deep down in a mine in the earth? They are mining out coal or gold or diamonds, but anyone flying or walking or traveling overhead may have no idea of what is going on in the depths of that hill. They would never know that deep within the earth there is an intelligent force at work bringing out jewels. That is what God does deep within us—and He works hidden and unseen.

But in our day we must be dramatic about everything. We don't want God to work unless He can make a theatrical production of it. We want Him to come dressed in costumes with a beard and with a staff. We want Him to play a part according to our ideas. Some of us even demand that He provide a colorful setting and fireworks as well!

That is how we want it, but God says, "No, no, no! You children of Adam, you children of carnality and lust, you who love a fair showing of flesh, you who have wrong ideas about my Son, I cannot do my work according to your prescription. I cannot do my work in you!"

How can God do His work in people who seem to think that Christianity is just another way of getting things from God?

I hear people testify that they give their tithe because God makes their nine-tenths go farther than the ten-tenths. That is not spirituality; that is just plain business. I insist that it is a dangerous thing to associate the working of God with our prosperity and success down here. I cannot promise that if you will follow the Lord you will soon experience financial prosperity, because that is not what He promised His disciples. Down through the years, following the Lord has meant that we count all things but loss for the excellency of the knowledge of Christ.

Some Christians prosper

"And don't some Christians prosper?" you ask.

We have many examples of Christian men whom God has been able to trust with unusual prosperity and as they continue to follow the Lord, they give most of it back to Him. But they haven't made Christianity just a technique of getting things.

I hear people testify about their search for the deeper Christian life and it sounds as though they would like to be able to get it in pill form. It seems that it would have been much more convenient for them if God had arranged religion so they could take it like a pill with a glass of water. They buy books, hoping to get their religion by prescription. But there isn't any such thing. There is a cross. There is a gallows. There is a man with bleeding stripes on his back. There is an apostle with no property, with a tradition of loneliness and weariness and rejection and glory—but there are no pills!

There are a thousand ways in which we try to use the Lord. What about that young fellow studying for the ministry, studying until his eyesight begins to fail, but he wants to use Jesus Christ to make him a famous preacher. They will ordain him, and he will get the title of Reverend and if he writes a book, they will make him a Doctor. But if he has been using Jesus Christ, he is just a common huckster buying and selling and getting gain, and the Lord would drive him out of the temple along with the rest.

Then there are some among us these days who have to depend upon truckloads of gadgets to get their religion going, and I am tempted to ask: What will they do when they don't have the help of the trappings and gadgets? The truck can't come along where they are going!

I heard a man boasting on his radio program about the equipment they were going to bring in from Pennsylvania and Ohio so they could better serve the Lord. I don't know of any fancy kind of equipment which will brighten your testimony or your service for God.

I think of the dear old camp meeting women who used to say, "This is my harp of 10 strings, and I praise the Lord!" I can see in my mind now those wrinkled hands with brown spots, but as they clapped those wrinkled, aging hands how their faces would shine! And their harp? Just those hands as they clapped and sang praises to God.

Who needs a bushel basket full of clap-trap in order to serve the Lord? You can worship God anywhere if you will let Him work in your being and suffer no rival. You may be still with arthritis so that you can't even get on your knees to pray, but you can look up in your heart, for prayer isn't a matter of getting on your knees. Prayer is the elevation of the heart to God and that is all a man needs to praise, to pray and to worship.

A strange thing

Now here is a strange thing. If you talk about mysticism in our day, every fundamentalist throws his hands high in the air with disgust to let you know that he considers the mystics dreamers, those who believe in the emotion and feeling. But all of those old saints and the fathers of whom I have read taught that you must believe God by a naked, cold intent of your will and then the other things follow along.

A naked intent unto God—those old saints were practical men. They have exhorted us to press on in faith whether we feel like it or not. They have exhorted us to pray—when we feel like it and when we don't. They never taught that we would always be lifted emotionally to the heights. They knew that there are times when your spiritual progress must be by a naked intent unto God.

Oh that we would have this naked intent to know God, to know Jesus Christ! To be able to put the world and things and people beneath our feet and to open our hearts to only one lover, and that the Son of God Himself!

Oh for the proper balance in all of our relationships! Husband and wife, father and son, mother and daughter, business man and partner, taxpayer and citizen—all of these in their proper place; but in the deep of the heart having only the One lover, He who suffers no rival.

Why has God insisted that it should be this way?

Because it is His intention that our understanding and our reason should be broken down and that our whole case should be thrown back on God. Many have known the time of darkness and oppression as they sought to go on with God and to be filled with His fullness. You believed God and you trusted Christ. Whether you felt like it or not, you went on and you believed and you obeyed. You prayed whether you felt like it or not. You straightened things out and you got adjusted in your relationships at home and in business. You quit the wrong things, the things that had been hindering you, whether you felt like it or not. This is faith—a naked intent unto God, and I must tell you this: out of our darkness and out of our stony grief, God will raise a Bethel. Out of the tomb, He will lift you into the sky. Out of darkness, He will lift you into the light!

This is what it means to love Jesus, to know Him just for Himself. How I pray that we may again recapture in our day the glory that men may have known of the beauty of Jesus.

In *The Cloud of Unknowing,* the old saint wrote that because God is a jealous lover, He wants us to be unwilling to think on anything but God Himself.

Jesus—Himself!

Now, this was the message of Dr. A.B. Simpson. He shocked and blessed a generation because of his central message: "Jesus—Himself!"

Dr. Simpson was asked to go to England to preach in a Bible conference. He discovered that he was to preach the third of three messages on sanctification—and that is a bad spot to be in. The first fellow said in his sermon that the way to be holy and victorious in the Christian life is to suppress "the old man." His was the position of sanctification by suppression. The second man got up and took the position of eradication, deliverance from the old carnal life by eradication. "Get rid of the old man, pull him up, turn up the roots to die!"

Dr. Simpson had to get in between there and he took just one word for his text: "Himself." Then he gave his testimony of efforts and struggles to get the victory. He said, "Sometimes I would think I had gotten it, and then I would lose it. What a blessedness when I came to the knowledge that I had been looking in the wrong place, when I found that victory, sanctification, deliverance, purity, holiness—all must be found in Jesus Christ Himself, not in some formula. When I claimed Jesus just for Himself, it became easy and the glory came to my life."

Out of that knowledge and out of that blessing, Dr. Simpson wrote his famous hymn, "Once it was the blessing, now it is the Lord. Once His gift I wanted, now Himself alone."

This is the basic teaching of the deeper Christian life. It is the willingness to let Jesus Christ Himself be glorified in us and through us. It is the willingness to quit trying to use the Lord for our ends and to let Him work in us for His glory.

That is the kind of revival I am interested in and the only kind—the kind of spiritual reviving and renewing that will cause people to tremble with rapture in the presence of the Lord Jesus Christ.

"Once it was the blessing—now it is the Lord!"

Dark, Dark Night
of the Soul!

"Remember how they nailed Jesus to a cross. Remember the darkness, the hiding of the Father's face. This was the path Jesus took to immortal triumph. As He is, so are we in this world!"

I AM CONVINCED that in New Testament Christianity the object of the Holy Spirit is twofold. First, He wants to convince Christians that it is actually possible for us to know the beauty and perfection of Jesus Christ in our daily lives. Second, it is His desire to lead us forward into victory and blessing even as Joshua once led Israel into the promised land.

The first is not too difficult. Most Christians will honestly confess that there are still spiritual frontiers before them which they have not been willing to explore. There is still ground to be taken if our object is to know Christ, to win Christ, to know the power of His resurrection, to be conformed to His death. If our object is to experience within our beings all of those things that we have in Christ judicially, we must come to the place of counting all things loss for the excellency of this knowledge.

We know our lack, but we are very slow in allowing the Holy Spirit to lead us into deeper Christian life and experience, that place where the intent of our heart is so cleansed that we may perfectly love God and worthily praise Him. In spite of our hesitation and delay and holding back God does not give up, because the Holy Spirit is faithful and kind and patient and ever seeks to lead us forward into the life of the special kind of Christian.

I well remember the caution of one of the old saints I have read who pointed out that "a persuaded mind and even a well-intentioned heart may be far from exact and faithful practice" and "nothing has been more common than to meet souls who are perfect and saintly in speculation."

Jesus did not say, "You will be my disciples by speculation." He did say that by your fruit and by your behavior you will be known. This is one rule that is never deceiving, and it is by this that we should judge ourselves.

God will sift out those who only speculate about the claims of Christ and He will lead forward those who by His grace see Him in His beauty and seek Him in His love.

Illustration of Gideon

The story of Gideon is an illustration of how God seeks His qualities within us and is not concerned with us just as numbers or statistics. Gideon was about to face the enemy and he had an army of 32,000 soldiers. But the Lord said to Gideon, "You have too many—let all who are afraid go back." So Gideon gave the word to the troops, and 22,000 of those men turned back. Then the Lord said to Gideon again, "There are still too many. I can see those among you who are not prepared for what we are going to do. You will never be able to make Israelite soldiers of them."

I presume that there are few preachers among us on the top side of this terrestrial ball who would have turned down those 22,000, but God was putting the emphasis on quality, on those who would cooperate in the performance of the will of God.

Then Gideon took the 10,000 men to the river and tested them as God had directed and when this sifting was all done, Gideon had an army of 300 men. God seeks out those who are willing that their lives should be fashioned according to His own grace and love. He sifts out those who cannot see God's purpose and design for our blessing.

Some of you know something of that which has been called "the dark night of the soul." Some of you have spiritual desire and deep longing for victory but it seems to you that your efforts to go on with God have only brought you more bumps and more testings and more discouragement. You are tempted to ask, "How long can this go on?"

Let me remind you of the journey of Jesus Christ to immortal triumph. Remember the garden where He sweat blood. Remember Pilate's hall where they put on Him the purple robe and smote Him. Remember His experience with His closest disciples as they all forsook Him and fled. Remember the journey up the hill to Calvary. Remember how they nailed Him to a cross, those six awful hours, the hiding of the Father's face. Remember the darkness and remember the surrender of His spirit in death. This was the path that Jesus took to immortal triumph and everlasting glory, and as He is, so are we in this world!

Few enter into the light

Yes, there is a dark night of the soul. There are few Christians willing to go into this dark night and that is why there are so few who enter into the light. It is impossible for them ever to know the morning because they will not endure the night.

In *The Cloud of Unknowing*, we have been told: "This work asketh no long time before it be truly done, as some men think, for it is the shortest work of all that men may imagine. It is neither longer nor shorter, but even according to the stirring that is within thee, even thy will."

The stirring within us often is not enough. There are too many other factors—there is not yet a vacuum within, a prepared place into which the Holy Spirit may come and be at home.

I think the more we learn of God and His ways and of man and his nature we are bound to reach the conclusion that we are all just about as holy as we want to be. We are all just about as full of the Spirit as we want to be. Thus when we tell ourselves that we want to be more holy but we are really as holy as we care to be, it is small wonder that the dark night of the soul takes so long!

The reason why many are still troubled, still seeking, still making little forward progress is because they have not yet come to the end of themselves. We are still giving some of the orders, and we are still interfering with God's working within us.

We struggle to keep up a good front, forgetting

that God says the most important thing is for us to be humble and meek as Christ gave us example. It seems that Christians are obsessed with keeping up that good front. We say we want to go to heaven when we die to see old Jordan roll, but we spend most of our time and energy down here just putting on that good front. It seems that many of us say to God, as did King Saul the apostate before us, "Oh God, honor me now before these people!"

Hiding our inner state

We also are guilty of hiding our inner state. The Bible plainly tells us to expose our inner state to God, but we would rather cover it up. God cannot change it if we cover it and hide it.

We disguise the poverty of our spirit. If we should suddenly be revealed to those around us on the outside as Almighty God sees us within our souls, we would become the most embarrassed people in the world. If that should happen, we would be revealed as people barely able to stand, people in rags, some too dirty to be decent, some with great open sores. Some would be revealed in such condition that they would be turned out of Skid Row. Do we think that we are actually keeping our spiritual poverty a secret, that God doesn't know us better than we know ourselves? But we will not tell Him, and we disguise our poverty of spirit and hide our inward state in order to preserve our reputation.

We also want to keep some authority for ourselves. We cannot agree that the last, the final key to our lives should be turned over to Jesus Christ. Brethren, we want to have dual controls—let the

Lord run it but keep a hand on the controls just in case the Lord should fail!

We are willing to join heartily in singing, "To God Be the Glory," but we are strangely ingenius in figuring out ways and means by which we keep some of the glory for ourselves. In this matter of perpetually seeking our own interests, we can only say that people who want to live for God often arrange to do very subtly what the worldly souls do crudely and openly.

A man who doesn't have enough imagination to invent anything will still figure out a way of seeking his own interests, and the amazing thing is that he will do it with the help of some pretext which will serve as a screen to keep him from seeing the ugliness of his own behavior.

Yes, we have it among professing Christians—this strange ingenuity to seek our own interest under the guise of seeking the interests of God. I am not afraid to say what I fear—that there are thousands of people who are using the deeper life and Bible prophecy, foreign missions and physical healing for no other purpose than to promote their own private interests secretly. They continue to let their apparent interest in these things to serve as a screen so that they don't have to take a look at how ugly they are on the inside.

So we talk a lot about the deeper life and spiritual victory and becoming dead to ourselves—but we stay very busy rescuing ourselves from the cross. That part of ourselves that we rescue from the cross may be a very little part of us, but it is likely to be the seat of our spiritual troubles and our defeats.

No one wants to die on a cross—until he comes to

the place where he is desperate for the highest will of God in serving Jesus Christ. The Apostle Paul said, "I want to die on that cross and I want to know what it is to die there, because if I die with Him I will also know Him in a better resurrection." Paul was not just saying, "He will raise me from the dead"—for everyone will be raised from the dead. He said, "I want a superior resurrection, a resurrection like Christ's." Paul was willing to be crucified with Christ, but in our day we want to die a piece at a time, so we can rescue little parts of ourselves from the cross.

There are men and women who beg and plead for God to fill them with Himself for they know it would be for their good, but then they stubbornly resist like our own spoiled children when they are not well and they want us to help them.

You try to take the child's temperature or give him medicine or call for a doctor and he will resist and howl and bawl. In the next breath he will beg for help, "Mama, I'm sick!" But he won't take a thing, he won't let you help. He is stubborn and spoiled.

Let God have His way

People will pray and ask God to be filled—but all the while there is that strange ingenuity, that contradiction within which prevents our wills from stirring to the point of letting God have His way.

It is for this reason that I do not like to ask congregations to sing one of the old songs, "Fill Me Now." I think it is one of the most hopeless songs ever written—gloomy and hopeless. I have yet to find anyone who was ever filled while singing "Fill me now, fill me now, fill me now." It just doesn't work that way—for if you are resisting God, you can sing all four verses and repeat the last one in a mournful melody but God will still have to wait for your decision on that part of yourself that you are saving from the cross.

Those who live in this state of perpetual contradiction cannot be happy Christians. A man who is always on the cross, just piece after piece, cannot be happy in that process. But when that man takes his place on the cross with Jesus Christ once and for all, and commends his spirit to God, lets go of everything and ceases to defend himself—sure, he has died, but there is a resurrection that follows!

If we are willing to go this route of victory with Jesus Christ, we cannot continue to be mediocre Christians, stopped halfway to the peak. Until we give up our own interests, there will never be enough stirring within our beings to find His highest will.

Why, then, does it take so long? Whose fault is it that we do not have the intents of our heart so cleansed that we may perpetually love Him and worthily serve Him, and that we may be filled with His Spirit and walk in victory?

I hope I have made it plain that it is our fault—and not God's! "This work asketh no long time before it be truly done, as some men think, for it is the shortest work of all that men may imagine, according to the stirring that is within thee, even thy will." If you are one of the fellows who is convinced it has to take a long time, you are wrong. It may be one of the quickest, shortest works that a man may know—just as short or as long as your own will decrees.

Many of us are hanging on to something, something that we hold dear to ourselves, something that comes between us and the Lord.

Some of you as young people may have a tiny baby that has now become your dearest treasure on earth. Perhaps you have heard the still small voice of the Lord saying, "Will you commit that tiny life back to me? Will you take your own hands from the direction of that life and put that direction over into the hands of the Holy Spirit?"

God deals with us all about His highest will for ourselves and for our children. Years ago when our two oldest boys were small I was away from home on a preaching mission. God dealt with me plainly about my possessiveness of the treasure which I had in those two sons. God spoke to me and asked me if I would give them up to Him, and I thought He meant that He wanted them to die. I was prostrate on the floor beside my bed and kicked my toes on the carpet and cried out to God—and I finally gave those two boys back to God. I have been able to see since then in raising those boys and the rest of the children that God doesn't ask for our children for Himself—He just wants to bring us out into a place of surrender so that our children and our earthly possessions do not possess our wills to the point of worship. God puts us through these times because there ought not to be anything in our earthly lives that we would knowingly hold back from God.

I confess that I went through this matter of dying after each child that God gave us. When our little girl came to us, we dedicated her to the Lord in a morning service, but that was nothing. My own personal dedication of that child was a prolonged, terrible, sweaty thing. I finally said to God, "Yes, Lord, you can have her." I knew that God wasn't going to let her die, for I had learned that lesson years before with her two older brothers.

But the thing was this—I didn't know what He wanted, and it was a struggle to give up, to yield.

Later, in giving a testimony in our church, I said, "The dearest thing we have in the world is our little girl, but God knows that He can have her whenever He wants her."

After the service someone came and said, "Mr. Tozer, aren't you afraid to talk like that about your little girl?"

"Afraid?" I said, "Why, I have put her in the hands of perfect love and love cannot wound anyone and love cannot hurt anyone. I am perfectly content that she is shielded in the life of Jesus Christ, His name being love and His hands being strong and His face shining like the beauty of the sun and His heart being the tender heart of God in compassion and lovingkindness."

Treasure possession

We who are Christians go through these times of testing and proving as our Lord seeks to deal with us about our treasures possessing us on this earth. With some it may be the commitment of a favorite boyfriend or girlfriend to God for His highest will. Some people have put life's highest value upon their job and their security in this life. With some it may be a secret ambition, and it is driving a wedge between you and the Lord. Others may be possessed by the amount of your nice little nest egg lying there in the bank, and you just cannot bring yourself to quit calling it yours. You just cannot let go and that is in spite of the fact that you know you can perfectly trust the Lord and the leading of His Spirit.

Do you remember a rather comic character by the name of Sancho Panza in that well-known book, *Don Quixote?* There is an incident in the book in which Señor Panza clung to a window sill all night, afraid that if he let go he would plunge and die on the ground below. But when the morning light came, red-faced and near exhaustion, he found that his feet were only two inches above the grass. Fear kept him from letting go, but he could have been safe on the ground throughout the long night.

I use that illustration to remind us that there are many professing Christians whose knuckles are white from blindly hanging on to their own window sill. The Lord has been saying, "Look on me and let go!" But they have refused.

Paul said we should be "straining toward what is ahead" (Philippians 3:13b)—but many are afraid. Happy are the men and women who have given God His way—they "press on toward the goal to win the prize for which God has called me heavenward in Christ Jesus" (v 14).

God Heard Elijah Because Elijah Heard God!

"Oneness with Christ means to be identified with Him in crucifixion—then going on to be identified with Him in resurrection power!"

WE URGENTLY NEED A NEW KIND of reformation throughout our Christian churches—a reformation that will cause us not only to accept the will of God but to actively seek it and adore it!

At one point in history concerned believers sought a reformation that would bring the Bible back to the church. They got it.

Again, the church needed a reformation that would demonstrate that men could be forgiven, converted and transformed. This came about in reality under the Wesleys.

The reformation we need now can best be described in terms of spiritual perfection—which reduced to its simplest form is no more and no less than doing the will of God! This would expose us all at the point of our need, no matter how sound we think we are in doctrine and no matter how great our reputations.

I long for the positive and genuine renewal which would come if the will of God could be totally accomplished in our lives. Everything that is unspiritual would flee, and all that is not Christlike would vanish, and all that is not according to the New Testament would be rejected.

If this ever happens, it will come because Christians are finally willing to look on the Savior and let Him work, and each will take his own cross with such gladness that he can breathe, "Oh cross, oh good cross, I embrace thee!"

As believers, our relation to the will of God may be twofold: passive and active. In the passive sense we are resigned to God's acts, and in our day when we mention the will of God, we almost invariably mean this kind of resignation to God's will.

We see this resignation in the New Testament account in which God revealed Himself to Mary. He told her what He was going to do and Mary said, "May it be to me as you have said" (Luke 1:38b). God promised that He would perform a great miracle and she accepted it as the will of God, indeed.

But the second aspect of the will of God is one which we rarely consider—the active side of the will of God. Do we voluntarily and actively observe God's commandments, making positive changes in our lives as God may indicate in order to bring the entire life into accord with the New Testament?

That is the active aspect of the will of God that I would own as reformation in the church, and it would surely result in revival.

Many are content to sit around in the pews singing, "Have Thine Own Way, Lord." They are resigned to this interpretation of the will of God: "Whatever God wants to do is fine with me." They are passively resigned.

But are they willing to hear the voice of God and obey His bidding and do what He wants them to do? That would become active participation and acceptance of the will of God. It would mean bringing the entire life into accord with New Testament teaching.

Can't separate the two

Some people in reading the Bible say they cannot understand why Elijah and other men had such active power with the living God. It is quite simple. God heard Elijah because Elijah had heard God. God did according to the word of Elijah because Elijah had done according to the word of God. You cannot separate the two.

When we are willing to consider the active will of God for our lives, we come immediately to a personal knowledge of the cross, because the will of God is the place of blessed, painful, fruitful trouble!

The Apostle Paul knew about that. He called it "the fellowship of Christ's sufferings." It is my conviction that one of the reasons we exhibit very little spiritual power is because we are unwilling to accept and experience the fellowship of the Savior's sufferings, which means acceptance of His cross.

How can we have and know the blessed intimacy of the Lord Jesus if we are unwilling to take the route which He has demonstrated? We do not have it because we refuse to relate the will of God to the cross.

All of the great saints have been acquainted with the cross—even those who lived before the time of Christ. They were acquainted with the cross in essence because their obedience brought it to them.

All Christians living in full obedience will experience the cross and find themselves exercised in spirit very frequently. If they know their own hearts, they will be prepared to wrestle with the cross when it comes.

Think of Jacob in the Old Testament and notice the direction from which his cross came—directly from his own carnal self. It took Jacob some time to discover the nature of his own heart and to admit and confess that Jacob's cross was Jacob himself.

Read again about Daniel and you will discover that his cross was the world. Consider Job and you will find that his cross was the devil. The devil crucified Job, the world crucified Daniel, and Jacob was crucified on the tree of his own Jacobness, his own carnality.

Study the lives of the apostles in the New Testament and you will find that their crosses came from the religious authorities.

Likewise in church history we look at Luther and note that his cross came from the Roman church which makes so much of wooden crosses, while Wesley's cross came from the Protestant church. Continue to name the great souls who followed the will of God, and you will name the men and women of God who looked forward by faith and their obedience invariably led them into places of blessed and painful and fruitful trouble.

I must point out here the fallacy of thinking that in following Jesus we can easily go up on the hillside and die—just like that! I admit that when Jesus was here on earth, the easiest and cheapest way to get off was to follow Jesus physically. Anyone could get out of work and say goodbye with the explanation, "I am going to follow Jesus." Multitudes did this. They followed Him physically, but they had no understanding of Him spiritually. Therefore, in that day the cheapest, easiest way to dispose of the cross was to carry it physically.

But, brethren, taking our cross is not going to mean the physical act of following Jesus along a dusty pathway. We are not going to climb the hill where there are already two crosses in place and be nailed up between them.

Our cross will be determined by whatever pain and suffering and trouble which will yet come to us because of our obedience to the will of God. The true saints of God have always borne witness that wholehearted obedience brings the cross into the light quicker than anything else.

Identified with Christ

Oneness with Christ means to be identified with Christ, identified with Him in crucifixion. But we must go on to be identified with Him in resurrection as well, for beyond the cross is resurrection and the manifestation of His Presence.

I would not want to make the mistake of some preachers who have never gotten beyond the message of death, death, death! They preach it so much that they never get anyone beyond death into resurrection life and victory.

I recall that when I was a young man and getting along well spiritually, having been wonderfully filled with the Holy Spirit, I read a book about the cross. In that volume, the author put you on the cross in the first chapter, and you were still hanging on the cross in the last chapter. It was gloomy all the way through—and I had a difficult time shaking that off because it was death, death, death! I was greatly helped at that time by the radiant approach of Dr. A.B. Simpson to the meaning of the cross and death to self. He took one through the meaning of the cross to the understanding that beyond the cross there is resurrection life and power, an identification with a risen Savior and the manifestation of His loving Presence.

The old 15th-century saint whom we have quoted declared that "God is ingenius in making us crosses."

Considering that, we have to confess that when Christians say, "I am crucified with Christ by faith," they are merely using a technical term and are not talking about a cross in reality. But God wants His children to know the cross. He knows that only spiritual good can come to us as a result of our identification with the Lord Jesus. So, He is ingenius in making crosses for us.

The quotation continues: "He may make them of iron and of lead which are heavy of themselves. He makes some of straw which seem to weigh nothing, but one discovers that they are no less difficult to carry. A cross that appears to be of straw so that others think it amounts to nothing may be crucifying you through and through.

"He makes some with gold and precious stones which dazzle the spectators and excite the envy of the public but which crucify no less than the crosses which are more despised."

Christians who are put in high places, Christians who are entrusted with wealth and influence, know something about the kind of cross that may seem dazzling to spectators and excites the envy of the public—but if they know how to take it, it crucifies them no less than the others.

It seems that He makes our crosses of all the things we like the best so that when they turn to bitterness we are able to learn the true measure of eternal values.

It appears, also, that it often pleases God to join physical weakness to this servitude of the Spirit.

"Nothing is more useful than these two crosses together," the quote from the old saint continues. "They crucify a man from head to foot."

I confess that when I read that it came like a shock to my soul, realizing anew that Jesus Christ was crucified from head to foot! When they nailed Him there, He was crucified in every part of His body and there was no part of His holy nature that did not suffer the full intensity of those pains on the cross.

The children of God must be ready for everything the cross brings or we will surely fail the test! It is God's desire to so deal with us about all of the things that the world admires and praises that we will see them in their true light. He will treat us without pity because He desires to raise us without measure—just as He did with His own Son on the cross!

The Apostle Paul gave us this wonderful assessment of the will of God concerning the person and the earthly work of Jesus Christ:

Your attitude should be the same as that of Christ Jesus:

> Who, being in the very nature God,
>> did not consider equality with God
>>> something to be grasped,
> but made himself nothing,
>> taking the very nature of a servant,
>> being made in human likeness.
> And being found in appearance as a man,
>> he humbled himself
>> and became obedient to death—
>>> even death on a cross!
> (Philippians 2:5–8)

But notice the next word: "Therefore."

> Therefore God exalted him to the highest
>> place
> and gave him the name that is above every
>> name,
> that at the name of Jesus every knee should
>> bow,
> . . . .
> and every tongue confess!
> (vv 9–11)

This is why I believe that God will crucify without pity those whom He desires to raise without measure! This is why we believers have to surrender to Him the full control of everything that we consider to be an asset in terms of human power and talent and accomplishment. God takes pleasure in confounding everything that comes under the guise of human power—which is really weakness disguised! Our intellectual power, our great mind, our array of talents—all of these are good if God has so ordered, but in reality they are human weaknesses disguised. God wants to crucify us from head to foot—making our own powers ridiculous and useless—in the desire to raise us without measure for His glory and for our eternal good.

Dare we realize what a gracious thing it is that the Lord of all creation is desirous of raising us into a position of such glory and usefulness? Can we conceive that God would speak to angels and all the creatures who do His will and say of us: "The lid is off for this child of mine! There is to be no ceiling, no measure on what he can have, and there is no limit to where I may take him. Just keep it open. Without measure I will raise him because without pity I have been able to crucify him!"

You who are parents and you who have had the care of children know what it is to chasten without pity and yet at the same time discipline and punish with both love and pity. What do you do when you want your child to be the very finest example of manhood and character and citizenship? You pray for him and you love him so much that you would give the blood out of your veins for him—yet without pity you apply the rod of discipline and chastening. It is actually pity that makes you punish him without pity!

That sounds like a beautiful mix-up, but that is the character and desire of our God for us if we are His children. It is the love and the pity of God for His children that prescribes the chastening of a cross so that we may become the kind of mature believers and disciples that He wants us to be.

Be completely separated

I earnestly believe that God is trying to raise up a

company of Christians in our day who are willing
to be completely separated from all prejudices and
all carnal desires. He wants those who are ready to
put themselves at God's disposal, willing to bear
any kind of cross—iron or lead or straw or gold or
whatever—and to be the kinds of examples He
needs on this earth.

The great question is: Is there a readiness, an
eagerness among us for the kind of cross He wants
to reveal through us?

Often we sing, "Hold Thou Thy cross before my
closing eyes,/ Shine through the gloom and point
me to the skies."

What a pathetic thing to see the cross so misunderstood in sections of Christianity. Think of
poor souls who have never found the evangelical
meaning and assurance of atonement and justification, cleansing and pardon. When they come to the
time of death, the best they know is to clutch some
manufactured cross to the breast, holding it tightly
and hoping for some power to come from painted
metal or carved wood to take them safely over the
river.

No, no! That is not the kind of cross that helps.
The cross that we want is that which will come to
us from being in the will of God. It is not a cross on
a hill nor a cross on a church. It is not the cross that
can be worn around the neck. It must be the cross
of obedience to the will of God, and we must embrace it, each believer for himself!

Willingness to suffer for Jesus' sake—this is what
we have lost from the Christian church. We want
our Easter to come without the necessity of a Good
Friday. We forget that before the Redeemer could

rise and sing among His brethren He must first bow His head and suffer among His brethren!

We forget so easily that in the spiritual life there must be the darkness of the night before there can be the radiance of the dawn. Before the life of resurrection can be known, there must be the death that ends the dominion of self. It is a serious but a blessed decision, this willingness to say, "I will follow Him no matter what the cost. I will take the cross no matter how it comes!"

Out of my own experience at this point I wrote a few words years ago which have long been my constant prayer:

"Oh God, let me die right, rather than letting me live wrong.

"Keep me, Lord, from ever hardening down into the state of being just another average Christian.

"Lord, I would rather reach a high point and turn off the light than to live a poor, useless life on a low level."

As individuals we often say that we want revival to come. Revival will come to us and within us when we really want it, when we pay the price.

Have you come to the place of heart-searching, of travail in the Spirit, the place of blessed pain and trouble for Jesus' sake?

Without that decision and that commitment, you can pray on for revival to your dying day. You can join groups and stay up and pray for revival all night but exercise is all you will gain and sleep will probably be all you will lose!

We must dare to pray, "Oh God, crucify me from head to foot—I lay in dust life's glory dead!"

This is the reformation that we need!

Don't Throw Your Head Away—You'll Need It!

"I am concerned about the attempts of some evangelicals to equate Christianity with all learning and all philosophy and all science!"

THERE IS A GREAT MISUNDERSTANDING in Christianity today about the value of human effort and human ability in relation to the knowledge of God and fellowship with Him as His flock on this earth.

If you are longing after God with the expectation that you are going to be able to think your way through to Him, you are completely mistaken. This is a hunger that cannot be filled by human effort and our travail cannot be in the area either of our wits or our imagination, for in all of this there is an element of "unknowing," a deep, divine abyss of the Godhead. We dare not settle for anything less!

This is why I am concerned about the attempts being made by some evangelicals to equate Christianity with all learning and all philosophy and all science. If they continue on in their blind ways, they will find themselves ultimately in the camp of the theological liberals and under the cold frown of Almighty God.

Many of them apparently overlook the fact that the Spirit of God never promised to fill a man's head. The promise is that God will fill the heart, or man's innermost being. The Word of God makes it very plain that the church of Jesus Christ will never operate and minister and prosper by the stock of knowledge in the heads of Christian believers but by the warmth and urgency of God's love and compassion flowing through their beings.

Now, don't throw your head away—you are going to need it! I am convinced that God has made it plain that man alone, of all the creatures on earth, is created so that he can have fullness of knowledge about the earth and all the wonders and glories that it holds. I believe that through grace man can have a fullness of knowledge even about the works of God—but this certainly does not mean that we find Him and know Him and love Him through thought processes and human wisdom.

It is utterly and completely futile to try to think our way through to knowing God, Who is beyond our power of thought or visualization. This does not mean that it is impossible for us to think about Him—but it does mean that we cannot think around Him or think equal to Him or think up to Him!

This can be illustrated with one of the dangers of our times. A young man, for instance, has a hunger within himself for the knowledge of God and perhaps for the service of God. He goes to see a teacher who says, "Let's think this thing through." So the young man goes away saying, "Thank you, Doctor." He thinks he is all fixed up, but he hasn't received a thing. He has been taught in his head but his heart has not been satisfied, and he goes away still hungry.

If we are not in love with Christ Himself and if we are satisfied with a knowledge of the works of God and of systems of theology, our hunger for God will not be satisfied.

Now, I know that there is an intellectual element in the Gospel, for one of the attributes of deity is intellect. We call this element theology or doctrine. Human thought may engage theology, and it may engage doctrine. These things are necessary and right in their place, but there must be a seeking of the heart and being which is beyond the intellect.

An old hymn says, "The Spirit breathes upon the Word and brings the truth to light." How much more glory we discover in the Scriptures when the Spirit breathes upon them. It is possible for the Scriptures to be "taught" merely as an intellectual exposition, and if the Spirit is not allowed to breathe the life of God into the truth, our teaching can be useless and perhaps harmful.

Know God Himself

When we sing, "Beyond the sacred page, I seek Thee, Lord," we do not mean that we are seeking contrary to or apart from the Word of God. The sacred page is not to be a substitute for God, although it has been made that by millions of people. The sacred page is not meant to be the end, but only the means toward the end, which is knowing God Himself.

In this current era many believers settle for knowing the text and having the text and arguing that because we have the text we must certainly have the experience.

The experience of God within the believer ought to result from the text, but it is possible to have the text and not have the experience!

This can be simply but plainly illustrated. Suppose a very rich man dies and leaves a will, the text of which passes on all of his millions to his only son. So the son and heir borrows the text of his father's will from the attorney and carries it around with him. He becomes ragged and hungry, begging on the street for a crust of bread.

But when someone says, "Poor fellow, you are in bad shape, weak and pale and sickly," the heir to the fortune reacts strongly.

"Don't talk to me like that," he says. "I have much more than I will ever be able to use!"

To prove it, he opens the will and reads: "Unto my dear son, Charles, I bequeath my property, my stocks and bonds, my bank accounts, my entire estate."

You see, Charles is completely satisfied with the text of the will. He has it and he holds it—but he has never had it executed, never had it filed for probate, never presented his legitimate claims to the inheritance. In actual experience, he has received nothing. He simply holds the text of the will.

In the same sense, a Christian may go around clutching the book of Ephesians and not realize that he is spiritually lean and hungry, pallid and weak, and ragged as well. If a pastor or an evangelist suggests that he could be in a more prosperous spiritual state, a strong, bristling reaction may result.

"Don't talk about me like that," he may say. "Am I not accepted in the Beloved? Do I not have everything in Jesus? Is not God my father and am I not an heir with God?"

How many of us does this portray, limping our ragged and lonely way down the street? It is one thing to have the text of the will—it is another thing to come into possession of the riches. The will of God is one thing but to have the will of God is another.

Old Testament illustration

God has seen fit to give us a powerful Old Testament illustration of the necessity for a divine illumination, an experience of supernatural transformation and understanding in the quickening of the soul. It is in the account of the progress of Israel's high priest into the Holy of Holies. First in the order which God established was the Outer Court, over which there was no roof or covering. When the priest was there, he was aided by the natural light of the sun.

Then he passed through a veil into the Holy Place. Here there was no light of nature, but an artificial light was kept kindled by the priests themselves.

Still beyond was the Holy of Holies where there was neither natural light nor artificial light. There was only the Shekinah glory, the supernatural light of God shining from the mercy seat. When the priest came into the Holy of Holies, there was nothing human upon which he could lean. The intellect was of no consequence. There was no ecclesiastical light nor associate preacher in long tails intoning in a ministerial voice.

Think about that man chosen to minister as the high priest in those days. He came into the Holy of Holies knowing that the God who made heaven and earth was dwelling in fire between the wings of the cherubim. He knew that this was the great and living God with His thousands of attributes and His sea of endless and boundless Being. This man, a human, knew that God dwelt there and that as priest he was to move into that Presence.

In the Outer Court, there was a light above to help him. That could represent our church and denomination—the natural things upon which we often depend.

Moving into the Holy Place, there was still the artificial light, and perhaps that could be a representation of our theology.

But he had to go on until there was no natural or artificial light—only a supernatural shining! There in that Presence he had nothing to assure him but the character of God, nothing to protect him but the blood which he presented.

Furthermore, he was all alone. No other person could go in with the priest. His helpers could aid him in getting the veils apart, but then they had to back away with their eyes averted. Only the high priest with the blood could enter into that holiest place of all. Without the protection of the blood he would have burned as a leaf burns in fire. There was no human reassurance, no human help or counsel. There was no other human to pat him on the back, no one to show him the text, no one to

help. He was all alone—but he had the character of
God to assure him!

It must be alone

Brethren, when we finally have our meeting with
God, it has to be alone in the depths of our being.
We will be alone even if we are surrounded by a
crowd. God has to cut every maverick out of the
herd and brand him all alone. It isn't something
that God can do for us en masse.

If it takes a crowd to get you converted, you have
not been converted! If it takes a crowd to get you
through the fullness of the Holy Ghost, you are
going to be disappointed.

I know that people do not want to be alone with
God, but if your longing heart ever finds the living
water, it will be alone. We humans want to help
each other and that is good insofar as we can, but
God wants us to press through to His Presence
where there is no natural or artificial help. Our
denominations have their place, but they cannot
aid us at this point of aloneness. He asks that we
come with a naked intent unto God. We must want
God Himself—and nothing more!

When we present ourselves to Him in this way,
what a blessing to have His assurance that God
Himself has removed all of the legal hindrances to
our access. It is a glorious hard core of fact that
Jesus Christ has removed all of the legal hindrances!

There are many legal reasons why I should not go
to heaven. There are governmental reasons why I
should not go to heaven. I believe that a holy God
must run His universe according to holy law—and I

do not belong there because I have broken every one of those holy laws in some way. Therefore, there has to be a redemption, a justification of some kind if I am to have God and He is to have me.

Thank God, it has been done! The New Testament language is plain as can be—in Jesus Christ and through His death and resurrection every legal hindrance has been met and taken away. There is nothing to stop you except yourself—no reason why we cannot enter into all the depths of the fullness of God!

Here I must repeat—too many people are trying to think their way in. The only way to get in is to believe Him with our hearts forevermore, crying after Him and looking unto Him with a naked intent of love! The time comes when all we can do is believe God—believe what He says, believe Him and love Him!

Thinking is not enough

The thinking process is not enough in this realm. The great God Almighty that fills the universe and overflows into immensity can never be surrounded by that little thing that we call our brain, our mind, our intellect—never, never, never! Never can we rise to face God by what we know and by what we are, but only by love and faith are we lifted thus to know Him and adore Him!

You know what a vacuum is—just an empty place where there isn't anything, not even air! They tell us that nature abhors a vacuum and unless the vacuum is surrounded by a hard casing of some kind, air or water or some other element will rush in and fill it. It should be happy knowledge to us

that the kingdom of God also abhors a vacuum—
and when you empty yourself, God Almighty
rushes in!

Someone has written:

"Drawn by my Redeemer's love,
After Him I follow fast;
Drawn from earth to things above,
Drawn out of myself at last."

Drawn out of myself at last! If we are not able to
make this confession, this becomes one of our
greatest problems. If we have not been drawn from
earth to things above, how can we be drawn out of
ourselves to be spent in God? What a happy hour it
becomes when we are drawn out of ourselves, and
into that vacuum rushes the blessed Presence. Our
subjection to Him is only because of our love for
Him and our resignation to His will is for His pleasure alone, for He wills and merits to be thus loved
and served!

The wonderful thing about the invitation of the
Holy Spirit of God is that He doesn't say different
things to different people. The Holy Spirit does not
say two things—He says one thing! He says the
same thing to all who are listening to Him.

He says, "Pour yourself out! Give yourself to Me!
Empty yourself! Bring your empty earthen vessels!
Come in meekness like a child!"

Drawn out of yourself by the Holy Spirit—for
who knoweth the things of God but the Holy
Spirit? Pulled out of the mud of your own ego, so
that you have stopped thinking that you are somebody, at last you are delivered from yourself and
are seeking God for Himself alone.

Think of that little woman centuries ago who pushed herself towards Jesus in the midst of a thronging crowd. Jesus was almost crushed in the crowd which pressed Him on every side. But one weak little woman completely ignored the pushing and the jostling, and as though she and the Savior were alone, she touched the hem of His garment—and was healed!

Jesus turned His head and said, "Who touched me?" There were those around Him who answered, "That's a foolish question. You are in the middle of a mob, crowded and pushed and jostled and you ask, 'Who touched Me?" But Jesus said, "I only asked who touched Me in faith? Who touched Me with love?" Many jostled Him—but this woman had really touched Him in faith and love and wonder—and she was made whole.

In our day there are still the crowds and the meetings and opportunities to reach out to Jesus in simple faith and love. But we have meetings where people revel in the crowd—and ignore the Lord. In the midst of our assemblies, isn't Jesus always waiting for someone to disregard the crowd and the circumstances and the traditions—and to push through in love and in faith to touch Him for His healing wholeness?

Oh, go back into the Word of God and consider how thirsty the friends of God were for God Himself! The great difference between us and the Abrahams and the Davids and the Pauls is that they sought Him and found Him and seeking Him still, found Him and sought Him—continually!

We accept Him—and seek Him no more and that is the difference!

In the Song of Solomon in the Old Testament there is the appealing story of the girl who is very deeply in love with a young shepherd. She is so beautiful that a king is attracted to her and demands her favors, but she remains loyal to the simple shepherd, her love, who gathers lilies in the dew of the night and comes to seek her and call to her through the lattice. In many ways it is a picture of the Lord Jesus, the shepherd; His love and care for His bride, the Church; and the world represented by the king demanding our love.

In the scriptural account the shepherd calls, "Arise, my darling, . . . the rains are over and gone. . . . the cooing of doves is heard in our land" (Song of Songs 2:10–12).

But she turns him away with excuses about the ointment on her hands and that she has already retired for the night. So he goes away in sadness. However, she is condemned in her heart and rises from bed to search for her shepherd lover. When she is unable to find him, she begs for help. She is asked by her friends, "How is your beloved better than others, that you charge us so?" (5:9b)

"Oh, he is altogether lovely!" she replies. "He came and called for me. I heard him but didn't have the heart to go. Now I know what I have missed and I must find him."

At last she is able to confess, "I have found him whom my soul loveth!" He had been grieved, but he was not far away. So it is with our Beloved—He is very near to us and He awaits our seeking!

Oh, a heart that is evermore crying after the One it loves is better indeed than the heart that has settled down to the little it already knows!

Forget That They Told You to Shut Up!

"Why do we not capture the divine illumination of Jesus Christ in our souls? Because there is a cloud of concealment between us and the smiling face of God!"

I CANNOT HELP BUT BELIEVE that in our generation there is a great, concealing cloud over much of the fundamental, gospel church which has practically shut off our consciousness of the smiling face of God.

Textualism, a system of rigid adherence to words, has largely captured the church, with the language of the New Testament still being used but with the Spirit of the New Testament grieved.

The doctrine of verbal inspiration of the Scriptures, for instance, is still held, but in such a way that its illumination and life are gone and rigor mortis has set in. As a result religious yearning is choked down, religious imagination has been stultified and religious aspiration smothered.

The "hierarchy" and the "scribes" of this school of thought have told us and would teach us that we ought to shut up and quit talking about spiritual longing and desire in the Christian church.

We have already seen the reaction to this among the masses of evangelical Christians. There has been a revolt in two directions, a rather unconscious revolt, like the gasping of fish in a bowl where there is no oxygen. A great company of evangelicals has already gone over into the area of religious entertainment so that many gospel churches are tramping on the doorstep of the theater. Over against that, some serious segments of fundamental and evangelical thought have revolted into the position of evangelical rationalism which finds it a practical thing to make its peace with liberalism.

This is why the message of spiritual perfection and longing after God sounds so strange to our generation. On one side the masses proclaim, "I have accepted Jesus—whoop de doo! Let's go and have fun!" On the other, serious and reverent men are thinking their way perilously near to the borders of liberalism. Meanwhile, the New Testament message, objectives and methods are allowed to lie dormant, spurned and forgotten.

I have read for many years in the old devotional classics of the desire of the saints of God to keep the candles of their souls burning brightly, day by day. They sought to feel the divine fire in their hearts, to experience the blessedness of reconciliation with God. They are on record as always willing to renounce everything worldly in order to possess the treasure buried in the field of their hearts.

This is not new doctrine and it ought not to sound so different and strange to us. Has not Christ made full atonement for us, and should we not renounce everything that would keep us from the conscious experience of knowing and receiving the Kingdom of God within us?

God's face is turned toward us. The famed Lady Julian wrote long ago, "The precious amends our Lord hath made for man's sin have turned all our blame into endless honor!" Paul said it in this way, "Where sin inceased, grace increased all the more" (Romans 5:20b).

It is glorious knowledge indeed that the smiling face of God is turned toward us. Why, then, do we not capture the wondrous, divine illumination of our Savior, Jesus Christ? Why do we not know the divine fire in our own souls? Why do we not strive to sense and experience the knowledge of exhilaration of reconciliation with God?

Cloud of concealment

Let me tell you why — it is because there is between us and the smiling face of God a cloud of concealment.

Some dismiss the subject by saying that it is all a matter of position with God — rather than possession! That is an answer as cold as dry ice and can only result in further coldness of soul.

I believe the smiling face of God is always turned toward us — but the cloud of concealment is of our own making.

The weather can be an illustration of these spiritual conditions which we allow and foster under a cloud. We are told that the sun is always shining somewhere. Since the day that God said, "Let the sun rule the day," the sun has continued to shine. On earth, however, there are cloudy days, dark and misty days. I have seen the daytime so dark that the chickens had gone to roost and the lights had to be turned on.

Yes, the sun was shining on those dark days, shining just as brightly as on the clearest day in June. You don't need to worry about the sun—it will always shine! But the dark concealing cloud comes between the radiance of the sun and the earth.

Apply this to the Christian life. All that can be done for our salvation has been done. Christ has died for us and has been raised from the dead. The face of God shines down on us, but as Christians we allow the clouds of concealment to form.

Sometimes it may be a cloud caused by our stubborn pride. You may be a child of God, heaven is your home—and yet for a lifetime you may go on without the wondrous, divine illumination of the Savior, Jesus Christ. You will not bend. You will yield neither to God nor man. Remember God's complaint against Israel. He said, "Your neck is brass and your forehead hard." He could not get Israel to bend, to yield to His will.

Self-will is a close relative of pride, and it will form a cloud that can hide the face of God. Actually, self-will can be a very religious thing for it can be accepted right into the church when you join. It can go right into the chamber with you when you pray. However, remember this—self-will is good-natured only when it can have its own way. Otherwise, it is grouchy and ill-tempered and cross. Under this cloud, we must examine ourselves and ask, "Is my surrender to God a complete surrender?"

Ambition can also bring the dark cloud of obscurity, and there is an ambition which operates in the area of religion. We claim things for ourselves—perhaps some place or recognition which is not in the will of God, some advantage for ourselves. If it is something that we refuse to yield, insisting it is ours, and that we own it, it will bring that cloud of obscurity that nothing can penetrate. This is not just a word to laymen, for it can happen to ministers as well. The preacher ought not to be settled comfortably in his place with all of his ambitions getting priority. The preacher who is ambitious for himself will be found out. His pastorate, his preaching, his position—everything must be on the block and ready to be released if he is to know the smile and blessing of God!

False presumptions

Then there is the matter of presumption. Some Christians recognize that the cloud of concealment is there—so they presume that they can fast and pray and thus penetrate the cloud. But you cannot pray through this kind of cloud and fasting in such a case is just another kind of stubbornness.

We have no word from God indicating that long prayers will make everything right. In fact, there are Bible instances when God had to stop prayer meetings because they were useless!

You may recall that at one point in the history of Israel, the prophet Samuel was trying to pray for King Saul when God said, "Samuel, don't pray any more for Saul. He is through!"

In another instance Joshua was lying prone, his face down, and he was praying. We would have written a tract about his saintliness in prayer, but

God said to him, "Joshua, what are you doing? I don't honor a man for complaining. Get up on your feet and deal with the situation in your crowd and then I will bless you!"

Genuine prayer is still the soul's sincere desire and God still answers. But we must give up this idea that we can hang on to those things that bring the cloud and still be able to pray the cloud away. You cannot do it.

Think with me about fear. Fear is always the child of unbelief. Unfounded fears, linked with unbelief, become a cloud of obscurity over your head. You are afraid that you may become ill with cancer. You are afraid that your child may be crippled. You are afraid you will lose your job. You are afraid of Russia's guided missiles. The Lord wants us to surrender all of our fears to Him. He has made full provision for us — it is for us to surrender and trust. He is able!

Self-love will also form the cloud. Humans like to joke about it, but self-love is not a joking matter. A person who has been converted and is a Christian can still keep a cloud of concealment over him simply by loving himself. Self-love, self-admiration and gratification of self in a variety of ways — these are all self sins. The modern "scribe" excuses them and assures us that no one can do anything about them. Yet, what is this groan, this cry within us, that the candles of our souls might burn brightly and that we might know the divine illumination?

We must not forget that there is also a cloud that arises over our attitude toward money and possessions of all kinds. Money often comes between men and God. Someone has said that you can take two small ten-cent pieces, just two dimes, and shut out the view of a panoramic landscape. Go to the mountains and just hold two coins closely in front of your eyes—the mountains are still there but you cannot see them at all because there is a dime shutting off the vision of each eye. It is not so much a matter of great wealth and riches, however. It is a matter of attitude and whether or not the Lord is allowed to lead us and guide us in stewardship of much—or of little!

Have you checked out your attitudes about people, about society, about traditions? Are you determined that you are going to "fit in"? Are you spending most of your time trying to adjust and conform? Are you busy teaching your children that getting along with people is the most important part of life? If these are your goals, you will have a cloud over your heart, my Christian friend.

The answer

What is the answer to this growing list of cloud-forming attitudes? I think it is the willingness to put the cloud which is above us under our feet by faith and through grace!

Paul gave us this example when he said, "Forgetting what is behind and straining toward what is ahead" (Philippians 3:13b). He considered that those things which were behind him would have shut out the face of God if allowed to remain in the foreground. He put them under his feet by forgetting—defeats, mistakes, blunders, errors, rebukes.

This is the place of victory for the Christian—putting the cloud under our feet so that we see the smiling face of God again. The blessed thing is that

He has been there all the time waiting for us to move up!

I had a vivid and memorable experience on an airplane leaving New York City some years ago. It was a dark, rainy afternoon and when we were aboard the plane, the relaxed, friendly pilot made a little speech about the miserable weather.

"We will be in the sunshine within 15 minutes after takeoff," he assured us. "The weather map shows that we will enjoy bright, clear weather all the way to Chicago after we get above the smog and the mist and the clouds."

As soon as we were in the air, the clouds became white under us and within a few moments we had put the clouds under our feet. The sun was shining brightly above and we flew those 900 miles in brilliant sunshine.

I didn't have to help that pilot at all, although I tried! I am the nervous type so I try to keep balancing the plane as we bank or turn. But that confident, smiling pilot doesn't have to count on my 159 pounds to balance that huge four-engine monster. He said he could get us up into the sunshine — and he did.

In the spiritual realm we have a Pilot who has promised us His sunlight, and if we will consent, He will put the clouds under our feet. He just asks that we be willing. If we let Him put the cloud beneath us, we find to our joy that He hides all of the past — all that has shamed and grieved and worried us! God waits for us to move upward into this place of spiritual restfulness and power.

"Into the sunshine in 15 minutes," the earthly pilot promised.

"Into the sunlight of God's will as soon as you are willing to put the clouds under your feet," our heavenly Pilot promises us now!

You will discover a marvelous deliverance from bondage, a great freedom!

You will find a new delight and confidence in the Word of God!

You will experience a radiance and an illumination and a fragrance that you have never known before!

Our greatest need is to be willing—we need to act in faith.

Dr. A.B. Simpson wrote a hymn which is rarely sung now—for two reasons: The first is that the tune is hard to sing, and the second is that very few have the experience of which he wrote.

These are the words:

"I take the hand of love divine,
    I count each precious promise mine
With this eternal countersign—
    I take—He undertakes!

"I take Thee, Blessed Lord,
    I give myself to Thee;
And Thou, according to Thy Word,
    Do'st undertake for me!"

This is the basic question for each of us—will we take from the hand of God all that He has provided? He has already undertaken for us. Will we "take the hand of love divine" and "claim each precious promise mine"?

Brethren, God waits for your faith and your love, and He doesn't ask whose interpretation of Scripture you have accepted. The New Testament tells of believers who met and prayed together, the strong taking the burdens of the weak, and all praying for those who had fallen. The place was shaken, and they were all filled with the Holy Ghost.

"Pay no attention to that," we have been told by "interpreters." "That is not for us." So it has been ruled out by interpretation and the blessed Dove has been forced to fold His wings and be silent.

Our hearts tell us that these modern scribes who are long on interpretation are wrong in spirit. Our own longing souls tell us that the old saints and hymn writers and the devotional giants were right!

Years ago Paul Rader preached a powerful sermon on the theme that "out of man's innermost being shall flow rivers of living water." Later, two men who had heard the sermon asked Mr. Rader to meet with them for a meal and for discussion. One man began by saying, "Mr. Rader, you preached a good sermon, but you are all wrong dispensationally." The other added, "Mr. Rader, you are a good preacher and a good brother—the problem is that you have the wrong interpretation."

I understand that Mr. Rader did not answer. They bowed their heads to pray before eating their meal, and when Mr. Rader finally looked across the table at the first brother, he saw that something had happened. Tears were streaming down the man's face, and his shoulders shook with emotion. Finally he was able to say, "Brother Rader, we have the interpretation, but you have the rivers of blessing!"

Some are going to continue to plod along with dryness—sticking to interpretation! But some of us want God's blessing and God's stirring and God's best for our lives at any cost! We have the Savior's Word that the Holy Spirit has come to us in our present world. He is mine and He is yours, our sweet possession!

No man can set up the rules as to how much you can have of God. The Lord Himself has promised that as far as He is concerned He is willing to keep the candles of your soul brightly burning!

11

Caution: Self-Will
Will Scratch Your Back!

*"If it were true the Lord puts the Christian believer
on the shelf every time he fails or does something
wrong, I would have been a piece of statuary by this
time!"*

MAN'S VERY HUMAN HABIT OF TRUSTING in himself is generally the last great obstacle block-
ing his pathway to victory in Christian experience.

Even the Apostle Paul, writing in his New Testament letters, confessed that his confidence in God
was in completely opposite ratio to his confidence
in himself. Paul made it very plain that it was only
after giving up the last inclination to trust in himself that he became immersed in the sufficiency of
Christ.

We can learn much from the experiences of Paul
and the humility of his testimony, "I know that
nothing good lives in me" (Romans 7:18a). He had
discovered that to be fully surrendered to God and
the will of God meant that first he must come to an
entire and radical distrust of himself.

After he became willing to look within his own
being, Paul had no further confidence in himself
and couldn't say enough against himself. But when

he went forth before men in the compulsion of ministry for Christ, he seemed to stand sure with a great cosmic confidence because he had met God and could honestly declare that "we have this treasure in jars of clay to show that this all-surpassing power is from God and not from us" (2 Corinthians 4:7).

Paul was being continually thrown into spiritual combat as he moved forward in his declaration of Jesus as Christ and Lord. He knew the blessing and the power of operating from a position of strength—the fact that he held no illusions about himself and depended completely upon the Spirit of God.

"By the grace of God, I am what I am" (1 Corinthians 15:10a), he said.

"I am the least of the apostles and do not even deserve to be called an apostle" (1 Corinthians 15:9), he wrote.

"Christ Jesus came into the world to save sinners—of whom I am the worst" (1 Timothy 1:15), he acknowledged.

This all adds up to a startling statement of truth held not only by Paul but by all of the great saints who have done exploits for God. They would all remind us that those who insist on trusting human self will never obtain the desired victory in spiritual combat, for they will presume vainly in their own strength!

To become effective men of God, then, we must know and acknowledge that every grace and every virtue proceeds from God alone, and that not even a good thought can come from us except it be of Him.

Self-trust is subtle

I think that most of us can glibly quote the Scriptures about the lessons that Paul learned without actually coming to this place of complete distrust of ourselves and our own strengths. Our self-trust is such a subtle thing that it still comes around whispering to us even after we are sure it is gone.

In our search for God and for victory, perhaps we have put away all the sins that have plagued us. We have tried to deal with all of the self sins that we know, allowing them to be crucified. At this point we have stopped boasting, and we are sure that we have stopped loving ourselves. It may be that in the process we have humbled ourselves and publicly gone forward to an altar to confess our need and to pray.

Now, this is my caution—after we have humbled ourselves there is a possibility that our subtle self-trust may prove to be stronger than ever, for it has a better foundation upon which to build! After we have put away our sins and given up our will and after we have taken a position of confession and humility, our self-trust is quick to whisper its consolation deep within us. Often when this has happened, Christians have made the mistake of believing that this whisper of consolation comes from the Holy Ghost—and that is why we are so weak when we think we are strong!

Just what is the whisper that is likely to come to us deep within our being?

"You have really come a long way, and you have advanced far ahead of others," self-trust is likely to whisper. "You have put sin behind you, and you have humbled yourself. You will be a power for you are not one of the dead ones. You may trust yourself now because you have left much behind, and parted with friends, and paid a price! You are really getting somewhere. You will have victory now—with God's help, of course!"

I call this a kind of back-scratching—and our old self knows just when to come through with it because it feels so good to us in terms of consolation and comfort. It is the process of reverting right back to self-trust, and almost all of the joy that the average Christian knows is the back-scratching that self gives him.

When self whispers an assurance to you that you are different—look out! "You are different," self whispers, and than adds the proof. "You have given up enough things to make you a separated Christian. You love the old hymns, and you can't stand the modern nonsense. You have a good standard—none of those movies and none of this modern stuff for you!"

You don't really know what is happening to you, but you are feeling pretty good about everything by this time. But the good feeling is strictly from being coddled and comforted and scratched by a self that has refused to die. Self-trust is still there—and you thought it had gone!

Our great encouragement

Now, what is our great encouragement in view of all that we know about ourselves? It is the fact that God loves us without measure, and He is so keenly interested in our spiritual growth and progress that

He stands by in faithfulness to teach and instruct and discipline us as His dear children!

I once wrote something about how God loves us and how dear we are to Him. I wasn't sure I should put it down on paper, but God knew what I meant. I said, "The only eccentricity that I can discover in the heart of God is that a God such as He is should love sinners such as we are!" God has that strange eccentricity but it still does not answer our wondering question, "Why did God love us?"

On this earth a mother will love the boy who has betrayed her and sinned and is now on his way to life in prison. That seems to be a natural thing for a mother, but there is nothing natural about this love of God. It is a divine thing—it is forced out by the inward pressure within the heart of God. That is why He waits for us, puts up with us, desires to lead us on—He loves us!

You can put all of your confidence in God. He is not angry with you, His dear child! He is not waiting to pounce on you in judgment—He knows that we are dust and He is loving and patient towards us.

If it were true that the Lord would put the Christian on the shelf every time he failed and blundered and did something wrong, I would have been a piece of statuary by this time! I know God and He isn't that kind of God. He will bring judgment when judgment is necessary, but the scriptures say that judgment is God's strange work. Where there is a lifetime of rebellion, hardened unbelief, love of sin and flagrant refusal of His love and grace, judgment will fall. But with His dear children, God watches over us for spiritual growth and maturity, trying to teach us how necessary it is for us to trust in Him completely and to come to a complete distrust of ourselves.

Completely distrusting ourselves

There are at least three ways that God may use to teach us this necessity of completely distrusting ourselves.

Occasionally this lesson from God has come by holy inspiration. I suppose the best and easiest way to find out that you are no good is to have God flash that knowledge suddenly into your soul. I know that it has happened to some people. I think of the writings of the saintly Brother Lawrence who testified that God gave him this vision and knowledge of himself in such a way that for years he was never out of the conscious presence of God!

"When I took the cross and decided to obey Jesus and walk in His holy way, I knew that I might be called upon to suffer," Brother Lawrence wrote. "But, for some reason, God never counted me worthy of much suffering. He just let me continue to trust in Him completely after I put all my self-trust away. It is a life of carrying His cross and believing that He is in me and around me and near me, and praying without ceasing."

Lady Julian, also, wrote in her book of the gracious experience when God, by holy inspiration, gave light to her heart so that she realized instantly that she was worthless in herself and that Jesus Christ was everything!

At this point someone is sure to say, "But Mr. Tozer, I already know that I am bad. I am a believer in total depravity!"

My reply is this: it is possible to be a confirmed believer in total depravity and still be as proud as Lucifer! It is possible to believe in depravity and still trust in yourself in such a way that the face of God is hidden and you are kept from victory.

We are dealing with something else here—not theological total depravity. We may not understand how we can inherit evil from our fathers, but there is no argument with the fact that as soon as we are big enough to sin, we go directly into the business of sinning. It has been true of every child of every race and of every nationality—we are born bad, and in that sense we are all alike.

The lesson that we are trying to draw here is the necessity of God revealing by the Holy Spirit the utter weakness of the child of God who is still putting trust in himself. A teacher can tell you that you are weak and that all of your righteousnesses are but filthy rags and you may still go through school and get a long degree and go out proudly to be a missionary or a preacher or a Bible teacher. Our selfish condition—if we are still trusting in ourselves—can only be demonstrated to us by the Holy Spirit. When the knowledge comes and we lean only on Him, we will know that "conscious presence" in which Brother Lawrence lived and rejoiced continually day by day!

Another way in which we may have to learn this lesson from God is with harsh scourgings. Perhaps this makes me appear to belong to the 17th century for it does not have a popular sound in our day. We are more likely to bring in the cow bells and try to give everyone a little bit of pleasure than to faithfully declare that our dear heavenly Father may use harsh scourging to teach His children distrust of self.

Actually, I would prefer to preach from the 23rd Psalm every Sunday for a year. Then I would take up the 53rd chapter of Isaiah and after a long time I would come to the 13th chapter of First Corinthians.

But if I should do that, what would happen to my congregation in the meantime? The flock of God would become the softest, sweetest and spongiest group of no-goods that ever came together!

We need a solid diet

The Lord does have to give us chastening and discipline and harsh scourging at times. None of you would feed your children continually on a diet of sugar cookies — they would lose their teeth! There must be a diet with solid stuff if they are to be vigorous and well.

We speak of harsh scourgings and immediately we think of that man Job in the Old Testament. We have a great deal of pity for Job and in human sympathy many people take Job's part against God — and certainly against his wife! But have you ever noticed that Job was far from being humble, even though he was a praying man and one who made sacrifices because his children might have sinned at their party the night before. But we finally hear him saying in that long discourse, "Oh, that I were as in months past, as in the days when God preserved me . . . when I went out to the gate through the city, when I prepared my seat in the street."

He was a "big shot," you know, and that is what

they did then. They had a place at the head of the street where the honored men were seated.

"When the young men saw me," he said, "they hid themselves; and the aged arose and stood up."

Who is this coming down the street? The honorable Mister Job!

"Oh, here I am now, lying in this ash pile," he said, "They have cast me out. No one would vote for me now, but there was a day when princes refrained from talking in my presence and laid their hands on their mouths."

Brother Job was no ordinary rag picker—he was a great man! But he knew it—and that was the trouble and that's why those harsh things happened to him. If you are great and you happen to suspect it, and you are God's child—things will start happening to you, too.

Finally, seeing God's majesty and power, Job said, "Oh God, I have been talking and talking and talking, but now I put my hand over my mouth—I am vile!" It was only then that the Lord could say to him, "All right, Job, now pray for the rest of them." So Job prayed for those who had tried to comfort him, and God gave back to him twice as much as he had possessed previously.

There is a third way, also, in which God may be trying to deal with our weakness of self-trust. We are familiar with this method if we study the Bible, for it is the discipline of manifold temptations.

Some Christians are prone to sink into discouragement when called upon to face temptations, but I think that these disciplines should become a spiritual encouragement to us. God does not allow the temptations and testings to come to us because He is trying to show us up—He is dealing with us through this means because we are Christians, we are His children! He is dealing with us in the midst of temptations because He has found our conscience is tender enough to listen and because we are willing to be drawn closer to Him. He is only trying to teach us this necessary lesson of distrust of self.

When temptations come, you are not to throw in the towel and say, "Oh God, I guess this proves that you don't want me!" Instead, it should be a sign to you as you come through the testing by His grace that you are nearer your eternal home today than you were yesterday!

There are scriptural examples of men of God who were sifted in the course of such testing experiences. Think of blustery Peter and his denial of the Savior when wicked men arrested Jesus and put Him through the mockery of a trial before taking Him out to Calvary to be crucified. What if Peter had taken his own actions as proof that he was not really a Christian disciple? It was a difficult course, but it was a most powerful lesson from the heavenly Father, revealing to Peter what an ineffective believer he would be if he continued to trust in his own strength.

God must expose us

None of us can really tell how weak and useless we are until God has exposed us—and no one wants to be exposed! But God knows so much better than we do that He must expose us for our own good.

Neither do any of us really know how unstable

we are until we have been exposed by the Holy
Ghost. Peter was a big, bold, strong fisherman, and
it seemed easy for him to say to the Lord, "Let
everyone else run away, but I will always stand by.
You can count on me, Master!" I am sure it was
hard for him to take the answer that Jesus gave
him: "Before the rooster crows tonight you will say
three times that you do not know me!" But Jesus
knew the instability of the man who still tried to
stand in his own strength and in his own self-trust.

We do not really know how unstable we are, and
we often refuse to admit the truth when we find
out, when we are exposed. That is why it is too
dangerous to trust our good habits and our virtues—and that is why our distrust of ourselves
must be the work of God's hand!

Oh, brethren, He is our God, and this is my advice—love Him and trust Him and depend only
upon Him! If we insist upon trusting ourselves,
our training, our education, our talents and our
human judgment—we make God less than He is
and we make man more than he is! We take the
glory from God and give it to our converted and
sanctified self—and that is shameful, because it
takes from God the ultimate and final trust. Even
when we say that we know that God is the source
and the fountain of all things, and we recite His
attributes and become expert in theology, we may
still believe in our hearts that we are more than we
really are!

This is where we need repentance and forgiveness. I recall that Brother Lawrence, writing about
the pattern of victory in the daily walk with God,
gave a simple and direct solution to failures and

wrong-doing. He advised that if we ever make a slip and do that which is wrong, we should not ignore it and let it remain unconfessed and unforgiven.

"I would go straight to the Lord and say, 'Now Lord, that's me—and if you don't forgive me and help me, that's what you can expect—for that's me!'" is what he wrote in essence. "God forgave me, and I went right on from there."

Some people insist that repentance and forgiveness must be a long, drawn-out affair, but I don't agree that it must necessarily be so. I believe the best repentance is turning to God and away from our sin—and not doing it any longer!

That is the best repentance in the whole, wide world. Why does it take us so long to put our complete trust in God when He has made it so simple and so rewarding to yield what we are to Him!

How Long Can You Slight the Christ of God?

"How long should it take us to yield completely to this One who has been made both Lord and Christ — yet loves us with an everlasting love?"

HAVE YOU EVER HEARD ONE of our modern, Christian activists say, "I am still busy looking around for the best doctrine on holiness," or "I don't know when I will find a doctrine of the deeper life that is satisfactory to me!"

There is really only one answer to this kind of a quest — turn your eyes upon Jesus and commit yourself fully and completely to Him because He is God and Christ, Redeemer and Lord, "The same yesterday, today and forever!"

In these matters of spiritual blessing and victory, we are not dealing with doctrines — we are dealing with the Lord of all doctrine! We are dealing with a Person who is the Resurrection and the Life and the Source from whom flows all doctrine and all truth.

How can we be so ignorant and so dull that we try to find our spiritual answers and the abounding life by looking beyond the only One who has promised that He would never change? How can we so readily slight the Christ of God who has limitless authority throughout the universe? How long should it take us to yield completely and without reservation to this One who has been made both Lord and Christ—and yet continues to be the very same Jesus who still loves us with an everlasting love?

I never want to come to a halt, pleading that I hold the right and proper doctrines—because I know that the only righteousness I can ever possess is His righteousness imparted to me. I claim nothing and my testimony is the same as Martin Luther's prayer: "Oh, Lord Jesus, Thou art my righteousness—I am Thy sin!"

The only sin Jesus had was mine, Luther's and yours—and the only righteousness we can ever have is His.

Christ does not change

It seems to be very hard for us to comprehend the importance of the fact that Christ does not change and that there is no fluctuation in His character, in His nature, in His resources, in His love and mercy.

Because change is everywhere around us at all times on this earth and among human beings, it is difficult for us to grasp the eternal and unchanging nature and person of Jesus Christ. We are well aware that if we elevate a man, giving him a high position with great influence and plenty of money—he is going to change! He may not realize it and often he will deny it, but he is not going to be the same in character and attitude and habits and manner of life. He will become proud—and probably aloof and unsympathetic! He will probably have his nose up in the air and it will be hard for him to recognize his old friends.

But nothing about our Lord Jesus Christ has changed down to this very hour. His love has not changed. It hasn't cooled off, and it needs no increase because He has already loved us with infinite love and there is no way that infinitude can be increased. His compassionate understanding of us has not changed. His interest in us and His purposes for us have not changed.

He is Jesus Christ, our Lord. He is the very same Jesus. Even though He has been raised from the dead and seated at the right hand of the Majesty in the heavens, and made Head over all things to the Church, His love for us remains unchanged. Even though He has been given all authority and power in heaven and in earth, He is the very same Jesus in every detail. He is the same yesterday, today and forever!

It is hard for us to accept the majestic simplicity of this constant, wonder-working Jesus. We are used to getting things changed so that they are always bigger and better!

An important man in the Old Testament represents all of us in our humanity. He was afflicted with leprosy and he wanted the prophet of God to come and strike a noble pose and in a very dignified and proper way say to the leprosy, "Be gone!" But the prophet said he should take his pride in hand and go to the Jordan river and bathe in the waters of the Jordan in order to be healed. In other words, God asked him to do something very simple.

You and I are not always satisfied with the manner in which God deals with us. We would very much like to do something new, something difficult, something big and dramatic—but we are called back. For everything we need, we are called back to the simplicity of the faith, to the simplicity of Jesus Christ and His unchanging person.

The very same Jesus—a Brother who bears your image at the right hand of the Father, and who knows all your troubles and your weaknesses and sins, and loves you in spite of everything!

The very same Jesus—a Savior and Advocate who stands before the Father taking full responsibility for you and being easier to get along with than the nicest preacher you ever knew and being easier to approach than the humblest friend you ever had.

The very same Jesus—His is the sun that shines upon us, He is the star of our night. He is the giver of our life and the rock of our hope. He is our safety and our future. He is our righteousness, our sanctification, our inheritance. You find that He is all of this in the instant that you move your heart towards Him in faith. This is the journey to Jesus that must be made in the depths of the heart and being. This is a journey where feet do not count.

Good at footwork

Many of our Christians are activists—they are good at footwork and they are engaged in many religious journeys, but they do not seem to move up any closer to Jesus in heart and in spirit. This modern religious emphasis on activity reminds me of the Japanese mice that I have seen in the windows of the pet store. Don't stop and look at them if you are the nervous type. I do not know why they call them dancing mice because they don't waltz—they just run continually. I think they must be fundamentalists, brethren—they are on the go all the time! Some Christians seem to feel that it is a mark of spirituality to attend banquets and seminars and workshops and conferences and courses, night after night, week after week.

This naturally brings up some lessons from the New Testament record concerning the sisters, Martha and Mary. I think it was plain that Martha loved Jesus but her concept of devotion was activity. She was an active girl and she believed that because she loved the Lord, she ought to be doing something all the time to show it. Mary also loved the Lord Jesus but with a different attitude in her devotion. She was fervently occupied in spirit about the love of His Godhead! Our Lord knew the difference then and He knows the difference today.

Actually, our craze for activity brings few enriching benefits into our Christian circles. If you look into our churches, you will find groups of half-saved, half-sanctified, carnal people who know more about social niceties than they do about the New Testament; and more about love stories and soap operas than they do about the Holy Spirit.

When they get together, they have no trouble in thinking up things to do, but there is a question in my mind as to whether all of these things ought to be done in the name of the Lord!

It is not enough just to be rushing somewhere to another meeting, another discussion, another dialogue. Jesus commended Mary for knowing the value of the one thing that is necessary—that God should be loved and praised above all other business which may occupy us bodily or spiritually. Mary was fervently occupied in spirit about the love of His Godhead. I like that—although I know it sounds strange and almost heretical to our modern activists.

My plea is that we will not be satisfied to continue on as "external" Christians. The extroverted Christian lives largely for the externals of Christianity, and therefore sadly neglects his inner life and growth.

Recall what happened when Jesus said to the disciples, "Go into all the world and preach the good news to all creation" (Mark 16:15).

Peter jumped up right away, grabbed his hat and would have been on his way, but Jesus stopped him, and said, "Not yet, Peter! Don't go like that. Tarry until you are endued with power from on high, and then go!"

I believe that our Lord wants us to learn more of Him in worship before we become busy for Him. He wants us to have a gift of the Spirit, an inner experience of the heart, as our first service, and out of that will grow the profound and deep and divine activities which are necessary.

Religious amateurs

Years ago I heard Dr. Oliver Buswell warn that our evangelical churches were beginning to suffer from what he called "a rash of amateurism." He didn't know what a prophet he was—for now we have religious amateurs running in all directions!

The first thing we tell our young converts, the babes in Christ, is, "Here is a handful of tracts—now get out and get busy!"

But the Lord did not say that. He spoke about the first thing that was needful—to be fervently occupied in spirit with the love of Christ's Godhead, and to love and praise Him above all other business, bodily or spiritual. That's what it means to love God, to be a spiritual person—to have an ordained and measured affection plainly directed unto God Himself! This is more than a flash of spiritual feeling or emotion—it doesn't necessarily have anything to do with goose-pimples!

An ordained and measured pouring out of our love and affection—and this cannot be done without some involvement of the emotions. But it is not like a rainy day when a cloudburst may pour itself out in a few hours—and then there may be a dry spell for weeks. It is a demonstrated love for the Lord Jesus Christ, continually pouring itself out, ordained and measured!

Knowing and loving the unchanging Christ with this kind of adoration will keep us from falling into a number of subtle traps which have long plagued unstable believers.

It will keep us from stumbling over "people." You will continue to have your longing after God, but you will no longer stumble over the imperfections of men and women around you. It was Thomas à Kempis who wrote in *The Imitation of Christ:* "If thou would'st have peace of heart, do not inquire too earnestly into other men's matters." If you spend time examining your Christian brother, you will find him lacking in some things. Don't forget that all idols have feet of clay.

We have plain teaching that the Lord does not want His children to become "saint-worshippers."

He doesn't want you to become a preacher-worshipper or a teacher-worshipper. God wants to deliver you from the best man you know so that man can die and be removed and you won't backslide!

Praises of people

Another thing we know is that this kind of love and devotion will keep you from stumbling over the praises of people. I am of the opinion that perhaps the praises people try to give us are more dangerous to our Christian walk than their blame.

The devil wants us to believe that we are saintly and superior to other Christians—that's the way he hooks us! That's why he gets other people to tell us how well we are doing—and how we are passing right by other Christians who are not humble and warm-hearted "like we are!"

Every time you take a new step forward for God the devil will have some means of communicating to you the fact that God is proud of you—and that you are wonderful! As soon as he can get you interested enough to say, "Yes, I guess that's true," you have had it, brother!

Now, what about the blame we often get from our fellow Christians? Are you hidden away in Christ Himself and so occupied in spirit that you take little heed of what men do or say about you?

I have observed that as long as we sit frozen to our chair, making no spiritual progress, no one will bother us. No one will come and put an arm around our shoulder and urge us: "Thou hast dwelt in this mount long enough—rise therefore and go across this Jordan!"

But, if we start to cross Jordan urged on by our

own spiritual thirst and desire, at least fourteen people will ask prayer for us in the concern that we are losing our minds.

During my ministry I have seldom been blamed for being cold when I was cold. People don't come to the pastor and say, "You are no longer warm-hearted—what has happened to your spiritual life?"

I have concluded that you can be backslidden, and in the rank and file of evangelical Christians no one will take any notice of it. There will be no rebuke.

On the other hand, they will jump down your throat and accuse you of showing off as soon as you start to seek God in earnest for victory and blessing! It does seem odd that we can be in the Christian faith and yet we are going to have bleeding fingernails and sore knees for every inch of ground that we take away from the devil!

That's why so many Christians are taking so little! Many of us had actually taken more spiritual ground when we were converted than we now possess.

I picked up a little piece of printed paper on a muddy road in West Virginia many years ago. I will never know who put it there, but I know God planned that I should see it and remember it.

There was only one paragraph and it said, "There are only two things know in this universe that are bigger when they were born than when they get their growth. One is a wasp and the other is a church member."

I don't know about the wasp, but I do know that many church members start out with a blaze, and then they look around and decide that they should be more like other Christians—just settle down. Soon they are as backslidden as the rest. The amazing thing is that so many people can be so backslidden and never know it!

What a sad condition for Christians who are in the church of the mighty Redeemer and Deliverer who is eternally the Victor, the Rock of Ages. Why can't we claim all that He has promised for us?

Christ is the same

In view of much of today's dispensational teaching about Bible interpretation, the apostles, miracles of God, and the fullness of the Spirit, I must remind you that the Lord Jesus Christ is the same yesterday, today and forever. That allows me to tell you something blessed and heartening which I have found to be true, and which I will stand by to the end of time.

This is my finding: there is nothing that Jesus has ever done for any of His disciples that He will not do for any other of His disciples!

Where did the "dividers-of-the-Word-of-Truth" get their teaching that all the gifts of the Spirit ended when the last apostle died? They have never furnished chapter and verse for that. When some men beat the cover off their Bible to demonstrate how they stand by the Word of God, they should be reminded that they are only standing by their own interpretation of the Word.

I find nothing in the Bible that says the Lord has changed. He has the same love, the same grace, the same mercy, the same power, the same desires for the blessing of His children. You will have to prove it to me if you take the position that Jesus Christ refuses to do for you something that He did for any other of His disciples! He is just the same toward everyone and everything.

His attitude toward the proud is unchanged. In the Bible record the proud men who came to Jesus got uniform treatment. Somehow, they were never able to discover that side of Jesus which is gentle and loving, kind and merciful. The proud always came up on the wrong side of Jesus, and they got that which the proud will always get from Jesus — justice and judgment, rebuke, warning and woe! It was the same with the self-righteous, the insincere, the hypocrites — they all came up on the wrong side of Jesus!

It is about time that the modern artists who paint pictures of Jesus should be told that He was not a pretty, curly-haired weakling. They should be told the truth — that He is the Christ of God and He will come riding through the skies on a white horse and with a sword at His side. He will judge the world, He will call all men to their feet and they will honor Him for His majesty, His power, His purity, and for creation itself.

He is the same Jesus — He will always be the same!

He is always the same to the meek, the mourner, the brokenhearted, the penitent sinner. His attitude is always the same towards those who love Him, the honest-hearted person. These are the people who come up to Jesus on the right side — and He never turns them away. He is ready with forgiveness. He is ready with comfort. He is ready with blessing.

He loves us

We cannot understand this readiness of Jesus to love us and help us and bless us—because He does not really need us. One of His attributes is omnipotence—so He doesn't need us. But the secret of this—He loves us!

Think of a man who is president of a great, thriving corporation. He has cars and airplanes at his disposal and hundreds of people who will carry out his orders immediately. This great man has a three-year-old daughter. Does he need her? No, of course not, but he loves her and he wants her! His heart is responsive to her needs and desires.

So it is with us. Before we were born, God was God, the Lord God Almighty! He has never needed us. None of our human talents and abilities are significant to Him. But He needs our love and wants our love!

The Apostle John leaned his ear against the beating heart of the Son of God and the Lord recognized His love and devotion and called him "the disciple whom Jesus loved." He loved the rest of the disciples, too, but He couldn't love them as much because they didn't reciprocate as much.

Jesus is still just the same towards those who seek His fellowship. He wants to be with those who are occupied with the love of His Godhead! Our relationship with Him is all summed up in this simple fact—everything you need is found in Jesus Christ, the Son of God!

He is God and He is the Son of Man. He is all the guilty sinner needs and He is more than the fondest expectation of the loftiest saint. We can never go

beyond Him. We can never learn all that He is able
to teach. We can never use all of the spiritual power
and victory He is able to provide.

It is good for us to remember how strong He is—
and how weak we are. I settled this issue a long
time ago. I tell you I have talked to God more than I
have talked to anyone else. I have reasoned more
with God and had longer conferences with God
than with anybody else.

And what did I tell Him? Among other things, I
told Him, "Now, Lord, if I do the things I know
I should do, and if I say what I know in my heart I
should say, I will be in trouble with people and
with groups—there is no other way!

"Not only will I be in trouble for taking my stand
in faith and honesty, but I will certainly be in a
situation where I will be seriously tempted of the
devil!"

Then, after praying more and talking to the Lord,
I have said, "Almighty Lord, I accept this with my
eyes open! I know the facts and I know what may
happen, but I accept it. I will not run. I will not
hide. I will not crawl under a rug. I will dare to
stand up and fight because I am on your side—and
I know that when I am weak, then I am strong!"

So I don't let anyone praise me and I try not to
pay attention to those who would blame me; I find
that this is not difficult, for I am only a servant of
the holiest man that ever walked the streets of Jerusalem—and they called Him a devil!

This is how I have learned to stand fast for Christ,
and all that He is to His own!

WHO PUT JESUS ON THE CROSS?

Twelve Sermons on Well-known Bible Texts

A.W. TOZER

**OM
publishing**

© Christian Publications 1975

This edition first published 1995
by arrangement with Christian Publications,
3825 Hartzdale Drive, Camp Hill, PA 17011, U.S.A.

01 00 99 98 97 96 95   7 6 5 4 3 2 1

OM Publishing is an imprint of Send the Light Ltd.,
P.O. Box 300, Carlisle, Cumbria CA3 0QS, U.K.

Scripture quotations are from the Authorized Version
(Crown copyright)

British Library Cataloguing in Publication Data

Tozer, A.W.
Who Put Jesus on the Cross?
I. Title
248.5

ISBN 1-85078-202-4

Printed in the U.K. by Cox and Wyman Ltd., Reading

Contents

Preface

Those who were friends and associates of Dr. A. W. Tozer during his lifetime knew of his very strong convictions against any kind of false profession or "phony" attitudes in the Christian life and ministry.

The reader of these sermons will note in several chapters the manner in which Dr. Tozer was willing to bare his own soul in affirmation of Christian honesty, candor and transparency among ministers and laymen alike.

In the chapter, "What Is It Costing You to Be a Christian?", Dr. Tozer asked his congregation to pray for him and the integrity of his ministry:

"Pray that I will not just come to a wearied end —an exhausted, tired, old preacher, interested only in hunting a place to roost. Pray that I will let my Christian standards cost me something right down to the last gasp!"

He never lost that insistent spirit on behalf of genuineness and truth. Just a few weeks before his unexpected death in 1963, Dr. Tozer was asked by an official of the National Association of Evangelicals to address the annual convention of the NAE in Buffalo, New York.

Because he had not been a proponent of Christian and Missionary Alliance membership in the NAE, Dr. Tozer asked frankly:

"Do you think I have something to contribute to your meeting—or are you just trying to 'butter' me up?"

Assured of the integrity of the invitation, Dr. Tozer consented and gave a memorable address on Christian commitment to the NAE convention delegates. It was his last public address and presentation of the claims of Christ outside of his own pulpit prior to his death in May 1963.

The Publisher

Chapter One

Who Put Jesus on the Cross?

"He was wounded for our transgressions, he was bruised for our iniquities: the chastisement of our peace was upon him; and with his stripes we are healed." Isaiah 53:5

There is a strange conspiracy of silence in the world today—even in religious circles—about man's responsibility for sin, the reality of judgment, and about an outraged God and the necessity for a crucified Saviour.

On the other hand, there is an open and powerful movement swirling throughout the world designed to give people peace of mind in relieving them of any historical responsibility for the trial and crucifixion of Jesus Christ. The problem with modern decrees and pronouncements in the name of brotherhood and tolerance is their basic misconception of Christian theology.

A great shadow lies upon every man and every woman—the fact that our Lord was bruised and wounded and crucified for the entire human race. This is the basic human responsibility that men are trying to push off and evade.

Let us not eloquently blame Judas nor Pilate. Let us not curl our lips at Judas and accuse, "He sold Him for money!"

Let us pity Pilate, the weak-willed, because he did not have courage enough to stand for the innocency of the man whom he declared had done no wrong.

Let us not curse the Jews for delivering Jesus to be crucified. Let us not single out the Romans in blaming them for putting Jesus on the cross.

Oh, they were guilty, certainly! But they were our accomplices in crime. They and we put Him on the cross, not they alone. That rising malice and anger that burns so hotly in your breast today put Him there. That basic dishonesty that comes to light in your being when you knowingly cheat and chisel on your income tax return—that put Him on the cross. The evil, the hatred, the suspicion, the jealousy, the lying tongue, the carnality, the fleshly love of pleasure—all of these in natural man joined in putting Him on the cross.

We may as well admit it. Every one of us in Adam's race had a share in putting Him on the cross!

I have often wondered how any professing Christian man or woman could approach the communion table and participate in the memorial of our Lord's death without feeling and sensing the pain and the shame of the inward confession: "I, too, am among those who helped put Him on the cross!"

I remind you that it is characteristic of the natural man to keep himself so busy with unimportant trifles that he is able to avoid the settling of the most important matters relating to life and existence.

Men and women will gather anywhere and everywhere to talk about and discuss every subject from the latest fashions on up to Plato and philosophy—up and down the scale. They talk about the necessity for peace. They may talk about the church and how it can be a bulwark against communism. None of these things are embarrassing subjects.

But the conversation all stops and the taboo of silence becomes effective when anyone dares to suggest that there are spiritual subjects of vital importance to our souls that ought to be discussed and considered. There seems to be an unwritten rule in polite society that if any religious subjects are to be discussed, it must be within the framework of theory—"never let it get personal!"

All the while, there is really only one thing that is of vital and lasting importance—the fact that our Lord Jesus Christ "was wounded for our transgressions; he was bruised for our iniquities; the chastisement of our peace was upon him; and with his stripes we are healed."

There are two very strong and terrible words here—*transgressions* and *iniquities*.

A *transgression* is a breaking away, a revolt from just authority. In all of the moral universe, only man and the fallen angels have rebelled and violated the authority of God, and men are still in flagrant rebellion against that authority.

There is no expression in the English language which can convey the full weight and force of terror inherent in the words *transgression* and *iniquity*. But in man's fall and transgression against the created order and authority of God we recognize perversion and twistedness and deformity and crookedness and rebellion. These are all there, and, undeniably, they reflect the reason and the necessity for the death of Jesus Christ on the cross.

The word *iniquity* is not a good word—and God knows how we hate it! But the consequences of iniquity cannot be escaped.

The prophet reminds us clearly that the Saviour was bruised for "our iniquities."

We deny it and say, "No!" but the fingerprints of all mankind are plain evidence against us. The authorities have no trouble finding and apprehending the awkward burglar who leaves his fingerprints on tables and doorknobs, for they have his record. So, the fingerprints of man are found in every dark cellar

11

and in every alley and in every dimly-lighted evil place throughout the world—every man's fingerprints are recorded and God knows man from man. It is impossible to escape our guilt and place our moral responsibilities upon someone else. It is a highly personal matter—"our iniquities."

For our iniquities and our transgressions He was bruised and wounded. I do not even like to tell you of the implications of His wounding. It really means that He was profaned and broken, stained and defiled. He was Jesus Christ when men took Him into their evil hands. Soon He was humiliated and profaned. They plucked out His beard. He was stained with His own blood, defiled with earth's grime. Yet He accused no one and He cursed no one. He was Jesus Christ, the wounded one.

Israel's great burden and amazing blunder was her judgment that this wounded one on the hillside beyond Jerusalem was being punished for His own sin.

The prophet foresaw this historic error in judgment, and he himself was a Jew, saying: "We thought He was smitten of God. We thought that God was punishing Him for His own iniquity for we did not know then that God was punishing Him for our transgressions and our iniquities."

He was profaned for our sakes. He who is the second person of the Godhead was not only wounded for us, but He was profaned by ignorant and unworthy men.

Isaiah reported that "the chastisement of our peace was upon him."

How few there are who realize that it is this peace—the health and prosperity and welfare and safety of the individual—which restores us to God. A chastisement fell upon Him so that we as individual humans could experience peace with God if we so desired. But the chastisement was upon Him. Rebuke, discipline and correction—these are found in chastisement. He was beaten and scourged in public by the decree of the Romans. They lashed Him in public view as they later lashed Paul. They whipped and punished Him in full view of the jeering public, and His bruised and bleeding and swollen person was the answer to the peace of the world and to the peace of the human heart. He was chastised for our peace; the blows fell upon Him.

I do not suppose there is any more humiliating punishment ever devised by mankind than that of whipping and flogging grown men in public view. Many men who have been put in a jail have become a kind of hero in the eye of the public. Heavy fines have been assessed against various offenders of the law, but it is not unusual for such an offender to boast and brag about his escape. But when a bad man is taken out before a laughing, jeering crowd, stripped to the waist and soundly whipped like a child—a bad child—he loses face and has no boasting left. He will probably never be the bold, bad man he was before. That kind of whipping and chastisement breaks the spirit and humiliates. The chagrin is worse than the lash that falls on the back.

I speak for myself as a forgiven and justified sinner, and I think I speak for a great host of forgiven and born-again men and women, when I say that in our repentance we sensed just a fraction and just a token of the wounding and chastisement which fell upon Jesus Christ as He stood in our place and in our behalf. A truly penitent man who has realized the enormity of his sin and rebellion against God senses a violent revulsion against himself—he does not feel that he can actually dare to ask God to let him off. But peace has been established, for the blows have fallen on Jesus Christ—publicly humiliated and disgraced as a common thief, wounded and bruised and bleeding under the lash for sins He did not commit; for rebellions in which He had no part;

for iniquity in the human stream that was an outrage to a loving God and Creator.

Isaiah sums up his message of a substitutionary atonement with the good news that "with his stripes we are healed."

The meaning of these "stripes" in the original language is not a pleasant description. It means to be actually hurt and injured until the entire body is black and blue as one great bruise. Mankind has always used this kind of bodily laceration as a punitive measure. Society has always insisted upon the right to punish a man for his own wrong-doing. The punishment is generally suited to the nature of the crime. It is a kind of revenge—society taking vengeance against the person who dared flout the rules.

But the suffering of Jesus Christ was not punitive. It was not for Himself and not for punishment of anything that He Himself had done.

The suffering of Jesus was corrective. He was willing to suffer in order that He might correct us and perfect us, so that His suffering might not begin and end in suffering, but that it might begin in suffering and end in healing.

Brethren, that is the glory of the cross! That is the glory of the kind of sacrifice that was for so long in the heart of God! That is the glory of the kind of atonement that allows a repentant sinner to come into peaceful and gracious fellowship with his God and Creator! It began in His suffering and it ended in our healing. It began in His wounds and ended in our purification. It began in His bruises and ended in our cleansing.

What is our repentance? I discover that repentance is mainly remorse for the share we had in the revolt that wounded Jesus Christ, our Lord. Further, I have discovered that truly repentant men never quite get over it, for repentance is not a state of mind and spirit that takes its leave as soon as God has given forgiveness and as soon as cleansing is realized.

That painful and acute conviction that accompanies repentance may well subside and a sense of peace and cleansing come, but even the holiest of justified men will think back over his part in the wounding and the chastisement of the Lamb of God. A sense of shock will still come over him. A sense of wonder will remain—wonder that the Lamb that was wounded should turn His wounds into the cleansing and forgiveness of one who wounded Him.

This brings to mind a gracious moving in many of our evangelical church circles—a willingness to move toward the spiritual purity of heart taught and exemplified so well by John Wesley in a time of spiritual dryness.

In spite of the fact that the word *sanctification* is a good Bible word, we have experienced a period in which evangelical churches hardly dared breathe the word because of the fear of being classified among the "holy rollers."

Not only is the good word *sanctification* coming back, but I am hopeful that what the word stands for in the heart and mind of God is coming back, too. The believing Christian, the child of God, should have a holy longing and desire for the pure heart and clean hands that are a delight to his Lord. It was for this that Jesus Christ allowed Himself to be humiliated, maltreated, lacerated. He was bruised, wounded and chastised so that the people of God could be a cleansed and spiritual people—in order that our minds might be pure and our thoughts pure. This provision all began in His suffering and ends in our cleansing. It began with His open, bleeding wounds and ends in peaceful hearts and calm and joyful demeanor in His people.

Every humble and devoted believer in Jesus Christ must have his own periods of wonder and amazement at this mystery of godliness—the willingness of the Son of Man to take our place in judgment and in punishment. If the amazement has all gone out of it, something is wrong, and you need to have the stony ground broken up again!

I often remind you that Paul, one of the holiest men who ever lived, was not ashamed of his times of remembrance and wonder over the grace and kindness of God. He knew that God did not hold his old sins against him forever. Knowing the account was all settled, Paul's happy heart assured him again and again that all was well. At the same time, Paul could only shake his head in amazement, and confess: "I am unworthy to be called, but by His grace, I am a new creation in Jesus Christ!"

I make this point about the faith and assurance and rejoicing of Paul in order to say that if that humble sense of perpetual penance ever leaves our justified being, we are on the way to backsliding.

Charles Finney, one of the greatest of all of God's men throughout the years, testified that in the midst of his labors and endeavors in bringing men to Christ, he would at times sense a coldness in his own heart.

Finney did not excuse it. In his writings he told of having to turn from all of his activities, seeking God's face and Spirit anew in fasting and prayer.

"I plowed up until I struck fire and met God," he wrote. What a helpful and blessed formula for the concerned children of God in every generation!

Those who compose the Body of Christ, His church, must be inwardly aware of two basic facts if we are to be joyfully effective for our Lord.

We must have the positive knowledge that we are clean through His wounds, with God's peace realized through His stripes. This is how God assures us that we may be all right inside. In this spiritual condition, we will treasure the purity of His cleansing and we will not excuse any evil or wrong-doing.

Also, we must keep upon us a joyful and compelling sense of gratitude for the bruised and wounded One, our Lord Jesus Christ. Oh, what a mystery of redemption—that the bruises of One healed the bruises of many; that the wounds of One healed the wounds of millions; that the stripes of One healed the stripes of many.

The wounds and bruises that should have fallen upon us fell upon Him, and we are saved for His sake!

Many years ago, an historic group of Presbyterians were awed by the wonder and the mystery of Christ's having come in the flesh to give Himself as an offering for every man's sin.

Those humble Christians said to one another: "Let us walk softly and search our hearts and wait on God and seek His face throughout the next three months. Then we will come to the communion table with our hearts prepared—lest the table of our Lord should become a common and careless thing."

God still seeks humble, cleansed and trusting hearts through which to reveal His divine power and grace and life. A professional botanist from the university can describe the acacia bush of the desert better than Moses could ever do—but God is still looking for the humble souls who are not satisfied until God speaks with the divine fire in the bush.

A research scientist could be employed to stand and tell us more about the elements and properties found in bread and wine than the apostles ever knew. But this is our danger: we may have lost the light and warmth of the Presence of God, and we may have only bread and wine. The fire will have gone from the bush, and the glory will not be in our act of communion and fellowship.

It is not so important that we know all of the history and all of the scientific facts, but it is vastly important that we desire and know and cherish the Presence of the Living God, who has given Jesus Christ to be the propitiation for our sins; and not for ours only, but also for the sins of the whole world.

Chapter Two

Are There Shortcuts to the Beauty of Holiness?

"Awake, O north wind; and come, thou south; blow upon my garden, that the spices thereof may flow out. Let my beloved come into his garden, and eat his pleasant fruits." Song of Solomon 4:16

I would like to be able to ask every Christian in the world this question: "Are you really interested in God's producing in you the beautiful fruits and fragrances of the Holy Ghost?"

For every affirmative answer, I would quickly recommend:

Then look to your own willingness to be regular in the habits of a holy life—for flowers and fruit do not grow in thin air! They grow and come up out of a root and "the root of the righteous yieldeth fruit."

For every beautiful garden that you see, whose fragrance comes out to welcome you, has its roots down into the hard earth. The beautiful flowers and blooms will grow and appear and flourish only when there are deep roots and strong stalks. If you take the roots away, the blossom and flower will endure perhaps one day. The sun will scorch them and they will be gone.

Now, we Christians, for the most part, reserve most of our interest for the fruit and the spice and the beauty of the garden. Most of us go to church, I think, for the same simple reason that a child climbs into its mother's arms after a long day at play, with many falls and bumps and frights and disappointments. The child wants consolation.

It appears that most people go to church for consolation. In fact, we have now fallen upon times when religion is mostly for consolation. We are now in the grip of the cult of peace—peace of mind, peace of heart, peace of soul, and we want to relax and have the great God Almighty pat our heads and comfort us. This has become religion.

This, along with one other item: the threat that if you don't be good the nuclear bomb will wipe out your modern civilization!

These seem to be the only two motives that remain in the wide world for religion. If you are not good, they warn, civilization will fall apart and the bomb will get us all, and if you do not come to the Lord, you will never have peace!

So, between fear and the desire to be patted and chucked under the chin and cuddled, the professing Christian staggers along his way.

My brethren, there is something better than this, something that has roots.

According to my Bible, there should be a people of God—they do not all have to belong to one church—but there should be a people called out by the Lord God and subjected to a spiritual experience given by God. Then they are to learn to walk in the way of the Truth and the way of the scriptures, producing the righteous fruit of the child of God whatever world conditions may be.

They know that those who destroy the body are not important—only those who destroy the soul. You can disintegrate a man, a saint of God, with a bomb and he is in heaven immediately with his Lord. The enemies of God have slain many Christians and sent them off quickly to be with God. They cast their

19

bodies aside as unclean things, but the souls of those men and women were immediately with the Lord.

Then there is the matter of constant consolation and peace—the promise of always feeling relaxed and at rest and enjoying ourselves inwardly.

This, I say, has been held up as being quite the proper goal to be sought in the evil hour in which we live. We forget that our Lord was a man of sorrow and acquainted with grief. We forget the arrows of grief and pain which went through the heart of Jesus' mother, Mary. We forget that all of the apostles except John died a martyr's death. We forget that there were 13 million Christians slain during the first two generations of the Christian era. We forget that they languished in prison, that they were starved, were thrown over cliffs, were fed to the lions, were drowned, that they were sewn in sacks and thrown into the ocean.

Yes, we want to forget that most of God's wonderful people in the early days of the church did not have peace of mind. They did not seek it. They knew that a soldier does not go to the battlefield to relax—he goes to fight. They accepted their position on earth as soldiers in the army of God, fighting along with the Lord Jesus Christ in the terrible war against iniquity and sin. It was not a war against people but against sin and iniquity and the devil!

There was much distress, many heartaches, painful bruises, flowing tears, much loss and many deaths.

But there is something better than being comfortable, and the followers of Christ ought to find it out—the poor, soft, overstuffed Christians of our time ought to find it out! There is something better than being comfortable!

We Protestants have forgotten altogether that there is such a thing as discipline and suffering. We live within an economy that enables us to have plenty. We live under a political system that enables

20

us to believe anything we want or nothing at all and still not be in trouble with the law. The result is that we have concocted a religion of sweet wine which we drink eagerly in the hope that we can walk around in a state of pleasant intoxication.

Now is that what God really wants to do for men and women?

No. God wants to bring us the fruit of the Spirit—love, joy, peace, longsuffering, gentleness, goodness, faith, meekness and temperance. The apostle Paul made it very plain in his language to the Ephesians that God wants to do something within every one of us that will cause us to love everybody, letting all bitterness and wrath and clamour and evil speaking be put away from among us, assuring that we will be kind to one another, tenderhearted, forgiving one another, even as God has, for Christ's sake, forgiven us.

That is what God wants to do: to bring out the likeness of Christ in the heart and life of the redeemed man. That is the purpose of God—not to make him happy, although in that condition he is likely to be happy. Not to make his civilization safe, although if there are enough people like that in the world, civilization has a better chance to survive.

So, this is our difficulty, brethren. We try to arrive at the fruits of Christianity by a shortcut. Of course, everybody wants peace and joy and love, goodness and gentleness and faithfulness. Everybody wants to be known as being spiritual, close to God, and walking in the Truth.

So, this is the answer. Every flower and every fruit has a stalk and every stalk has a root, and long before there is any bloom there must be a careful tending of the root and the stalk. This is where the misunderstanding lies—we think that we get the flower and the fragrance and the fruit by some kind of magic, instead of by cultivation.

There is something better than being comfortable

and lazy and relaxed, and Paul is good authority for it: "Be ye therefore followers of God, as dear children; and walk in love, as Christ also hath loved us, and hath given himself for us an offering and a sacrifice to God for a sweetsmelling savour." This is the likeness of Christ in the human heart and life—and our neighbors are waiting to see Him in our lives!

Now, I want to be practical and down-to-earth, and mention a few of the things which I consider to be necessary roots of true Christian living, out of which the fruits and the flowers of deep spirituality appear.

I am thinking first of such necessary spiritual roots as loyalty and faithfulness to God and to His church, the body of Christ on this earth.

Many people boast of their loyalty to their own denomination, but I refer to something greater and more basic than that. I refer to a loyal and prayerful identification with the very cause and truth of Jesus Christ as Lord to the point that we are willing to sacrifice for it. Most Christian churches are already showing signs of a great breakdown in loyalty in these modern times. Every church must have its few who are completely loyal to the implications of Jesus Christ actually being Saviour and Lord and are willing to suffer, if need be, for their love and faith.

Loyalty is surely interwoven with faithfulness, and we do well to remember that Jesus promised His disciples that God would reward us for our faithfulness. In a parable of the kingdom of heaven, Jesus taught that the master, upon his return from the far country, said to his faithful servants, "Well done . . . enter thou into the joy of thy lord."

I know that faithfulness is not a very dramatic subject and there are many among us in the Christian faith who would like to do something with more dash and more flair than just being faithful. Even in our

Christian circles, publicity is considered a great and necessary thing, so we are prone to want to do something that will be recognized, and perhaps get our picture in the paper. Thank God for the loyal and faithful Christians who have only one recognition in mind, and that i 'o hear their Lord say in that Great Day: "Well done . . . enter into the joy of thy Lord."

It is a plain truth that goodness and faithfulness are at the root of much of the consistent fruit-bearing among the witnessing children of God!

In God's Word, the Lord has always placed a great premium on the necessity of faithfulness in those who love Him and serve Him.

Noah was faithful in his day. If old Noah had been a baseball fan or had taken an early retirement or had placed some other interest in his life above God's work, there would have been no ark, no seed preserved and no human race.

Abraham was faithful in his day. If, in his wanderings, Abraham had struck uranium or gold and had given up the idea of going down to Palestine and establishing a people there from whom Jesus Christ would come, what would have happened to God's great plan? If Abraham had turned aside and built himself a little city, making himself mayor and living on the fat of the land, where would we be today?

Moses was faithful in his day. The scriptures leave no doubt about the faithful spirit and ministrations of Moses as God's man for his day and time—"Choosing rather to suffer affliction with the people of God, than to enjoy the pleasures of sin for a season; esteeming the reproach of Christ greater riches than the treasures in Egypt: for he had respect unto the recompence of the reward."

What do we need to say about the faithfulness of our Saviour, Jesus Christ? The world threatened Him all around. The devil was there with his lies and his temptations, offering Jesus the world if He would not go to the cross. But Christ was faithful to His Father and to us. Should we not be faithful to Him? Faithfulness is a wonderful, productive root and out of it comes much fruit.

When we look to our spiritual roots, we dare not dismiss the emphasis of the Word of God on plain, downright honesty and God-ordained goodness in our daily lives.

Honesty that can be trusted and respected is a very fragrant flower in the life of the Christian. Honesty has never yet grown in a vacuum—it is a blossom and a fragrance that grows and develops with spiritual care and nurture. There is a great deal of carelessness about the truth even among Christian believers. Some are surely guilty of stretching the truth about certain things even when they give their Christian testimony. Preachers and evangelists have been known to have exaggerated the numbers and the results of their Christian assemblies.

We joke about such things and forgive the brethren on the basis that their exaggeration was really "evangelistically speaking." But on behalf of God-honoring honesty in our daily lives, it needs to be said that any lie is of its father, the devil, whether it is told in a church service or anywhere else.

God's work does not need pious lies to support it. Rather we ought to follow the spirit of the old saying, "Tell the truth and shame the devil!" In our Christian fellowship, we should be known for being perfectly frank and wholly honest, for honesty has a good root that will also produce other sterling Christian virtues.

Do you know that one of the things that marked the lives of the original Quakers was their honest handling of the truth? They would not lie and they would not stretch the truth. They would not steal and they would not use flattering words. Someone in history wrote about the lives of the Quakers and commented that they "astonished the Christian world

24

by insisting upon acting like Christians." In England they were often kicked around and some languished in jail because they insisted on honoring only God and refused to bow down to people who did not deserve it. In the midst of professing Christians who generally acted like the world, the honest, God-honoring Quakers were considered queer because they sought to live as Christians should.

Many people in our day seem to dream of becoming great while there are far too few who spend any time in concern about being good. The Bible tells us about many good men and few of them would be considered great men. One of them was Jabez, a good man in the Old Testament who is mentioned in only three verses. Saul and Ahab came to places of leadership, and while they were considered great and important men of their times, they were not good men.

The Bible makes it plain to us that our Lord always placed the emphasis upon goodness, rather than upon greatness. Inherently, man does not have a good nature, and that is why Jesus Christ came to this earth and wrought the plan of salvation that makes bad men good. Christ died to wipe away our past sins, to give us new birth, to write our names in the Book of Life, to introduce us to the Father in eternal life.

When we say that Christ died to make us good, we are not being liberal in theology—we are being scriptural. What more can you say about any man than the tribute that he was a good man and full of the Holy Ghost?

Now, let me return to the root of this whole matter—are we Christians willing to be regular in the habits of a holy life, thus learning from the Holy Spirit how to be dependable and faithful, unselfish and Christ-like?

The crops in the fields are regular, and the birds and the animals have a regularity of life. We see it in the rising and the setting of the sun, and in the regularity of the phases of the moon.

The Old Testament revelation itself was built around regularity. It is said of the old man of God that he went into the temple of God in the order of his course and everything in the temple was laid out in order.

God has ordained, as well, that order and regularity may be of immense value to the Christian life.

You should learn to be regular in your prayer life, in your giving to God and His work, and in your church attendance.

But there are too many in the church who say, "I believe in Christ and I have had a spiritual experience and I have the right doctrine"—and then after that go to pieces and become whimsical, and pray according to impulse and give according to the way they feel at the moment, attend church when the weather is good, and do what they do with whimsical irregularity. No wonder they do not carry the sweet fragrance of the Spirit when they come to worship.

It is because people have neglected the root, and the flowers have died. The root of regularity has been forgotten, with the result that when the root is gone, the flowers die shortly thereafter.

But I can hear someone protest, saying, "I wanted to get into the Christian life, the spiritual faith, in order that I might be freed from necessity and from a law of having to do things regularly."

Well, you have missed it, my brother! You might as well close your Bible and walk out because you are in the wrong church and the wrong pew and the wrong dispensation! God would have His people learn regular holy habits and follow them right along day by day.

He doesn't ask us to become slaves to habits, but He does insist that our holy habits of life should become servants of His grace and glory.

Now, of course, this kind of order and regularity in our Christian lives must be tied in with the reality of dependability.

Nature again is the great example of dependability. If you plant corn, you will reap corn. Plant barley and you get barley, not wheat or corn. Set a hen on hens' eggs and you will get chickens, not guinea hens. So with everything after its kind.

Everything is dependable in nature—except man, and even in human society there is a certain amount of dependability.

If your car fails you a few times, you get rid of it, for you need a dependable car. You women know that your refrigerator and freezer must be dependable or the food will spoil unknown to you.

Our monetary system must be dependable, or there would be chaos. What would happen if the dollar was worth a dollar in Chicago, but worth only 75 cents in Milwaukee, 32 cents in St. Louis and in Detroit they wouldn't take it at all?

So, in society we have to know dependability, with the mail and with the milkman and with the schools. You have to be able to trust somebody. The sad thing about it in our human society is that people, as a rule, are trusted and dependable because they get something out of it.

The milkman doesn't come around every morning just because he is a nice fellow; he comes because he is getting paid for it. The mailman doesn't deliver the mail just because he is interested in you and hopes you get a card from Aunt Mabel; he's paid for doing it. The people who make your car build dependability into it because they want you to buy another one, which you won't do if it proves undependable.

How sad to think that it is only at the altar of God that men and women can't be depended upon. Why is it that it is so difficult to find people in the sanctuary who can be depended upon?

27

The root of dependability is dead in most churches, except for a faithful few, and these few have to take abuse from the unfaithful, undependable ones. The faithful few can always be depended upon and are always in evidence, so they are criticized for wanting to run the show.

Now, I want to ask you a question, and it is not something new and original. Think about your religious life, your holy habits, your church attendance, your giving to the Lord's work, your pattern of dependability during the past 12 months.

Now, be honest with yourselves, and ask an answer of your own heart: "If everyone in this church had been exactly as dependable as I am, where would our church be today?"

That's a question we ought to ask on our knees with tears and with sorrow, praying that God will help us to be dependable. When you are asked to do something, even if it is something simple, do it. It seems that so many of us only want to do the dramatic things—no one wants to be known as being dependable.

If you are waiting until you can do something with a flourish and a flair, something big and grand in the church of God, the chances are that you never will, and if you do, it will simply be a flash in the pan, a rainbow without any meaning, having no final stability!

Why doesn't anyone want to be dependable in the work of Christ?

Brethren, remember that sweet flowers are beautiful to look at and very fragrant to smell, but someone has to be out there on his knees in the dirt, long before there are any blossoms—fertilizing and digging, and going back and doing it again, watching the weather and watering when it gets too dry, and looking after that root.

One of the roots of the Christian life is dependability, and you cannot have spirituality without dependability any more than you can have a begonia without a begonia stalk.

Now, this is probably the place to consider punctuality in the work of God, also.

Isn't it strange that the very fault that would wreck a business, sink a ship, ruin a railroad, is tolerated at the very altar of God?

Why is it that in the church of God so few are concerned about lack of punctuality? The carelessness they show about the work of God would wreck a business or upset the economy, or if done in our bodies would ruin our health.

Now, punctuality is a beautiful thing, but Sunday school teachers don't realize it. Many a Sunday school superintendent has found his hair turning gray because of his worries about getting teachers who will be on time on Sunday morning. Everything we do for God should be done with beautiful precision.

We have a sacred duty. In church and Sunday school, we have in our hands the teaching of immortal souls. We have character to mold and souls to win and the work of God to do.

I have been around a long time and I am convinced that generally people are not spiritual at all if they are not punctual. If they are so lacking in self-discipline and so selfish and so inconsiderate of others and their time that they will not be punctual in the service of God and His church, they are fooling nobody! I repeat it again—if you are not punctual, you are not spiritual!

Everyone can be excused for the emergencies of life—there are accidents that will at times keep any of us from meeting our appointments. But I am trying to show my concern about those who practice the art of not being punctual until it has become a habit in their life.

There isn't anyone important enough to justify that kind of behavior, and anybody that is not punctual, habitually, is guilty of deception and falsehood.

He says he will be there—then he fails to appear!

Punctuality is a beautiful thing. You can't have a rose without a rose bush, and punctuality is the bush on which the rose grows!

So, love and faith, joy and peace may bloom in the heart of the Christian. Beautiful is the Christian character and the sweet smile of the holy man or woman, but that holy life is not by accident nor by coddling. Rather it comes by the bearing of strong burdens, by putting the yoke on his own neck and saying, "For Christ's sake, who bore the cross for me, I will take this self-imposed yoke."

Therefore, let us settle for being good, spiritual people—and let those be great who can! Let us seek first that we might be good, remembering that goodness grows from the roots of obedience, prayer, Bible reading, and surrender. Amen!

Chapter Three

Why Do Men Refuse the Streams of Mercy?

". . . this people refuseth the waters of Shiloah that go softly . . ." Isaiah 8:6

There are, in the Bible, many references where God has used the precious, reviving and life-sustaining qualities of streams of water to give us a true and adequate figure of the gracious, life-giving salvation which He offers all mankind.

He has promised, "I will give you streams of living water."

You will find these scriptural allusions to water and refreshment and cleansing and fruit-bearing in figures of speech, in God's gracious invitations, some spoken in poetic terms.

In the very last chapter of the Bible—in Revelation—God tells us that the Spirit and the bride say "Come," adding that whosoever will may come and "take of the water of life freely."

The historical reference in this text in Isaiah is to the quietly-flowing waters of Shiloah, a stream sometimes wrongly called Siloam.

Shiloah is said to have been the only perennial stream in the city of Jerusalem, the only one that did not dry up seasonally. It seems to me that it is exquisitely named. God Himself must have named it, because this Shiloah means tranquility and rest.

The waters of Shiloah are the waters of tranquility, the peaceful waters that go softly.

The Bible repeats important things often and it is certainly repetitive in making plain that water is one of man's necessary and most valuable assets. It is old and familiar truth that three-fourths of the world's surface is covered with water and that the composition of the human body is 70 per cent water. There is a large water content in our food, as well. Without water there could be no births, no growth, no digestion, no cleansing, no plants, no animals, no atmosphere. Take away water from the face of the earth and this globe we now call our familiar earth would be little more than a parched and ghastly death's head flying endlessly and meaninglessly through space.

But, even above and beyond the scientific interest is the dependence of every farmer and every gardener upon the availability of water.

I recall that when I was a boy I thought the heavy snowfall which covered the fields would smother and freeze the winter wheat and rye, but my father would actually express his thanks, to no one in particular, for the heavy snow cover on the fields. He knew that a good spring crop depended largely upon the heavy snow that kept the ground warm and that the slow melting of the snow in the early spring provided the right kind of moisture.

In some areas of our country, the productivity of the arid land is completely dependent upon the availability of water for irrigation. Farmers everywhere know that they will experience futility and emptiness if there is no water. The crops and fruits and vegetables will never come to fruition without the necessary supply of water. The man tending his herds of animals is in the same situation—for unless he has a place for his cattle to water he cannot use the grazing grounds.

The traveler, too, knows what it would mean to

go into the desert without a supply of water and without a guide. It means to invite death. The simplest way to commit suicide, although not the most painless, would be to walk out across the Sahara or any of the other great deserts of the world without a guide and without sufficient water.

Oh, the precious nature of water—as precious as our blood, of which it is a large part. If there is no water, as in the case of fatal necessity on the desert, there will be a certain and speechless death. This is a strange fact—no one dies crying for water. As he nears death, the poor victim has such swollen tongue and dryness of mouth and cracking of lips that it is impossible to form any words. So, without water, it is not just death but a speechless death—a death that cannot even cry!

When the Lord keeps referring in the scriptures to the precious and necessary streams of living water, He is trying to bring attention and emphasis to the great spiritual needs of the inner man. He is continually hopeful that men and women will heed His truth and admonitions, learning that if streams of water are so vitally important to the well-being and health and welfare of the outer and physical man, how much more should a person be responsive to God's offer of the streams of spiritual life for the immortal part of his being, the soul?

Actually, we find a great preoccupation today with man's physical needs throughout the world. I suppose there never has been a time in the history of the world when there was more interest in the human body than there is today. You can flip open any magazine or periodical and you will find many articles and a great deal of advice about caring for your body, but only occasionally will you find any help for your soul or spirit.

Actually, many people are getting rich, cashing in on our great love for our physical bodies. I must confess that when I read about the many ways in

33

which the human body is groomed and fed and pampered I think about the publicity for Julius the First, a young Angus bull featured in the livestock shows.

You may not believe it, but the owners or handlers of Julius the First brush his teeth every day. They curl the hair on his forehead just like a young fellow brushing himself before he takes off to see his girl. Julius is just an Angus bull, but they brush him and groom him and watch his weight in the hope that he will win the top prizes in the show ring.

What a picture of our humanity! Men and women are brushed and groomed and massaged, intent upon diets and vitamins, completely preoccupied with the outer man, the physical body. The irony of it all is expressed in the fact that in the livestock auction, Julius the First will bring a price of about $16,000— and you know you could not begin to get anything like that for your human body, even in youth, with strength and energy and beauty at their maximum!

Oh, it is the inner man that really matters, for the outward man must perish and go back to the elements from which it was taken, but the inner man lives on and on after the physical body drops away in death.

That body of yours, to which you give so much thought and care, is only the outer tabernacle. The apostle Paul told us about the importance of the inner man and he said he was willing to let the outer man die a little at a time in order that the inner man might be renewed. Throughout the Bible, God emphasizes the value and worth of the inner man, although certainly not to the exclusion of His concern for our physical bodies. We do well to remember the scriptural balance, for the Bible does say that "the Lord is for the body." Certainly, we are putting the emphasis in the wrong place if we become too physical in our outlook, insisting that the most important concern is for the body.

Well, we know for certain that God is much more

concerned with the inner man than with man's outer tabernacle, so He gives us water—the sweet waters, the soft-flowing waters of Shiloah. These are streams of tranquility and peace and He gives them to the inner man.

What a gracious truth—that there is an inner and spiritual man!

Jacob once said, "I go down to Sheol, mourning for my son." Yet, when Jacob died and was buried, they could tell you where his body was. Jacob did not say, "My body will go down." When he said, "I will go down," he was referring to the inner man, that part of him that was the soul, the real Jacob.

On the cross Jesus cried out, "Father, into Thy hands I commit my spirit." They laid His body in the grave and it was there three days, but His inner man, the spirit, was committed unto the Father.

Judas, it is said, went unto his own place—yet we know what happened to his body. It was buried in a field, but Judas himself went unto his own place. There was a Judas, an inner man apart from the body. There was a Jacob apart from the body. There was a Jesus apart from the body.

Abraham's body had been lying in the cave of Machpelah with the dust of centuries upon it when the rich man, Dives, lifted up the eyes of the inner man after his own death and discerned the beggar, Lazarus, resting on Abraham's bosom. It was the real Abraham he discerned—the immortal inner man—there in paradise and it was the real Lazarus who had gone to be with Abraham.

Brothers and sisters, there is a real sense in which we will never know each other until we shuck off this old earthly tabernacle of deception. There is a sense in which our bodies actually veil us from one another. We are uncertain. We shake a hand and look at a face. The influence of that hand or face is a physical thing—and the real you, the inner man, is deeper than that, and beyond and past all of that.

What did it actually mean for mankind when Jesus Christ came into our world?

No one should think for even one second that He came just to bring a state of peace between nations, or that He came merely to give prosperity so we would all have richer food to eat, softer beds in which to sleep and finer homes in which to live!

God's Word leaves no doubt about it—Jesus came in order that our spirits might prosper! He came that our inner man, the eternal and undying part of us, might prosper! He died to open a fountain of such gracious nature that to partake and drink means a spiritual transformation, never to hunger and thirst again for temporal and passing things.

Now, what is this water, this softly-flowing stream of peace and tranquility and rest? God wants us to be sure—either we know or we do not know!

If this is not a reality, it is simply poetry with which I am regaling you to earn my living.

I ask you: can you not put aside all of the poetry and figure and metaphor and get through to something basic and solid and real, where you can say, "Thank God there is mercy and forgiveness and cleansing and eternal life for the guilty soul, the inner man who has sinned!"?

I heard the voice of Jesus say,
Behold, I freely give
The living waters; thirsty one
Stoop down and drink and live!

I came to Jesus, and I drank
Of that life-giving stream,
My thirst was quenched, my soul revived,
And now I live in Him!

There it is—there is the mercy of God! Man's great difficulty is that we have religion without guilt, and religion without guilt just tries to make God a big "pal" of man. But religion without guilt is a religion that cannot escape hell for it deceives and finally destroys all who are a part of it.

Religion without any consciousness of guilt is a false religion. If I come to Jesus Christ without any confession of guilt, simply to gain some benefit, I still have woe upon me, as did the Pharisees before me! But if my guilt drives me to Jesus, then I have my guilt taken from me and I find mercy. Oh, the mercy of God! We sing about the mercy of God, and I hope we know what we are singing about: "O depths of mercy, can it be, that gate is left ajar for me."

The good mercy of God—that is the water to a thirsty man—the man whose conscious guilt and sin are causing him pain and anguish.

That thirsty man can come to the Lord Jesus and drink of the waters of Shiloah—the waters of mercy!

My brother, you will never have inward peace until you have acknowledged your guilt. This is something you cannot dodge and evade, because you have a conscience and your conscience will never let you rest until you get rid of the guilt!

Guilt must be dealt with and taken away! Oh, you can be smoothed over and given a little theological massage, patted on the head and told that it is all right, but that treatment will not take away guilt and condemnation. Sins that you thought were absolved by religion will always come back to haunt you.

Only the Redeemer and Saviour, Jesus Christ, can forgive and pardon and free from guilt—and the sins He has forgiven will never come back to haunt you as a child of God—never while the world stands! He forgives and forgets, burying your old load of guilt so that it no longer exists. God has promised, "I will not remember thy guilt." Since God is able to remember everything, the only way to figure this

37

is that God beats that guilt and condemnation back out of being so it does not even exist any more! The sin that God pardons is no longer an entity—it is gone forever!

Christians have often talked about the "covering" of our sins and I know it is a common phrase. I have used it myself, but it is a figure of speech—for sin is not covered. The sinner must be cleansed. Let me explain. In the Old Testament, sin was covered as they waited for the Lamb to come and die on the cross! But in the New Testament sinners could look back on the finished work already done by Christ, blood already spilled. Sins are not covered now. They are cleansed and forgiven! That is why the believing Christian can have inward peace and joy.

There it is—the water of grace, the flow of mercy to the sinner, poverty stricken and spiritually bankrupt. The grace of our Lord Jesus Christ flows like the waters of Shiloah—the quiet waters that are so readily available.

Did you know that sheep cannot drink from noisy, running water? A sheep's nostrils are so close to his mouth that if he starts to drink and the water is moving, he will choke and could perhaps drown. It is necessary for the shepherd to dam the stream until a quiet pool is formed, and the moving water becomes still. Then the animal can put his muzzle into the water and drink without choking and gasping for air. When David wrote about our Lord being our shepherd, he said, "He leadeth me beside the still water."

The grace of God is like the still, quiet pool of water. The water flows softly! Oh, Grace of God, how you have been wounded in the house of your friends! Grace of God, how you have been made into a fetish before which modern men bow in worship. The sweet grace of God—how it has been used to hide what people really are. The grace of God has been preached in ways that have damned men instead of saved them. Yet it is still full and free—the grace of God!

If God could not extend us His mercy and grace, and treated us exactly as we deserved, there would be only one course for Him to follow. God would have to turn an angered face to us in life and He would have to turn His back to us in death. That would happen to the best human beings that ever lived, if we should receive only what we deserve.

But, oh, the grace of God! God through the plan of salvation in Jesus Christ will go beyond our merits, beyond that which we deserve. Even if our sins have been like a mountain, it is the grace of God that assures our forgiveness. There is cleansing for the defiled, gracious and satisfying cleansing—a beautiful element in Christianity as revealed by the Lord Himself, and not just abstract theology.

I saw a magazine cover which pictured four men. It was an unusual picture for it showed the youngest man preaching his first sermon, for he had just come out of prison where he had received Christ—a redeemed, converted, transformed follower of Jesus, now determined to tell others the good news. With him was the pastor of the church in which the young man was preaching, the lawyer who had been the prosecutor in his trial, and the judge who had sentenced him to prison. Many judges and lawyers will admit that when most criminals are returned to a happy and useful life it is because they have purgation in the blood of the Lamb, the power of Christ to change a man, to cleanse from defilement, to transform his life and character.

This is a beautiful thing—that a former car thief can stand with a big grin on his face and hold an open Bible in his hand, and witness to the power of the Christian gospel.

Men will ask: How can it be? Because the blood of Jesus Christ cleanses from all sin. Because there is a fiery purgation in the Christian message that can take any sinful man and make him clean and make him good, for Christ's sake!

Knowing the power of this gospel, I am willing to put myself on record that I would rather be preached to by a converted car thief than be lulled to death by the educated gentlemen who have reduced Christianity to nothing more than a psychology of comfort. Even their church ads woo men and women with the appeal, "Come to church and be comforted."

Brothers and sisters in Christ's church, you do not want consolation and comfort—you want to know the facts, you want to know where you stand before God Almighty!

In recent days I have had two persons come to me personally to tell me that my preaching has been cutting them to pieces, making them miserable and desirous of something better God has for them in their lives.

I think that is a beautiful thing and I thank God that I am worthy of that. People should not come to Christ and to His church with the expectation that all spiritual problems are consummated in comfort and consolation. If that is all people want in their church going, they will find a large number of preachers waiting to rock them to sleep with the consolation, "Bye, bye now, and here's your bottle!"

What do we know about today? Any of us can have a sudden heart attack and be called from this life. How will it be with our souls and where will we go—those are the things we want to know for sure. Following Christ, we want to know how we can go on to be holy and live holy and be right with God, turning our backs on sin and living in the Spirit!

Men are always faced with choices and decisions as the loving and eternal God deals with them, now in mercy and in patience.

I must confess as a pastor and minister that I

have had to say "Goodbye" to people in some instances when they have said: "We cannot worship here. You are too strict. Your standards are too strict for this day and age. Your message is too strict!"

My only apology is that I am still not as strict as the Bible is. I have to confess that I am still not up to the standard of the scriptures. I am trying, but I am not that strict.

But, occasionally, we have to say farewell to someone who says they have to find a different kind of church, an easy-going church, a church that majors in relaxation.

What did Jesus say to us? He said that unless we are ready to turn from everything and follow Him with devotion, we are not yet ready to be His disciples, and unless we are ready to die for Him, we are not ready to live for Him. The whistle is going to blow for us one of these days and then we will have to appear and tell God how we carried on His work, how we conducted ourselves in the light of what Jesus said.

So we cannot afford to let down our Christian standards just to hold the interest of people who want to go to hell and still belong to a church. We have had carnal and fleshly and self-loving people who wanted to come in and control young people's groups and liberate us from our spiritual life and standards and "strictness."

I would like to know why people of that kind of disposition want to go to church. I know what I would do if I were determined just to eat, drink and be merry—I would never want to show up among people who are devoted to Jesus Christ and to His saving gospel. If I were of that mind and disposition and found myself at church, I would at least go to the furnace room and stay there until church was over!

I thank God for Christian men and women who want to know the facts and the truth as it has come from God. Thank God, they are not just looking for someone to give them a relaxing religious massage! These are the facts—the blood of Jesus Christ cleanses. There is a purging element in Christianity. Then there is the Holy Spirit, the blessed Spirit of God who brings us the peace and tranquility of the waters of Shiloah.

The living God invites us to this stream, the only perennial stream in the world, the only stream that never runs dry, the only stream that never overflows and destroys.

Yet, the prophet Isaiah went on to record the fact that he could not understand how the people of Israel could refuse the soft-flowing waters sent by the Lord.

The prophet voiced his incredulity and amazement: "How can it be? Israel refuses the soft waters of Shiloah sent by the Lord; the healing, tranquilizing stream that brings peace to the heart and conscience. They refuse it and turn to men like themselves instead."

Isaiah then warned that those who refuse the still and peaceful streams from God have only one thing to anticipate—the overflowing torrents of judgment. He said, "If ye choose to turn away from the soft waters of Shiloah, the Lord God bringeth upon you the waters of the river, strong and many, and he shall come over all his channels, and go over all his banks."

I do not think we are overly-serious in our approach. I do not think we have made extreme statements, statements that need modification, in light of New Testament truth given by our Lord Jesus Christ. I do not think we are as severe as God would have us be in the facing of coming judgment, for it was Jesus Himself who told the Jews in His day, "The Father . . . hath committed all judgment unto the Son."

Chapter Four

How Can a Moral Man Ever Find Saving Truth?

*"Jesus said unto him, If thou wilt be perfect, go
and sell that thou hast, and give to the poor, and
thou shalt have treasure in heaven: and come and
follow me.*

*"But when the young man heard that saying, he
went away sorrowful: for he had great possessions."*
Matthew 19:21-22

I have never felt that it was my ministry to personally expose or defrock those whose religious views
happen to fall far short of the New Testament demands of Jesus Christ, but I do believe there is one
man in the New Testament record whose "debunk-
ing" has been delayed almost 2,000 years.

I refer, of course, to that person who has become
so well known to Bible students and to Christian
audiences as "the rich young ruler" who came to
Jesus to talk about the terms of eternal life.

Christian congregations throughout the years
have heard a countless number of sermons in which
this young religious leader has been portrayed as
a Sir Galahad of his time—"whose strength was as
the strength of ten because his heart was pure."

Personally, I have found it strangely amazing to
look back into the records of scholars and preachers

and find that great ranks of religious people down the years have misunderstood the manner in which Jesus dealt with this inquirer.

Almost everyone has gone over to the side of this young man in accepting his word as valid testimony when he said: "The commandments? All of these I have kept from my youth up!"

"I have kept them," he said. So there is a great chorus of moral applause and for centuries that nameless man has been preached and praised as a paragon of morality and a sincere seeker after truth.

There are several things for us to review as we consider this incident in the earthly life of our Lord. Perhaps the most common misunderstanding about the "rich young ruler" is the presumption of many that he was a political or government leader, but the gospel records indicate that he was a religious leader among the Jews, probably in one of the synagogues. The word *ruler* should not indicate to us a man with crown and scepter and a robe—it simply means that the man was a chairman, a president, a leader of a local worshipping group.

Another thing to notice is that even though he was recognized among those in religious circles, he was still trying to satisfy the uncertainties of his own inner life. I mention this because it makes it appear that things have not changed a great deal in 2,000 years. Personally, I have never before had a year in which so many persons of high place and status in church circles have sought me out for counsel regarding their own spiritual condition and problems. The point I make is this: these are not beginners in the faith. They are not unbelievers. Some are highly placed in our own evangelical circles.

What can be wrong when religious leaders are uncertain and shaken and miserable? I say that they have been brought into the Christian faith without any confrontation with total commitment to Jesus Christ as Lord, without any instruction that Christian victory means complete abandonment of our self and person to Jesus Christ!

Now, this review of the gospel record: This young Jewish leader came to Jesus, asking, "Good master, what good thing shall I do, that I may have eternal life?"

Jesus answered, "Why do you call me good? There is only one who is truly good and that is God; but if you will enter into life, keep the commandments."

Then, looking into Jesus' face, he asked: "Which commandments? Are you teaching some commandments that I do not know about?"

The answer Jesus gave him was direct: "No, I am talking about the regular commandments with which you are familiar as a religious Jew. God's commands: Thou shalt do no murder, thou shalt not commit adultery—you know them all."

It was then that the young man, looking into the face of Jesus Christ, said: "All of these things I have kept from my youth—what lack I yet?"

Jesus then gave him the opportunity for spiritual decision—the opportunity of self-renunciation, the privilege of putting spiritual things above material things, the complete abandonment of himself as a follower and disciple of Jesus, God's Son, and messianic provision for lost men.

There follows one of the sad and depressing statements of the New Testament record: "But when the young man heard that saying, he went away sorrowful, for he had great possessions."

Let us notice a great truth here—a religious life and religious practice have never provided the eternal assurance for which the heart longs. This young man was in religious leadership and yet he came to Jesus to discuss the void in his own being. He wanted something more than a conclusion drawn from a text. He was undoubtedly groping for the knowledge in his own heart that he had entered into a state of eternal benediction—we refer to it now as the assurance of eternal life.

His question to Jesus was: "What good thing must I do?"

Remember that our Lord Jesus Christ had never studied the books, but He was a master in dealing with people. He was a master psychologist, which means simply that He knew the ways of men and how their minds work. That is the basis of true psychology, anyway.

Jesus heard what this young man said and immediately was able to appraise him. Jesus knew that he was a religious leader. Jesus knew that he read the Hebrew scriptures and that he lifted his hands to God and led the people in their ancient prayers. Yet Jesus knew that he was not satisfied, that he was still miserable because of the aching lack within his own being.

In dealing with him, Jesus took him where he found him, and for the sake of the argument, He accepted him at his own estimate.

"You have come to talk to me, and you lay this matter of your relationship to God and eternal life on the foundation of doing good things to obtain life," Jesus reminded him.

"Just how good would that good thing have to be?" Jesus continued. "You do know there is only one good and that is God, and if you are going to do something good enough to move God to give you the gift of eternal life, how good must your action be?

"Seeing there is only one good, and you do not believe I am God, for you called me good master and good teacher, all in the same breath, what could you do that would be good enough? How are you going to be good enough if there is only one good and that is God? To win anything from God on the devil's terms, you would have to do something good enough for God to accept.

"So, young man, if you insist on buying your way in, I have the answer: Keep the commandments. That is the way you will have to do it."

The reply to Jesus was, "All of these I have kept from my youth up."

Now, we will all agree that without doubt this young man had kept certain of the commandments from his youth. I doubt that he had ever murdered anyone. He had probably never committed adultery. I suppose it had never been necessary for him to steal. Probably he had honored his father and mother, for the Jews did this, as a rule.

This young man has been praised so often in sermons because he was what we call "a moral man." Let me tell you what a moral man really is: he is good enough to deceive himself and bad enough to damn himself!

This young man did not realize the danger of being a moral man. He was self-deceived—and because his goodness prevented him from knowing his badness, he turned his back on God and walked away.

It is plain in every age that many men and women deceive themselves by accepting the idea that any kind of religion is all right, any kind of religion will do.

Is any kind of old mustard plaster all right in dealing with cancer in the body?

Is any kind of food all right for the health and growth of a tiny baby?

Is any kind of old beat-up airplane all right for transporting men and women through the skies, several miles above the earth?

No, my friends. Sometimes, having anything is worse than having nothing. Frankly, I would much rather have no religion at all than to have just enough to deceive me.

This was the downfall of this rich young ruler.

He had just enough religion to delude himself and deceive himself. He was just good enough to make himself think that he was all right, to answer that he had kept God's laws.

I am going to ask you to decide whether he had—or not.

The Bible says, "Thou shalt have no other gods before me."

I believe that Jew and Catholic and Protestant all would agree that whatever comes before God is god to them, and that whatever shuts out God and stands between the soul and God is an idol, a god.

This young man knew very well the command that God must have first place in our lives. Yet, he was very rich and when our Lord put to him on his own terms the question of selling everything and giving it away, making God first in his life and becoming a disciple, he turned his back on it.

He turned his back on God because he had another god that he loved, although he would not admit it. He was able to lead the people in worship and in prayer and in the songs of Zion, but unknown to them, he had a god, an idol, tucked away. When the chips were down, he chose the god of gold instead of the God of his fathers.

I say that the rich young ruler was not a keeper of the law. He shattered and smashed the first one like a glass on the pavement. When the God of his fathers instructed, "Sell everything and follow me," he turned his back and walked away.

Again, our Lord summed up all of the commandments in His words: "Thou shalt love the Lord thy God with all thy heart."

When this young man came face to face with the vital question of his love for God or his love of wealth, he went away because he had great possessions. So, he broke and shattered this summation of all of the commandments of God.

Jesus also coupled with love of God the command

that "thou shalt love thy neighbor as thyself."

Even as this young man talked with Jesus, the poor and the beggars and the crippled and the starving were all around them. Old men and women in poverty, little children without enough food to eat, lepers trying to find roots and grasshoppers and snails in an effort to keep their emaciated and ailing bodies from falling apart.

Yet, knowing the reality of human need for countless thousands, this young man could stand in the temple and pray and lead out in song in an effort to glorify his God and Abraham, Isaac and Jacob. When Jesus suggested that, as a condition of following Him, he distribute his earthly goods, the young man flatly refused.

Surely, he did not exactly love his neighbor as himself. But in his own eyes he was a noble keeper of the law. He could stand and say to Jesus, "All of these I have kept." I do not believe he was lying—but he was terribly deceived.

The last commandment in the decalogue says to every man: "Thou shalt not covet."

This means a great many things, for the word *covet* in the rest of the Bible, in both the Old and New Testaments, clearly means wanting anything with inordinate desire.

The young man shattered that one wide open, even as Jesus talked with him: "Distribute thy goods, and come and follow me—like Peter and the rest. We may be known as poor, but we owe nothing. I owe nothing. Come and go with me—for there is a regeneration taking place."

But he refused. He was unable to leave his bank accounts and his properties. So, he was a covetous man. He was a lover of self instead of loving his neighbor. He was a lover of his own wealth rather than loving God with his innermost being. The living God was not first in his life and in his love—and so the commandments were broken.

There is an important teaching for each of us here.

It is entirely possible for us to imagine ourselves to be all right when we are not all right. It is entirely possible to jockey our souls around over the checkerboard of our conscience to make everything appear to be all right.

That's what this moral young man was doing as Jesus talked to him and instructed him. It is well to note that our Lord plainly faced him with the terms of eternal salvation: full acknowledgement of sin rather than a defensive attitude, complete trust in the person of Jesus Christ, and utter abandonment to His Lordship alone.

Actually, there have never been any other terms laid down for salvation anywhere or at any time. Men with their multitudes of petty gods are still like this young man—ready to declare their own goodness even while standing knee-deep in broken laws.

A man who truly comes to God in repentance and contrition of heart does not work up a defense on the basis that he has not broken every law and every commandment. If he is truly penitent in seeking pardon and forgiveness, he will be so overcome with the guilt of the commands that he has broken and the sins he is confessing that he will be down before the great God Almighty, trembling and crying out, "Oh, God, I am an unclean man and I have sinned against Thee!"

Remember, an outlaw is not a man who has broken all the laws of his country—he may actually have ignored and flouted and violated only a few. The bandit Jessie James may have broken only a couple of laws—those that say "You shall not kill" and "You shall not steal." But he was a notorious outlaw with a price on his head, even though there were thousands of other laws on the books which he had not violated.

Brethren, when I come before my God as an outlaw, returning home as the prodigal, returning from

50

the pig pen, I will not be dickering and bargaining with God about the sins that I did not commit. I will not even be conscious of those—for the fact that I have broken any of God's laws or committed any sins will so overwhelm me that I will go before God as though I were the worst sinner in all the wide world.

The defensive attitude of "moral" men and women is one of the great problems confronting Christianity in our day. Many who are trying to be Christians are making the effort on the basis that they have not done some of the evil things which others have done. They are not willing to honestly look into their own hearts, for if they did, they would cry out in conviction for being the chief of all sinners.

Look at the record of the apostle Paul. He took an honest look at his own sinful nature, and the fact that he had committed any sin at all bit down so hard on him that it crushed him like an eggshell.

Paul could testify that as far as conscience was concerned, he had tried to honor it. As far as was humanly possible, as a member of one of the strictest sects, he had been concerned with keeping the laws of God. Actually, no one can go into the record and try to pin the awful, daily variety of gross and heinous sins on Paul, for, in most ways, he was a strong and noble and moral man. He did the best he could in his own unregenerate state before he met Jesus Christ. But out of his own crushed heart, after experiencing the transformation that Christ brings within, Paul confessed that he saw his own being as God had seen it: "I am chief of sinners. I have been the worst sinner in the world!"

Oh, the difference Jesus Christ makes in our attitudes!

Because Paul finally saw himself as the worst man in the world, God could make him one of the best men in the world and in history.

The rich young ruler never had this sense of his

own sin and unworthiness. He dared to stand before Jesus Christ, of whom he was inquiring the way of eternal life, and defend himself.

"I am no heathen," he said. "I have kept God's laws."

Oh, how wrong he was. The very fact that he could remember that he had kept any of God's laws disqualified him instantly for eternal life. He trusted in his own moral defense rather than acknowledge his sin and his need.

Now, the matter of complete trust in the person of Christ.

No man has any hope for eternal salvation apart from trusting completely in Jesus Christ and His atonement for men. Simply stated, our Lord Jesus is the lifeboat and we must fully and truly be committed to trusting the lifeboat.

Again, our Lord and Saviour is the rope by which it is possible to escape from the burning building. There is no doubt about it—either we trust that rope or we perish.

He is the wonder drug or medication that heals all ills and sicknesses—and if we refuse it, we die.

He is the bridge from hell to heaven—and we take the bridge and cross over by His grace or we stay in hell.

These are simple illustrations, but they get to the point of the necessity of complete trust in Jesus Christ—absolute trust in Him!

I wonder how many people in our own day really trust Christ in that way. There are so many who want to trust Christ plus something else. They want to trust Christ and add their own morals. They want to trust Christ and add their own good works. They want to trust Christ and then point to the merits of their baptism or church membership or stewardship.

Let me tell you straight out that Jesus Christ will never stand at the right side of a plus sign. If you will insist upon adding some "plus" to your faith in Jesus Christ, He will walk away in His holy dignity. He will ever refuse to be considered the other part of a "plus" sign. If your trust is in the plus—something added—then you do not possess Jesus Christ at all.

The rich young ruler thought that he possessed all of the necessary plus signs. The truth was that he possessed nothing that really mattered.

Then, a man's salvation involves utter abandonment to Jesus Christ. Our Lord taught this fundamental truth throughout His earthly ministry, so it was not a new concept proposed for the rich young ruler. Jesus skillfully got that man into a place where He could clearly and plainly tell him this great fact of the spiritual life: "Do not keep anything in your life that is more important than God Himself; come and follow me in complete trust and abandonment!"

I wonder also how many Christians in our day have truly and completely abandoned themselves to Jesus Christ as their Lord. We are very busy telling people to "*accept* Christ"—and that seems to be the only word we are using. We arrange a painless acceptance.

We are telling people that the easiest thing in the world is to *accept* Jesus Christ, and I wonder what has happened to our Christian theology which no longer contains any hint of what it should mean to be completely and utterly abandoned to Jesus Christ, our Lord and Saviour.

I think it is a good sign that we are having a restlessness and a dissatisfaction among professing Christians concerning their own spiritual state. I find that we are having to start all over with many of them because they have never been taught anything but "the acceptance of Christ." They need the plain statement of the terms of eternal salvation: acknowledgement of sin and complete trust in Christ and utter abandonment to Him and His Lordship.

At this point, the rich young ruler was not interested. These were terms that he had not anticipated and he could not accept them at all. So, we read in the scripture: "He, sorrowing, went away."

You see, like all men, he had a basic interest in eternal life, but there were other things that he wanted more! No doubt he had some urge to follow Christ as the Messiah, but there were other things he wanted more!

Let me point out here something I feel about this young man and many others like him who live around us today.

I do not believe that every person who is spiritually unbelieving and lost is morally careless. We all know men and women who care very deeply about life, about evil conditions and changing moral standards. Many of them work and teach and try to do the best they can—but they are still lost because they have never acknowledged God's terms for eternal salvation and they are not abandoned to Jesus Christ, our Lord.

It is not only the careless who perish. Those who are careful and busy about many good things will perish as well. The rich young ruler took the human way and perished, even though he cared enough to come to Jesus and ask the way of life in a reverent and tender question.

He was a religious man of his day—but he was a lost man. He was a sinner, a law-breaker, a rebel—and the Lord quickly brought the truth to the surface.

It is actually true that many people engage in earnest prayers on their road to perdition. In a way, they want God, but they don't want Him enough. They are interested in eternal life, but they are still more interested in other things. They know that they should follow Jesus in true faith, but other things keep them from that decision.

I hope that God can burn this frightful fact into our souls—the truth that men and women can be respectable and religious and prayerful and careful and eager and ask the right questions and talk about religion—and still be lost!

In our churches today, we feel that we have found a real treasure if we find someone who appears to be eagerly seeking the truth of God. Actually, we rarely find anyone who seems to be as eager as the rich young man who came to Jesus.

They don't seem to be coming to us in the churches. We have to go out after them—joke with them, talk with them about their sports, try to find some common ground, and then gingerly tell them that if they will receive Jesus they will have peace of mind, good grades in school and everything will be all right. Amen!

Now, that is a fair run-down on modern Christianity, and it explains why there are Christians who ask, "What's the matter with me, brother? What's the matter with me?"

They have not come into the kingdom of God through repentance and trust and abandonment. The result is exactly what we would expect in those who have been "leaked" into the kingdom of God, taken in between the cracks, crawling in through a side window. There is no inner witness. There is no assurance. There is no inward peace.

When we think we have found someone who is a seeker, we settle back and say, "That's wonderful! He will be all right—he is a seeker."

Here is the caution, brethren: if you could see all the seekers who are in hell today who were seekers while they were on earth, you would know that many have sought and found out what they had to do—and then refused to do it.

This rich young ruler was a seeker. The church today would have put his name down on a card and would have counted him among the statistics. But he walked away and turned his back on the offer and the appeal of Jesus Christ.

Every faithful pastor can tell you, with great sorrow and concern, the stories of young people and men and women who walked away from the church and straight Bible teaching and warm Christian fellowship to have their own way. When the old nature stirred, they turned their backs on God and walked away. They went into questionable marriages. They went into worldly alliances. They took jobs in which there was no chance to please and glorify God. They went back into the world.

Now, they did not walk out of the house of God because they did not want God—but because they found something they wanted more than God! God has given men and women the opportunity for free will and free choices—and some are determined to have what they want most.

The rich young ruler made his decision on the basis of what he wanted most in life. The last thing we know about him is the fact that he turned from Jesus and walked away. He was sorry about it and sorrowful, because he had great earthly possessions. But Jesus looked upon him as he walked away and Jesus was sorrowful, too.

Those who walk away from Christian fellowship, leaving the church and the choir, directly into the arms of sinners, do not actually leave with happiness and great joy. I have had some of them who came back to counsel and consult with me. I believe they are trying to get a pastoral excuse or rationalization for the manner in which they turned their backs on God.

I have committed sins in my day which I believe the blood of the everlasting covenant has cleansed and blotted away forever—but that kind of rationalization is not one of them. I can say that I have never told anyone, "It will be all right; don't worry about it," when it was not all right, in fact. There are many virtues as a minister that I do not have, but those who have turned their backs on God and wanted me to give them some excuse have found that they have never succeeded in softening me up.

People often come to me to find out where they have missed the secret of the victorious and joyful Christian life. Generally, I discover that they want to live in two worlds. They want to live a holy life like Dr. A. B. Simpson, but at the same time they want to be as worldly as the heathen. They aspire to the saintliness of the saintly McCheyne, but they are satisfied to be as worldly as the world—and it is impossible to have both!

I admit that there are parents who counsel me about the danger of losing the young people from our church life because I am faithful in preaching against this present world and the worldly system in which we live.

I can only say that I am concerned and I will stand and cry at the door when they decide to go, but I will not be guilty of deceiving them. I refuse to deceive and damn them by teaching that you can be a Christian and love this present world, for you cannot.

Yes, you can be a hypocrite and love the world.

You can be a deceived ruler in the religious system and love the world.

You can be a cheap, snobbish, modern Christian and love the world.

But you cannot be a genuine Bible Christian and love the world. It would grieve me to stand alone on this principle, but I will not lie to you about it.

The rich young ruler wanted God, but he turned back to his money and possessions. He was grieved within himself that he had to pay such a price— the true knowledge of eternal life—in order to keep the things he loved the most.

How about the men and women all around us who seem satisfied with their choice of this present world, having turned their backs on God? They are determined to have and to hold what they love the most, but they are actually grieved at the knowledge of what it has cost them to have their own way. They choose and take what they want, but they grieve for the God they have deserted.

We have many like the rich young ruler among us still. It is not enough to inquire about the power of the crucified life and the Spirit-filled life. It is not enough to want it—it must be desired and claimed above everything else. There must be an abandonment to Jesus Christ to realize it. The individual must want the fullness of Christ with such desire that he will turn his back on whatever else matters in his life and walk straight to the arms of Jesus!

So much for the case of the rich young ruler. His veil was taken away and he turned from Jesus Christ. He was still the hypocrite, still a covetous man, a money-lover, a breaker of the law. Above all, he was still a sinner, and Christless.

He had to pay a great price to keep what he loved most. Actually, he had to sell Jesus even as Judas Iscariot sold Him. Judas sold Him for 30 pieces of silver. We have no idea in terms of money and land and possessions what the rich young ruler paid in his refusal to follow Jesus.

I do not think I have been over-serious in this appraisal of what it means to become a true and devoted disciple of Jesus Christ. I do not think I have been as severe as the New Testament actually tells it. And I do not think I have said as much as Jesus said when He laid down His terms of discipleship in the New Testament.

What about you? If you are a seeker after Jesus Christ in truth, He is saying to you: "It is not enough to inquire. Give up that which is the dearest thing you hold in life; and come, and follow me!"

Chapter Five

What Is It Costing You to Be a Christian?

"And then shall appear the sign of the Son of man in heaven: and then shall all the tribes of the earth mourn, and they shall see the Son of man coming in the clouds of heaven with power and great glory."
Matthew 24:30

It is very easy in our day to discern a glaring inconsistency among many well-groomed and overfed evangelical Christians, who profess that they are looking for Christ's second coming and yet vigorously reject any suggestion that Christian faith and witness should be costing them something.

I have come to believe that when we discuss the prophetic scriptures and the promises of the Lord Jesus Christ that He will return, we must necessarily examine the kind of love we really have for Him in our hearts.

If we are soon going to look upon His blessed face, should we not be expecting that He will search out the true nature of the love and adoration which we profess?

The Bible makes it plain that the love of many shall wax cold in the terrible and trying period just before Jesus does return to earth. It is well, then, to face up to a searching question:

"How ardent, how genuine, and how meaningful is your love for the Lord Jesus Christ?"

A second question follows in quick succession:

"What are you doing to prove your love for the Saviour? What is your faith and witness of Jesus Christ actually costing you in your daily life?"

I confess that a preacher cannot bring this kind of message to laymen without making a request for prayer on his own behalf. I do believe that we are living in those times that Jesus said would come when the love and concern of many would wax cold.

Will you pray for me as a minister of the gospel? I am not asking you to pray for the things people commonly pray for. Pray for me in light of the pressures of our times. Pray that I will not just come to a wearied end—an exhausted, tired, old preacher, interested only in hunting a place to roost. Pray that I will be willing to let my Christian experience and Christian standards cost me something right down to the last gasp!

It is impossible for us to dismiss the explicit teachings of our Lord Jesus concerning the end of this age and His return to earth. It is impossible to dismiss the emphasis of the entire Bible concerning God's plan for this earth and the consummation of all things. A large percentage of Bible truth is actually predictive in nature, telling us what will come to pass. Some of these passages are already fulfilled. Others remain to be fulfilled.

When the World Council of Churches held one of its most important international assemblies in Evanston, we were struck by the unusual significance of the theme, "Christ, the Hope of the World."

It turned out that many of the American and European leaders of the World Council were embarrassed when many of the representatives of overseas Christian groups interpreted the theme to mean that the hope of the world lies in the second return of Christ to our earth.

Actually, the leaders were embarrassed because they had been playing down any emphasis upon the prophetic scriptures for years, and because they denied all reality in relationship to a visible and specific return of Jesus Christ to this earth.

I can think of at least three reasons why the strenuous effort was made to contain the discussions and to keep the world delegations from coming out with a clear-cut statement on the second coming of Christ as the world's greatest hope.

First, there are many churchmen and church organizations which have their own ideas for society and for their own nations. Bible prophecy concerning the return of Christ does not fit in with those ideas at all.

Second, these men and their groups are well aware of the spiritual implications of Christ's prophecies, and to believe sincerely in His return would necessitate a willing separation from this world system and its ungodly practices.

Third is the immediate rejection of any kind of link with literal Bible prophecy because of those who have made themselves ridiculous by insisting upon their own wild speculations and by going far beyond the bounds of interpretation set in the scriptures themselves.

Some basic things should be very clear to all. Our Lord taught that He would come back to earth again. The chosen apostles taught that the Saviour would come back to earth to reign. For centuries the church fathers emphasized that Jesus would return to earth as the final and ultimate hope and consolation of the Christian church.

At the time of the ascension of Christ, the angelic message assured that "this same Jesus, which is taken up from you into heaven, shall so come in like manner as ye have seen him go into heaven."

Most of us have encountered the glib explanations

of those who refuse any literal interpretation of the prophetic words.

Through the years, some have taught that the return of Christ was fulfilled in the destruction of Jerusalem. That is so ridiculous that I see no reason for attempting to refute it.

Others have been satisfied to believe that Christ's promise of returning to the earth has been fulfilled over and over again when Christians die. However, the scriptures plainly teach that in God's great plan for humans and for this earth, there would be only two advents—one, to die; and the other, to reign. If Christ were keeping His promise to return to earth every time a Christian dies, it would leave no basis for the clear instructions He gave concerning two climactic and significant advents to earth.

Well, it is evident that no one can study the implications of the prophetic scriptures without realizing that in our generation we are living in days which are not only grave and sobering, but are grand days, as well.

Grave and grand—dramatic days! Greater days than you and I realize. Solemn days in which we are to give heed to the prophetic scriptures.

Now, I do not say that any of us can stand and proclaim and predict the world developments as if by schedule. The Bible does not have a schedule like the local train—giving the name of every stop and the time it will arrive and the time it will leave.

For anyone to say that the scriptures can be interpreted in that way is to distort and misinterpret prophetic truth. The Bible is a book of great and grand outlook and scope, and it tells us of the future, but it tells us in great, sweeping strokes like an artist painting a picture across the sky. The size would be so tremendous that you would have to retreat to a point far away to sense it and take it in. There would be no place in that kind of painting for tiny details, with vast brush strokes that would start with one star and extend across to another.

So, we cannot predict for one another what may come tomorrow. Not even the angels know that—our tomorrow is in the knowledge only of our Father in heaven.

It is not only the little fellow, the common man, who is helpless to predict how things may fall in the future—the great leaders in world society are just as helpless.

Leaders and groups and nations often think they have something great and enduring and superior going for them in human society, and because we don't jump on the bandwagon and remark, instead, that "This, too, will pass away," we get a look of anger with the comment, "You are a cynical pessimist."

Let me say that it is very difficult to have any brains in this day in which we live and not get blamed for it. It is hard to have any insight and not be considered a cynic. It is hard to be realistic and not be classed with the pessimists.

But with most men and their methods and movements in society, a few months, at the most a few years, bring an entirely new perspective. People who disagreed with you and were engaged in flag-waving for someone's scheme or speech six months ago are probably looking back on that same thing and see it now just as you foresaw it.

It is a wonderfully exhilarating thing to be able to anticipate and foresee just a little bit—but it is also an ability that will bring you much criticism and hostility from those with lesser foresight and judgment.

Well, the great men of the earth are still only men. Think what they would be willing to give for a supernatural gift of foretelling events of the future! The world leaders must be great men in some respects; otherwise, we would be there and they would be here!

But, if I am not mistaken, it will be the great

men of the earth who will be crying for the mountains to fall on them in the coming day of judgment, according to the book of Revelation.

Again, if I am not mistaken, there was not one man considered great in human leadership and ability that recognized the plan and Presence of God when He was incarnated in the womb of the Virgin. Not one great man recognized what God was doing. Then, when Jesus ministered, it was only the plain people who heard Him gladly.

I believe there is something inherent in human greatness and fame and recognition that works subtly against the quality of fine spiritual insight in the human mind. World leaders as a rule do not possess spiritual insight.

The leaders in most of the nations make a great deal of their desires and their campaigns for peace. There are few people anywhere in the world who are not interested in nations being able to live in peace and harmony. We could all wish that nations would beat their cannons and guns into implements of agriculture and peaceful production.

But such hopes for peace among nations are fleeting. The leaders who call for peace and tranquility have not done their homework in the study of the Bible and what it has to say about the future.

Even the so-called diplomats and statesmen have little knowledge and even less control over the day-to-day incidents that bring tension and violence among the nations. The story has been told of one of our own State Department officials saying to another as they arrived at the Washington offices in the morning, "Well, what is our long-range, unchanging foreign policy going to be today?"

We may smile at that, but it does illustrate the point that men and nations are completely uncertain about each new day's events. National strategy becomes sort of a game of expediency—we act or we react according to whatever another nation has done or said. In that sense, it is like a game of chess among the nations. You do not sit down and think the whole game of chess through ahead of time. You do what you are forced to do one move at a time according to the moves the other fellow makes.

I have only heard one prediction made by a world statesman in recent years that was absolutely foolproof, and that was a remark that the next war will be fought in the future!

Well, there are no certainties, but it is sobering to realize that this present world with its great store of bombs and weapons is a powder keg, indeed. It will take only greed or lust for power or thoughtlessness on the part of some careless man to toss the match that will set it all off again.

Where will the blame fall—on politics? on religion? on morals?

I think it is possible that these three elements of national life and world society are so intertwined that they cannot be separated.

After all, what most any nation is at its heart depends upon its religious heritage and background.

It follows that the moral life and standards of a nation will also follow the pattern of its religious instruction.

As for the ultimate politics of any given nation, you may be sure that governmental and political decisions will very likely follow the national pattern seen in the religious and moral teachings and standards.

All of these things are on the human and natural side of the growing suspicions and uncertainties among nations—and there is no prediction of man that can be counted upon as a certainty for tomorrow.

But our Lord Jesus Christ does have a certain word for us and the Bible does offer us a more sure word of prophecy.

The words of Jesus spoken to His disciples concerning the signs and evidences of His soon return at the end of the age have come down to us in the scripture record.

In this twenty-fourth chapter of Matthew's Gospel, we will note several characteristics in human society in the days just before His return.

Jesus told His followers to watch out for a growing pattern of messianic delusions.

"For many shall come in my name saying, I am Christ, and shall deceive many," Jesus warned.

He continued with the cautions that "Many false prophets shall rise and shall deceive many," and "There shall arise false Christs, and false prophets, and shall shew great signs and wonders; insomuch that, if it were possible, they shall deceive the very elect."

Now, Jesus was not saying that it would be a new kind of thing for false prophets and false Christs to appear in the end of the age, for history records that this type of fanatic and self-proclaimed prophet and redeemer has appeared quite often through the centuries. The emphasis that Jesus made was this: there will be a great number of false messiahs as though the end of the age and the perilous times that will exist will bring about an open season for this kind of false proclamation.

We may expect a greater concentration of these false prophets as the second appearing of Jesus Christ nears and the distress of nations becomes worse. These are some of the promises we will hear: "I am the Christ." "I have the answer." "I can bring peace to the world." "I can lead you into Utopia —the Promised Land." "Tomorrow the Millennium —Prosperity for all!"

A great many of these so-called "saviours" will be religious. Others are certain to be political in promise and program. Their numbers will increase as the world hastens into the vexing political, social and economic tangle of the end-time.

We note, also, that a part of the warning that Jesus gave His disciples had to do with war and violence and revolt, famines and pestilence. He said to them: "Ye shall hear of wars and rumours of wars: see that ye be not troubled: for all these things must come to pass, but the end is not yet. For nation shall rise against nation, and kingdom against kingdom: and there shall be famines, and pestilences, and earthquakes, in divers places."

In all of the teachings of Jesus concerning the conditions on earth prior to His return, there are indications of increasing dependence upon military power among the nations.

Some of us have lived long enough to see how the war and anti-war pendulum swings. Soon after World War I, there were strong anti-war movements among the people of many nations. Many preachers found it very fitting and convenient to take leading roles as pacifists and "ban-the-war" leaders.

As a result, the people of many church congregations were carried along with ministerial leaders who declared, "We outlaw war!" and who issued manifesto after manifesto to prove that mankind had learned its most important lesson with this result: "There will be no more war!"

As a result, a generation started growing up in the twenties believing that a great war could never break out again. So, we sold our unwanted scrap iron to Japan and they turned it into weapons and bombs and threw it back on us at Pearl Harbor. Almost the whole world was on fire like a tenement house and the blaze and destruction continued throughout the years of World War II. Then, the notorious A-bombs were dropped on the Japanese cities and the great war came to its costly, grisly end.

The United Nations came into being, and men and nations assured themselves once more: "Mankind has really learned his lesson this time—war must certainly be outlawed now. We will find a better way."

I ask only one question: who holds the power behind nearly every government in the world in our time?

I am sure you know the obvious answer: the military leaders!

I think back into the history of our own country. Our government is established upon the principle that the civilians—the people—will rule themselves and direct the destiny of the nation. It was long repugnant to Americans that so many nations were virtually armed camps, with generals and admirals and other military people in full control.

I suppose it is because of the kind of world in which we live, but little by little we have seen a shifting of governmental emphasis. Military men speak for the necessity of great military budgets, and generals and admirals are among those who point out the way that we must take as a nation. It is enough to make thinking men wonder if we are drifting back into the very situation in which Europe found itself before the great conflagration of World War II and the decimation that brought European nations to their knees.

Many find it easy to consider the warnings of Jesus with the casual response that war is in the nature of man, and I question whether there has ever been a time of even 365 consecutive days since the time of Christ when all the nations and all the tribes and all the divisions of mankind were actually at peace with one another.

Brethren, I do not think Jesus was cautioning us about the minor feuds and arguments between small tribal groups. Jesus could foreknow the complexities of international relations of the last days of this age; He knew full well the conditions among nations that could spawn a hellish World War III overnight.

Reading again in Matthew 24, you will find that Jesus forewarned His disciples: "And then shall many be offended, and shall betray one another, and shall hate one another."

Just think with me of all the totalitarian states and nations in today's world. What kind of control do these states have over the lives of the people, the citizens?

An important part of the totalitarian technique for control and regimentation of the people is the employment of disloyalty and hatred and betrayal within every family unit.

It is my opinion that if all of the families in Russia could have maintained complete loyalty and concern for one another within the family circles, communism would have died out in ten years. But the very basic party line is built upon so subverting the minds of the individuals that they are willing to surrender and betray their family ties as well as their former ties to church and knowledge of God.

How sad and how perverted that millions of boys and girls have been willing to betray and sell out their parents in order to get a higher mark and a higher status in the party!

As in the case of the sign of false prophets and messiahs, Jesus does not point out hatreds and betrayals as a new manifestation among humans. Jesus is making the emphasis that when this happens in the very last days before His return, it will be a great worldwide "season" for betrayal. The philosophy of treason and disloyalty is becoming an accepted and successful technique throughout the whole world.

Persecution is linked to this philosophy among modern man and Jesus said about the time of the beginning of sorrows, "Then shall they deliver you up to be afflicted, and shall kill you: and ye shall be hated of all nations for my name's sake."

I need not recite for you the well-known terror

and horror which have marked the persecutions taking place in our world since Hitler came to the European scene and turned his hatred and fury against the Jews of the world. I do not have to document for you the persecutions, regimentations and strictures which have taken place in such modern nations as Spain, Argentina and Colombia. I do not have to tell you that persecution is one of the techniques of totalitarianism, both in church and state. Jesus seemed to be pointing to a "season" for an outbroken philosophy of persecution as one of the signs of His near return.

Speaking of the last days of this age, Jesus also instructed the disciples that "because iniquity shall abound, the love of many shall wax cold."

Jesus plainly connects the increasing of iniquity in the earth with a spiritual falling away and a coldness among the people of God.

Again, we return to the fact that Jesus was not speaking of normal times among men, but of a great, concentrated "season" for sin and lawlessness as well as a "season" for coldness and callousness among the professors of religion.

I believe that Jesus meant to shake us up!

I believe that He meant for us to consider seriously what it would mean and what it would cost to keep our lamps trimmed and burning brightly in a time of great lawlessness and apostasy.

Our Lord knew that in these times there would be those in our churches who are just highly-groomed show-pieces of Christianity—middle class and well-to-do, satisfied with a religious life that costs them nothing.

Oh, yes, we do tithe! But the nine-tenths that we keep is still a hundred times more than our mothers and fathers used to have. It is right that we should tithe because it is God's work, but it does not really cost us anything—it does not bring us to the point of sacrificial giving. An old prophet of God long ago said something for us all: "Shall I offer God something that costs me nothing?"

Brethren, what has our Christian faith and witness cost us this week?

Oh, yes, you have been to church twice this week. But you would have been just as hot if you had stayed home—so it did not cost you anything. You met your friends and it was a pleasure to go to church—that did not cost you anything. You gave your tithe but you had something left to put in the bank. That did not cost you anything.

Is it not time that we face up to the fact that most of us do only those things for the Lord and for His church that we can do conveniently? If it is convenient, we will be there. If it is not convenient, we just say, "Sorry, Pastor! You will have to get someone else."

It is a generally accepted fact that most Protestant Christians serve the Lord at their own convenience. We say we believe in such things as prayer and fasting but we do not practice them unless it is convenient. Very few of us are willing to get up before daybreak as many Catholics do in order to be present in their daily services.

I am not saying that we ought to be Catholics, but I am saying that we have great throngs of professing Christians who are the slickest bunch alive in getting their religion for nothing!

We are very willing to let Jesus do all the suffering and all the sweating, all the bleeding and all the dying. It seems a great bargain to us that simply by faith we may take over all the results of His agony and death. We pat ourselves on the back for making such a good bargain, and then go galloping along to our own convenient affairs and habits.

Brethren, I realize that this message will not win any popularity prizes in the Christian ranks, but I must add this based on my observations on the current state of the church: Christianity to the average evangelical church member is simply an avenue to a good and pleasant time, with a little biblical devotional material thrown in for good measure!

It is time that we begin to search our hearts and ask ourselves: "What is my Christian faith costing me? Am I offering to God something that has cost me absolutely nothing in terms of blood or sweat or tears?"

The members of many Christian churches dare to brag about being part of a "missionary-minded congregation," somehow failing to realize that it is the same old story—let the missionaries go out and suffer in the hard places. We say we are vitally interested in missions—and that seems to be true as long as it does not inconvenience us at home and the missionaries are willing to go and endure the hardships in the jungles overseas.

People in the Christian churches who put their own convenience and their own comfort and their own selfish interests ahead of the claims of the gospel of Jesus Christ surely need to get down on their knees with an open Bible—and if they are honest as they search their own hearts, they will be shocked at what they find!

Oh, brethren, have we forgotten that it was the smug, affluent, middle-class crowd that delivered Jesus to be killed when He came into our world the first time?

The poor and the oppressed and the outcasts—they heard Him gladly and they believed in Him. But how many of the poor and oppressed of our own day do we welcome into the ranks of our church fellowship with open arms?

A despised publican with his unsavory name and reputation believed in Him, and Jesus was criticized for dining with him.

But the middle-class folks, largely religious and proud and selfish, believed not and received Him not.

Well, we cannot leave these words of Jesus in

Matthew 24 without emphasizing His instructions that "this gospel of the kingdom shall be preached in all the world for a witness unto all nations; and then shall the end come."

There is no doubt that the outreach of Christian missionary activity is now greater and more extensive than at any other time in history. This should be a great rallying point for the believing children of God, and a source of strength and stability in this awful and unusual hour in which we live.

"The gospel of the kingdom shall be preached," Jesus said.

Now, let me ask you: what is a kingdom without a king? While men of this earth and the worldly kingdoms are in confusion and competition, concerned with persecutions, disloyalty and betrayal, God is in His holy temple and His throne is in heaven. In all of these situations of earth, God Almighty is trying us and testing us. He is trying the nations and the kings and the rulers of the nations.

Our Lord wants to hold us steady in these days and He asks us to look upward, for there is a kingdom, and there is a King sitting upon an eternal throne. God has promised that He will look after His people, and thus we are kept, and given His own spiritual calmness, even in the eye of the gathering storm.

Christian brethren, there will be multitudes in panic and distress because of world conditions before Christ returns as King of kings and Lord of lords. But there is a special provision for the believing Body of Christ, those who make up His church, for the angels of the Lord encamp around those who fear Him, and delivereth them. We do not yet have the heavenly understanding of all of God's promises, but there have been so many instances where true children of God in danger have been surrounded as by a wall of invisible fire that we dare to rest back on His deliverance.

I must confess that my soul delights in the words

and prophecies of our Lord Jesus, because I sense that He was able to look down the long corridor of all of the years of history, viewing the future as with a telescope, and telling us with such detail that we can be sure that He knows all things. He Himself was God and He had lived all of our tomorrows when He walked in Galilee, because He is God eternal. I delight in the inward knowledge that Jesus Christ, the Son of God and our coming Lord, will be sufficient for every situation which is yet to come to pass. We will never panic along with this present world system as long as we are fortified with our knowledge of who Jesus Christ really is.

The Word of God is the foundation of our peace and rest. Even in these dangerous and dramatic hours, "God is our refuge and strength, a very present help in trouble. Therefore will not we fear though the earth be removed, and though the mountains be carried into the midst of the sea; though the waters thereof roar and be troubled, though the mountains shake with the swelling thereof.

"There is a river, the streams whereof shall make glad the city of God, the holy place of the tabernacles of the most High. God is in the midst of her; she shall not be moved: God shall help her, and that right early.

"The heathen raged, the kingdoms were moved: he uttered his voice, the earth melted. The Lord of hosts is with us; the God of Jacob is our refuge. Come, behold the works of the Lord, . . . he maketh wars to cease unto the end of the earth."

Notice that this is the kingly strength and dominion of our Lord—not the United Nations!

He breaketh the bow and cutteth the spear in sunder. Be still and know that He is God.

In other words, get alone with God and His Word every day. I recommend that you turn off the radio and the television and let your soul delight in the fellowship and the mercies of God.

Be still and know that He is God. He will be exalted among the nations. He will be exalted in the earth. The Lord of hosts is with us. Fear not, little flock —it is the Father's good pleasure to give you the kingdom.

And the gates of hell cannot prevail against it!

Chapter Six

Do You Know about the Next Chapter after the Last?

". . . Fear not ye: for I know that ye seek Jesus, which was crucified. He is not here: for he is risen, as he said. Come, see the place where the Lord lay." Matthew 28:5-6.

The account of the life of Jesus Christ is the only biography known to man that does not end with death and burial—the only record of a human life that joyfully hastens on to the next chapter after the last!

The book of Matthew is biography—literally, the writing of a life. It tells the story of the birth and life and death of a man, and by common consent, we would include the burial. Every man knows that when the last tattered remnants of his body are finally taken to the grave, the last chapter of his life will have been written. The writing of the life ends where the life ends and at the burial the word *finis* closes out the human manuscript. The word *more* is no longer a consideration.

In any common biography of man, if there is any notation after the burial, it is not true biography. It may be editorial comment, it may be a summary of the man's teachings, it may be eulogy—but it is not biography. The writing of the life ends where the life ends and this is a fact by the logic of sad necessity. It holds true in every land, among all people and in the midst of every culture.

Many of the moral philosophers of the past dared to dream about a hope for tomorrow but they could never cope with the finality of death. They had always to take into account that fact that when a man is dead and buried he talks no more, he writes no more, he paints no more, he travels no more. No matter how beloved he has been, he speaks no more to his friends. The man is gone and that is the end. So, we write a respectful *finis* after the last word of the biography and it is over.

The man is gone and with the passing of the man no other chapter is possible. The last chapter has been written.

It is against this factual background that we come to the biography of Jesus. In the book of Matthew, it is a short sketch but it is a biography and it follows the common pattern of all biography.

Matthew begins with the ancestors of Jesus, back to Abraham himself, and then traces His ancestry forward to Mary. After identifying the mother of Jesus, he tells about the birth of the child, of the wise men coming from the East to see Him. Quickly Matthew proceeds to the manhood of Jesus, to the baptism with the Spirit descending like a dove and resting upon Him and preparing Him for the temptations offered by Satan in the wilderness.

The chapters that follow describe the beginning of His public ministry. Matthew records the Sermon on the Mount and then goes on to tell of the miracles of Jesus, the feeding of the 5,000, the raising of the dead, the stilling of the waves and the calming of the winds. There is a clear picture of His conflict with the hypocritical religious leaders of His day and the slow decline of His popularity with the people.

It is a striking record of the pressures of public hatred moving in to surround Jesus like the gradual falling of darkness.

Then follows the account of the arrest of Jesus by His detractors and the manner in which He was turned over to the Romans to be crucified. It is in Matthew's twenty-seventh chapter that Jesus is taken out to the hill and there, still wet with the bloody sweat of the previous night's agony, is nailed to the cross.

We learn in some detail the story of the six sad hours that followed and the humiliation of His death, the bowing of His wearied head and the words, "It is finished!" as He gave up His spirit—and He was dead.

The human biography comes to an end. Friends begged the body and tenderly placed it in a tomb and the Roman soldiers were there to place the official seal upon the grave in compliance with the Roman law. Jesus was dead—the grave was closed and sealed. His enemies were satisfied, moving on to their other interests.

There ends the human biography. This Man who had been proved to be of the seed of Abraham according to the flesh; this Man who had been declared to be the Son of God and proved so to be by His wonders and miracles and words; this Man who had struggled and fought His way with kindness and gentleness and love through the ranks of those who hated Him through three wonderful and terrible years; this Man who in love had gone out to die for His enemies is now finished. Human biography ends in the twenty-seventh chapter.

Amazingly, we find another chapter and it is there because for the first time in human history, it became necessary to get out that pen again and add another chapter—authentic biography!

Matthew 28 is not annotation! It is not composed of footnotes or summary! It is not an editorial comment or human eulogy! It is an authentic chapter in the biography of a Man who had died one chapter before.

How can this be? This Man is talking and eating, walking and making a journey with His friends on the Emmaus road. He is sharing truths about the kingdom of God and of His own coming and telling men to go into all the world preaching the gospel and witnessing of eternal life.

How can this be? His enemies and the world system had sealed the grave and written *finis*. They had satisfied themselves as well as they could that they would hear no more from this Man who had challenged their sins and their selfishness.

This is a new chapter because Jesus Christ, the Son of God, upset all of the old patterns of human life and existence. Jesus Christ took life into the grave and brought life out of the grave again and He who had been dead now lives again! For that reason, and for the first and only time in human history, it was necessary for the evangelist to add the chapter that has no ending.

Jesus Christ is alive again! This is the great truth that suddenly brought frantic confusion to those who had counted upon the old, reliable logic of death. This Man was alive again—not simply memories of Him, not just quotations from His lovely teachings, not words of commendation sent in by friends—but authentic and continuing biography!

They saw Him. They heard Him. They touched Him. They knew He was there. He stood among them. He said, "Mary!" He called His friends by name and looked at Peter and cooked fish on the sandy shore and said, "Children, have you any meat? I have some breakfast for you!"

Yes, it is an entirely new chapter. There is now a certainty of victory over death—death that had taken every man and traced him with that lipless, toothy grin; death that had waited as he went from cradle to the grave and then had written "The End."

Now it is death and the grave that are shaken with confusion for Jesus Christ is alive, having made a fool of death, and that toothless grin is as hollow now as the skull itself. Thank God there is another chapter, for He is risen. He is no longer in the grave!

We who are men must quickly ask: "What does this mean to you and me?"

Thankfully, it means for the believing and trusting Christian that the iron reign of death is ended! For those who are Christ's people, it means that the logic of death no longer applies. For Christ's believing children, it means that death is not the end—there is more to follow.

For an example of what it means, let's look at the experience of another man, the apostle Paul.

We have good biographical material here. Paul was born as other men and grew up through the maturing processes of life. He was educated at the feet of the finest teachers. He became a member of the Jewish Sanhedrin, which is equivalent to being a member of the Supreme Court in the United States. He stood high in his day as one of the orthodox Pharisees, the strictest sect among his people. But on the Damascus road he was suddenly and miraculously converted to believe and trust in the One whom he had hated. He was filled with the Holy Spirit, commissioned and sent forth to preach the gospel everywhere. He went from place to place preaching the Word, establishing churches, writing encouraging letters to the new churches.

Brought to trial one day, he was freed. On trial another day, again he was freed. Charged and tried again a third time, he was condemned.

It was then that Paul wrote a letter to a young friend, Timothy.

"The day of my departure is come and I am now ready to be offered," he wrote. He knew that death was near, so he wrote on:

"I have fought a good figh[...]

"I have finished my course"—[...]

"My testimony has been given. [...] and a witness. I have done all that I could[...] The war is over and I will take off my unifo[...] have completed God's plan for me on earth."

According to the logic of death, the next words should have been "The End," for within a few days, Paul knelt on the flagstones of a Roman prison and the executioner severed his head from his body with a sword.

He had written his last testimony, but he did not say, "This is the end of Paul." Instead, he had purposely added one of those conjunctive words that speaks of a yesterday and connects it to a tomorrow.

"I have finished my course; *henceforth* . . ."

Paul's judges and jailers and executioner would have said that Paul was in no position to talk about *henceforth*—which means from here on in! Using the old logic of death, they would have said that Paul was a man with no tomorrow. His head was off. His earthly course was finished.

The fact that death was near had not caused Paul to despair. He had grasped that pen again, tired and weary as he was, and wrote in faith: "Henceforth there is laid up for me a crown of righteousness. which the Lord, the righteous judge, shall give me at that day."

Now, if it were not for that word *henceforth*, I respectfully submit that Paul could be considered one of the great fools of all time.

Consider that he was a man who had highest status in the esteem of his own nation and countrymen. He was a man of great education, culture and judgment. The historians say he undoubtedly had some wealth. He testified that he had given up all of this, counting it but refuse, turning his back on his own people, stoned one day and beaten the next, thrown into jail and bound in stocks, beset with perils and

those who were trying
the garments he wore
thing else for Jesus' sake.
this aging man to lose his
on, his use of the word *hence-*
knew he had not been a fool,
to Jesus Christ and eternal life
in the sea and the floggings in
ation and damp rottenness in the
thing.

estifying: "All of these things were a
part of the human biography, but I am going on to
another and better and eternal chapter!" For Paul,
it was the blessed experience of coming to the next
chapter after the last!

Thus did Paul confuse his human biographers. He
knew what he was doing, for he had written: "If men
do not rise again from the dead, then we are of all
men most miserable"—and that is still the truth!

The promise of the resurrection makes the difference for the man who is a believing Christian. If men
are not to be raised from the dead, why not eat, drink
and be merry, for tomorrow we die!

But the Christian stands with Paul in the knowledge that there is another chapter because Jesus
Christ is alive. We stand in faith and expectation
alongside the martyrs, even though we have not been
called upon to share the extremes of their sufferings.
These are the believing saints of God who staunchly
insisted upon the reality of another chapter after the
last. They were thrown to wild beasts and were torn
limb from limb. Impaled on stakes, they were allowed to die in slow agony under the sun by day and
the stars by night. They were sewed into sacks and
thrown over the cliffs into the waves of the ocean
beneath. They were starved to death in prisons; some
were driven into the wilderness to slowly die of ex-
posure and starvation. The tongues of some were cut
out; arms and hands were severed. They were fas-

tened to carts and dragged to death through the streets while the crowds screamed with applause.

Was it worth all that?

If there had been no eternal tomorrow for those martyrs, no crown awaiting in a better land, then those torn and charred and tortured bodies would have screamed to high heaven above and hell below that Christianity is a fraud—only a cruel, treacherous story. But another chapter is waiting!

While we live in this world, we see only a few chapters of what men call earthly biography. Church history tells us that Timothy, to whom Paul wrote that final letter of triumph, died while being dragged through the streets at the tail of a cart. If that had been all for Timothy, everyone could have said, "Poor Timothy! It is too bad that he did not have sense enough to let Christianity alone!"

But you can be assured that God said to Gabriel and to those who write the records of the martyrs above: "This is not the end—just write 'More to follow!'" The divine Editor yonder in the skies knows that this is not the end of Timothy. There will be a long gap and there will be nothing written about him for a time, but this is only an episode. Another chapter follows and that chapter will have no ending!

It is God Almighty who puts eternity in a man's breast and tomorrow in a man's heart and gives His people immortality, so what you see down here really is not much. But when the bird of immortality takes to the wing, she sails on and on, over the horizon and out into the everlasting tomorrows and never comes down and never dies.

Thank God for the gracious chapter still being written, the chapter titled "Immortality." It is the chapter of God's tomorrows. It is the chapter of the *henceforths* known only to the children of God.

There is another day yet to be for there is to be a day of resurrection. I know this because there was once a Man, a lonely Man. They put Him in the grave and they sealed Him in. But the third day He arose again from the dead according to the scriptures, and ascended to the right hand of God the Father Almighty.

Besides this, I dare say that if all the books in the world were blank and were being written in by a multitude of angels until they were filled, they still would not be able to record all of the glorious deeds and words of Jesus Christ since the day evil men thought they had laid Him in the grave forever.

I want to tell you what I believe about the resurrection. When the grave that held the body of Jesus was sealed, I believe Death sat grinning beside the Roman seal, thinking, "I've got another one!" But the Life that could not stay dead broke that seal as easily as we break the seal on a letter, and Jesus walked forth, alive!

I believe that so completely that I believe it all the time. This is not an Easter "thing" that I try to believe once a year. I believe it so fully and so completely that it is a part of my being, every moment of every day. I stand humbly in this faith with all of God's dear children who are convinced that God has promised another chapter after the last.

I think often of the earthly biography and ministries of dear old Dr. R. A. Jaffray, that great missionary pioneer and statesman in the Far East and in the Pacific islands. After many fruitful years of vision, sacrifice and compassion, pressing on into all of the most forbidding and unlikely places of earth with the gospel of Jesus Christ, the last chapter of his earthly life was spent languishing in a wartime concentration camp, prisoner of the Japanese. The man who occupied the next cot while they were housed in a virtual pig pen said of Dr. Jaffray: "I never saw such godliness in any man in my lifetime."

But now, starved and sick and exhausted, Dr.

Jaffray curls up on that poor little prison cot, thousands of miles away from his nearest friends, and his human life ends. His biography says that he died. It does not say that that was the end, for Dr. Jaffray knew a gracious tomorrow in Jesus Christ and anticipated the chapter yet to come. All that he earned for himself by the grace of God will be his in the tomorrows and the complete life of Jaffray has not yet been written.

Brethren, you and I are the plain and ordinary Christians, but this shining hope relates to every one of us. We are not martyrs. We were not among the great reformers. We are not apostles.

We are the plain, everyday Christians in the family of God and there is a gracious word for us from the Saviour about our next chapter after the last. One by one we also break from the ranks and slip away.

There is nothing heroic about our passing, leaving families and friends, but then, death is never heroic and it is never kind. Death is never artistic, always much more likely to be crude and messy and humiliating.

The preacher who once stood with strength and keenness to preach the living Word of God to dying men is now in his bed, his cheeks hollow and his eyes staring, for death is slipping its chilly hand over that earthly tabernacle.

The singer whose gifts have been used to glorify God and to remind men and women of the beauty of heaven above is now hoarse, dry-lipped, whispering only a half-spoken word before death comes.

But, brethren, this is not the end. I thank God that I know that this is not all there is. My whole everlasting being, my entire personality—all that I have and all that I am are cast out on the promises of God that there is another chapter!

At the close of every obituary of His believing children, God adds the word *henceforth*! After every biography, God adds the word *henceforth*! There will be a tomorrow and this is a reason for Christian joy.

The Romans thought they had seen the last of Paul, but they were wrong. The Jews thought they had seen the last of Jesus, but they were wrong. The Japanese thought they had seen the last of Jaffray, but they were mistaken. Thank God, the Christians will be around again! This world gets rid of us, buries our bodies in the ground, charges for the trouble, and presumes that we are gone forever—but we are not! Perhaps a neighbor that hated you because you loved God will say when you die, "Well, that fellow is out of my hair. He was always giving me a tract or suggesting that I go to church. And he bored me stiff." Oh, he doesn't know that you will be around again! Yes, God's people will be around again. Paul will be back, Stephen will be back, and Timothy, who was dragged at the tail of that cart, will be back. Dr. Simpson will be back. Wesley will be back—no longer gray and weak, but in the bloom of his youth! In fact, the whole believing family of God in Christ. This is the eternal promise of God!

I recall that there was a good man of God by the name of Samuel Rutherford, whose witness shone like a star in dark England in days gone by. He was a poet, an author, and a great preacher—a man who loved Jesus probably better than any man of his times. His convictions were unpopular and he was in trouble because he refused to conform his preaching to the dictates of the state church. When he was an old man, the officials decided to try him as a criminal because he would not submit to the rules of the state church. The date of his trial was set, and he was notified by Parliament that he must appear for trial.

Rutherford knew that he was on his deathbed and so he wrote a letter in reply. He said, "Gentlemen,

I have received your summons, but before I got yours, I received one from a higher source. Before the day of my trial, I will be over there where very few kings and great men ever come. Farewell!"

That was Samuel Rutherford, witnessing to all of England that an entire new chapter awaits the Christian when our Lord says, "Welcome home!"

And "the kingly King to His white throne, my presence does command, where glory, glory, glory dwellest in Emmanuel's land." Ah, yes, there is another chapter, friends. There is a tomorrow for the people of God because there was a tomorrow for Jesus Christ our Lord. "For if we believe that Jesus died and rose again, even so them also which sleep in Jesus will God bring with him. . . . For the Lord himself shall descend from heaven with a shout, with the voice of the archangel, and with the trump of God: and the dead in Christ shall rise first: Then we which are alive and remain shall be caught up together with them in the clouds, to meet the Lord in the air: and so shall we ever be with the Lord." Then he added rather climactically, ". . . comfort one another with these words."

Ah, what a comfort this is! It is a promise to every Christian that has bid goodbye to loved ones in Christ. You will see them again! They will be around. There is another chapter, and it will have no ending. The bird of immortality is on the wing. Thank God for our faith that begins with our sins and ends with our glorification!

Chapter Seven

What Is the Supreme Sin of a Profane Society?

"He was in the world, and the world was made by him, and the world knew him not." John 1:10

The Bible tells us in a variety of ways of an ancient curse that lingers with us to this very hour —the willingness of human society to be completely absorbed in a godless world!

It is still the supreme sin of unregenerate man that, even though Jesus Christ has come into the world, he cannot feel His all-pervading Presence, he cannot see the true Light, and he cannot hear His Voice of love and entreaty!

We have become a "profane" society—absorbed and intent with nothing more than the material and physical aspects of this earthly life. Men and women glory in the fact that they are now able to live in unaccustomed luxury in expensive homes; that they can trade in shiny and costly automobiles on shinier and more costly automobiles every year; and that their tailored suits and silk and satin dresses represent an expenditure never before possible in a society of common working people.

This is the curse that lies upon modern man—he is insensible and blind and deaf in his eagerness to forget that there is a God, in his strange belief that materialism and humanism constitute the "good life."

My fellow man, do you not know that your great sin is this: the all-pervading and eternal Presence is here, and you cannot feel Him?

Are you not aware that there is a great and true Light which brightly shines—and you cannot see it?

Have you not heard within your being a tender Voice whispering of the eternal value of your soul—and yet you have said, "I have heard nothing"?

This is, in essence, the charge that John levels at human kind: Jesus Christ, the Word of God, was in the world, and the world failed to recognize Him.

Now, our word *world* in the English needs a bit of definition. In the Bible it has three distinct meanings, and two of them concern us in this passage in John's Gospel. *World* here means nature and mankind—both coming from the very same Greek word. They are used together without clear distinction, so that when the Bible says, "He was in the world, and the world knew him not," the two meanings are apparent. You must check the context to learn which meaning is which, because they come from a precise word in the original.

In the Bible, the word *world* comes from a root word meaning to tend and take care of and provide for. Then, it also means an orderly arrangement plus a decoration.

As far as I am concerned, everywhere I look in His world I see God and my soul is delighted. I look into a dry, old book that looks like a telephone directory gone mad—we call it a lexicon—and I find that in the New Testament the word *world* means "an orderly arranged system, highly decorative, which is tended, cared for, looked after and provided for." It is all there in that one word.

Anyone who knows God, even slightly, would expect God to make an orderly world because God Himself is the essence of order. God was never the author of disorder—whether it be in society, in the home, or in the mind or body of man.

I have noticed that some people let themselves go to seed in a number of ways, thinking it makes them more spiritual—but I disagree. I think it is proper to comb your hair, if you have any. I do not think it is a mark of deep inward spirituality for a man to forget that a soiled shirt is easily cleaned and that baggy trousers were originally meant to have an orderly crease in them. I am sure God is not grieved when His Christian children take a little time every day to present themselves in clean and orderly appearance.

Some of the saints of God also insist upon completely informal and spontaneous worship. I do not think our Lord is grieved by a service of worship in which we know what we are going to sing—because God is a God of order.

So the word *world* has this idea of order in it, and we can expect God to be orderly because it is necessary to His nature. The world is a mathematical world and the essence of mathematics is order—it has to be that way.

Those who have gone on to know God better will also expect that God would make a beautiful world and that is exactly what the Bible teaches. God has made an orderly and beautiful world, and He is looking after it, providing for it, and tending it.

I think this is a delightful thing—God can take an old, dry word which has been dead for hundreds of years and speak to the bones and they get up and stand and sing a solo. That is what God has done here with the word *world*.

You will think about this the next time you are asked to sing: "For the beauty of the earth, For the glory of the skies, / For the love which from our birth over and around us lies, / Lord of all, to Thee we raise This our hymn of grateful praise. / For the wonder of each hour Of the day and of the night, / Hill and vale, and tree and flower, Sun and moon, and stars of light, / Lord of all, to Thee we raise This our hymn of grateful praise."

Let me tell you that the man who wrote that was not simply having himself a poetical time. He was putting in harmonious language a truth—and that truth is that God made a world beautiful in its order.

At this point I anticipate a word of argument from Mr. Worldly Wiseman, the man who has more brains than he has heart, who thinks more than he prays, and who tries to understand and measure the unapproachable glory of God with his poor little peanut head.

He is likely to say, "Now, wait a minute. You are talking about God making the world so beautiful, but don't you know that *beauty* is a word only—a word we use to describe that which happens to please us? If a person likes the way something looks, he says it is beautiful. On the other hand, if we don't like the way something looks, we say it is ugly. So, nothing is beautiful or ugly in itself—it just depends upon whether we happen to like it or not!"

So, Mr. Worldly Wiseman tells us that this idea that God made a beautiful world is all wrong. He is of the opinion that such an idea is only the figment of an over-heated religious imagination.

Frankly, Mr. Worldly Wiseman does not frighten me by his learned criticism and I am not looking for a place to hide, because I think that he is the dumb one, after all.

Listen, brethren. God made us in His image and in His own likeness and there is a similarity between the minds of men and the mind of God, sin being excepted. Take sin out of the mind of man and the similarity to God is there because God made man in His image. I repeat—if the human race would only see that God made us in His image, we would stop wallowing in the gutter and try to behave like God ordained when He made us in His own image and likeness.

When He made us in His image, part of that was mental and aesthetic so that my mind is somewhat like God's mind as soon as I get sin out of it. There is no doubt that when God makes a thing beautiful and orderly, it pleases the mind of God.

I say that it is only a half-educated man who insists that *beauty* is only a word that we give to something that happens to please us. The simple fact is that God made things to please Himself and for His pleasure they are and were created. Why should we apologize because we have the God-given ability to like what God likes and to be pleased with that which pleases God?

Now, I think that God first makes things orderly for utility. Whenever He made something in this universe it was because He had a purpose for it. I do not believe there is anything in the universe that just got here by accident. Everything in the universe has a meaning.

My father was philosophical about many things and I remember that he used to sit during the summertime and ponder why God made the mosquitoes. I still do not have the answer, but I am just a human being, and just because I do not have that answer, I am not going to accuse the Creator of making a cosmic blunder. I know the mosquito is not a blunder—he is just a pest. But God made him.

The same principle is true of a great many other things. I do not know why God does some things, but I am convinced that nothing is accidental in His universe. The fact that we do not know the reason behind some things is not basis enough for us to call them divine accidents.

If I am allowed to go into an operating room in a hospital, I find many strange and complex things all around me. I am completely ignorant as to what most of them are and how they are supposed to be used. But the surgeon knows—and all of those tools and instruments are not there by accident.

If I could step into the cab of one of the great, powerful diesel locomotives, I would be perplexed and confused trying to figure out why there are so many buttons and handles and bars. I could wreck the whole thing in a few minutes if I started pushing buttons and pressing bars. But the engineer knows—and he gets the proper results when he pushes the right buttons.

So, when God Almighty stepped into the cab of His locomotive, which we call the cosmos, He was at the controls and He has always pushed the right buttons. Just because there are things in the universe beyond my human explanation does not allow me to accuse God of making a lot of unnecessary truck to clutter up the universe. God made everything for some purpose.

I have mentioned utility in this regard. In the book of Genesis, we find that usefulness was God's first plan. God said, "Let there be light," and He saw that it was good and that it had a purpose. So He divided the light from the darkness, and called the light day and the darkness night.

God did the same thing with the waters and throughout those two chapters of Genesis there is a beautiful exercise in utility—God making an orderly world for a purpose, with everything having a reason for existence.

With God usefulness was first, and so it is with people.

Whenever a pioneering man has gone out to the undeveloped plains to get himself a homestead, a little plot of ground which is to become his home, he does not think about beauty but about utility and usefulness. He knows he must have a log house or some kind of safe dwelling before the blizzards come. You will still find many such plain, often ugly houses scattered throughout the West. It is a place to live, it is home, it is a place to rest when a man is tired. It may be primitive, but it fulfills its purpose.

In the second place, God added decoration. That is the expression that is actually in the Greek root. The word *decorative* is in it. First, He created for utility and purpose and then added decoration and beauty. There probably is a sense in which we could get along without the decoration, but it is a lot better to have it. There is that which is in the mind of God that desires to be pleased—not only satisfied. Order and usefulness and purpose bring satisfaction, but God desired that there should be beauty in His work.

I think it would be a great thing if more human beings discovered the truth that it does not cost any more to have things pleasing and beautiful than it does to have them useful and ugly. We could start out right here in our own city. You start to drive out of the city in almost any direction and you soon wonder if there is anything beautiful left in the world. Smoke stacks and smell and the sprawling apparatus for making gasoline out of crude oil—ugly, ugly, ugly! But, of course, the utility is inherent in our factories and foundries and refineries. If it were not for that kind of utility, many of you could not have driven to church—useful but not beautiful.

Well, perhaps the day will come in the millennium when we will make things beautiful as well as useful. I still think it does not cost any more to add the beauty and the pleasure and the delight. It costs no more to raise a beautiful daughter than to raise a homely daughter, and a beautiful wife does not eat any more than a homely wife.

You choose two men and give each of them a pot of paint, and one of them will turn out a masterpiece to hang in a gallery, and the other will turn out a horrible insult to the human imagination. All of that with just the same amount of paint and just the same amount of time. One is an artist and the other is a dauber.

Give two architects a free hand, each with a carload of bricks, and one will come up with a monstrosity—like some church buildings I have seen—while the other will add a touch entirely pleasing and satisfying. The costs will be the same—it is just a question of beauty in arrangement.

God could have made a river to go roaring right down to the sea—a plain, straight, ugly-looking channel. It would have fed the fish and done its job. But I think God smiled and made it to meander around under trees and around hills, a stream that catches the blue of the sky and reflects it to those nearby. People are intrigued by the meandering stream and comment, "Isn't it beautiful?" And God says, "Thank you for seeing it. I made you to see it." God is able to make things useful and beautiful. That is what the word *world* means.

Now, you say, what is this—a lecture on art?

No, it is a theological talk on what the word *world* means in the Bible—the created world which is God Almighty's decorated order which He watches and tends.

The other use of this word *world* is that which means mankind—the organized world and society of men and women.

When God reports that Christ was in the world and the world neither recognized nor knew Him, He was not referring to the created clouds and hills and rocks and rivers. He was referring to human society, the world of mankind, and it was this organized world of man that knew Him not.

John testified that God's Word, His only begotten Son, became flesh and dwelt among us. What was He doing in our kind of world, in our kind of fallen society?

Before the incarnation, He was the all-permeating

Word of God moving creatively in His universe. When Jesus Christ became man, God incarnate in a human body, He did not cease to be the all-permeating Word of God. To this very day, the all-permeating Word still fills the universe and moves among us.

How few men there are who realize His presence, who realize that they have Him to deal with. He is still the Light of the world. It is He that lighteth every man that cometh into the world. After His ascension from Olivet's mountain, He still remains as the all-permeating, vitalizing, life-giving Word operative in the universe.

What is He doing in the universe?

The scriptures tell us that "by him were all things created, that are in heaven, and that are in earth, visible and invisible, whether they be thrones, or dominions, or principalities, or powers: all things were created by him, and for him: and he is before all things (in time), and by him all things consist (or hold together)." The all-permeating Word which is in the world is the adhesive quality of the universe. That is why we do not fall apart. He is, in a very true sense, the mortar and the magnetism that holds all things together.

That is why He is here, for this is not a dead planet that we inhabit. Sin is the only dead thing. This is a living world we inhabit and it is held together by the spiritual presence of the invisible Word. He was in the world and the world was made by Him.

The scriptures continue speaking of Him: "Who being the brightness of his (God's) glory, . . . and upholding all things by the word of his power, when he had by himself purged our sins, sat down on the right hand of the Majesty on high." He is upholding all things by the word of His power.

When a little child looks up into the starry sky at night there may be a natural and childish fear that the sky will fall down. The parents laugh and pat the child on the head and apologize that he is tired—but the child is not as dumb as we might think.

Why doesn't the sky fall down? Why is it that stars and planets do not go tearing apart and ripping off into chaos?

Because there is a Presence that makes all things consist—and it is the Presence of that One who upholdeth all things by the word of His power. This is basically a spiritual explanation, for this universe can only be explained by spiritual and eternal laws. This is why the scientists can never manage to get through to the root of all things and never will, for they deal only with the things that they can see and touch and taste and mix in the experimental test tubes.

The scientist does not know how to deal with this mysterious Presence and Force that holds all things together. He can mix elements and chemicals and note the reactions that take place and then write an article and say, "I did not see God in the formula." But the scientist is only able to come up with dependable and consistent formulas because of God's faithfulness and power in holding all things together.

The scientist announces that a certain star will be in a definite place in the universe after another 2,510 years and twenty minutes! Then he sits back from his computer and boasts, "I have run God out of His world! I can predict where the stars will be in the future."

Oh, what a foolish man! The stars would all grind themselves to powder unless God in His faithfulness continues to keep them in their courses and in their systems. He upholds all things by the word of His power.

Again, we read in the scriptures: "Lift up your eyes on high, and behold who hath created these things, that bringeth out their host by number: he calleth them all by names by the greatness of his might, for that he is strong in power; not one faileth."

We lose a good deal of the expression of this passage in our English translation, but it is still one of the most beautiful in the Bible. It is a companion piece to the twenty-third Psalm, dealing with the astronomical host instead of His care for human beings.

The man of God says, "Lift up your eyes on high, and behold who hath created all these things." He is referring to that great display of shining, bright, diamond things that look down upon the country and the city and reflect on the waters of the sea. These stars yonder—who has created these things that bring out their host by number?

Why do they bring out their host?

Because they are like sheep, and this is the figure of a shepherd bringing his sheep out by number and calling them all by name, counting them as they come out and naming every one, and leading them across the green grass of the meadows and beside the still waters.

So, the shepherd-minded poet, Isaiah, saw that the starry hosts above were like a flock of sheep and that God, the great Shepherd, called and they came sailing out through the inter-stellar space as He numbered them and said, "They are all here!" Then He called them by their names, throughout the boundless universe, and because He is strong in power, not one faileth!

I believe that this can be said to be the most majestic and elevated figure of speech in the entire Bible—with no possible exception. We still know so little about the far reaches of the universe, but the astronomers tell us that the very Milky Way is not a milky way at all—but simply an incredible profusion of stars, billions of light-years away, and yet all moving in their prescribed and orderly directions.

We delight in the fact that it was God who called them all out, who knows their numbers, and He calls them all by name as a shepherd calls his sheep. What a lofty, brain-stretching illustration of what God is doing in His universe, holding all things together in proper courses and orbits.

He is that kind of Creator and God—yet the world knew Him not. That is mankind. He is still in the world, but mankind scoffs in its ignorance of Him, almost completely unaware of His revelation that the Word can be known and honored and loved by the humble human heart.

Now, the Word in His Presence can be known by mankind of the world. I am not conferring salvation upon every man by this statement. I mean to say that an awareness and consciousness of the Presence of God has often been known among men.

May I put it like this?

In the early days of America, when our founding fathers were writing constitutions and drafting laws and making history, many of the men in high places were not believing Christians. As a nation, we have been dreamy-eyed about some of those old boys and have made them out to be Christians when they were not.

I recall that Benjamin Franklin, who often said that he was not a believing Christian, suggested prayer to Almighty God at a time when the young nation was being threatened. The leaders did pray and they got out of the tight place.

Now, Franklin was not a Christian, but he believed there was a God operative in the world and he did not deny the awareness of that Presence. Daniel Webster confessed that the profoundest thought he had ever entertained in this life was his "responsibility to a holy God."

Surely, our fathers were not all fundamental Christians and many were not born again, but most of them were men who held a reverent and profound belief in the Presence of God in His world. A modern generation considers them old-fashioned and laughs at them, but they drafted far-sighted legislation and a world-renowned code of personal and national ethics and responsibilities that remain to this day.

Standing up for the awareness and consciousness of a Creator God did not save them, but it stamped them in character and manhood as apart from some of the poker-playing, whiskey-drinking rascals who have never given any thought to the idea of God and His Presence in our day. The Word is in the world and the world knows Him not—but it is possible to know.

A Moslem falls down on the ground five times a day in reverence to God in heaven—and a lot of people laugh at him. The Hindu measures himself painfully on the way to the Ganges river to bathe himself—and a lot of people comment, "How foolish can you get?"

But I would rather be a Moslem or a Hindu or a primitive tribesman living in a cootie-infested hut in Africa, kneeling before bones and feathers and mumbling some kind of home-made prayer, than to come into judgment as a self-sufficient American businessman who ruled God out of his life and out of his business and out of his home.

Many an unthinking, secular-minded American would reply: "I'm willing to take my chances!"

What foolish talk from a mortal man!

Men do not have the luxury of taking their chances—either they are saved or they are lost. Surely this is the great curse that lies upon mankind today—men are so wrapped up in their own godless world that they refuse the Light that shines, the Voice that speaks, and the Presence that pervades.

If you can stop this modern, self-sufficient man long enough to talk, he will assure you that preaching is for the down-and-out bum on Skid Row. He will assure you that he has never robbed a bank, that he is a good husband and a good citizen.

Citizenship is not the final issue with God. Morality and obeying the law are not the final issues with God. The Spirit of God tries to speak to this modern man of the great curse that lies upon his heart and life—he has become so absorbed with money and bank accounts and profit and loss and markets and loans and interest that any thought of God and salvation and eternity has been crowded out. There are dollar signs before his eyes and he would rather close another deal and make a neat profit than to make his way into the kingdom of God.

Many others in our human society are completely hooked on fame and notoriety and public attention. A well-known actress and singer recently told the press about her long career and the fame and fortune which have come to her, and she summed it all up in these words: "Fate made me what I am!"

After an entire life absorbed in a godless world and society, no better answer than some kind of esoteric, weird fate. She has lived only for the kind of fame and notice that men can give, and she would rather have her name on the marquee of a theater than to have it eternally inscribed in the Lamb's Book of Life. The Voice has been here with us, but she has never heeded it. The Light is here, but she has never seen it. The Presence is in our world, but she cannot feel it.

Money and profits, fame and fortune—and with millions of others it is a complete addiction to pleasure. Flesh contacts, nerve endings, sensuous delight, carnal joy—anything to take the seriousness out of living, anything to keep humans from sensing that there is a Presence, the Way, the Truth and the Light.

Brethren, do not charge me with acting like a mystic.

Instead, hear again these words of scripture: "In him was life; and the life was the light of men. And the light shineth in darkness; and the darkness comprehended it not." And "in the beginning was the

Word," and the Word "was in the world."

Now, there is the Word—and He is the Voice and He is the Light.

And the Word "was in the world"—there is His Presence. This is not poetry. This is the truth of God. And because our generation does not recognize the Voice and does not perceive the Light and has no sense of the Presence, we have become a profane generation. We dote on things—secular things—until we mistakenly assume that there is nothing in the universe but material and physical values. The profane man has come to the conclusion that he alone is important in this universe—thus he becomes his own god.

It is sad but true that a great and eternal woe awaits the profane and completely secular man whose only religion is in the thought that he probably is not as bad as some other man. I think that there is an Old Testament portion in the book of Job that fits modern, profane man very well: "Woe is me, that I was ever born, that my mother ever conceived me. Let the stars of the twilight of that night be as darkness. Oh, that I might have been carried from my mother's knees to the grave, where the wicked cease from troubling and the toil-worn are dressed."

I am thinking actually of men who give lip service to the church and some mental assent to religion, but they have forgotten that they were created, that they have a responsibility to God, and they have ignored Jesus Christ—His Presence, His Voice, His Light.

Actually, you can be too bright and too educated and too sophisticated, and thus fail to hear and to heed God's entreaty. But you cannot be too simple!

I was an ignorant 17-year-old boy when I first heard preaching on the street, and I was moved to wander into a church where I heard a man quoting a text: "Come unto me, all ye that labour and are heavy laden, and I will give you rest. Take my yoke upon you, and learn of me; for I am meek and lowly in heart: and ye shall find rest unto your souls."

Actually, I was little better than a pagan, but with only that kind of skimpy biblical background, I became greatly disturbed, for I began to feel and sense and acknowledge God's gracious Presence. I heard His Voice—ever so faintly. I discerned that there was a Light—ever so dimly.

I was still lost, but thank God, I was getting closer. The Lord Jesus knows that there are such among us today, of whom He says: "Ye are not far from the kingdom of God."

Once again, walking on the street, I stopped to hear a man preaching at a corner, and he said to those listening: "If you do not know how to pray, go home and get down and ask, 'God, have mercy on me, a sinner.'"

That is exactly what I did, and in spite of the dispensational teachers who tell me that I used the wrong text, I got into my Father's house. I got my feet under my Father's table. I got hold of a big spoon and I have been enjoying my Father's spiritual blessings ever since.

Actually, I have paid no attention to those brethren pounding on the window outside, shouting at me and beckoning to me, "Come on out of there, boy. You got in by the wrong door!"

Dispensations or not, God has promised to forgive and satisfy anyone who is hungry enough and concerned enough and anxious enough to cry out, "Lord, save me!"

When Peter was starting to sink under those waters of Galilee, he had no time to consult the margin of someone's Bible to find out how he should pray. He just prayed out of his heart and out of his desperation, "Lord, save me!" And his Lord answered.

Brethren, why don't we just let our hearts do the praying? If a man will just get his heart down on its knees, he will find that there is an awful lot that he does not need to know to receive Jesus Christ!

He is here now. "The Word became flesh and dwelt among us." He went away in His human body, but He is still with us—the everlasting, all-permeating Word—still with us to save! He only waits for a child-like prayer from a humble and needy heart—"Oh, Lamb of God, I come, I come!"

Chapter Eight

Is It True that Man Lost His Franchise to the Earth?

"In my Father's house are many mansions: if it were not so, I would have told you. I go to prepare a place for you." John 14:2

When the followers of Jesus Christ lose their interest in heaven they will no longer be happy Christians and when they are no longer happy Christians they cannot be a powerful force in a sad and sinful world. It may be said with certainty that Christians who have lost their enthusiasm about the Saviour's promises of heaven-to-come have also stopped being effective in Christian life and witness in this world.

I still must lean in the direction of the old camp meetings songs in which happy and effective Christians gloried in the promises of a heavenly home where there is no need of sun or moon because the Lamb is the light thereof! Those enthusiastic souls were much nearer the truth than today's dignified theologians who discourage us from being too pragmatic about the joyful prospects of our future home.

It is very clear in Bible revelation that God created all things to display His own glory and then ordained that man should be the supreme instrument through which He might display those glories.

It was for that reason that man was made in God's own image and likeness—a description of man alone and a term never used concerning any other of God's creatures.

There is no doubt that man was created for this earth. For reasons known only to God, God chose the earth as man's sphere of activity. He made man of the dust of the ground and adapted our nature to earth's conditions.

Did you ever stop to thank God that you are adapted to the environment around you? You could not live on the moon. You could not live on any of the heavenly bodies, as far as we know, but you can live on this earth. God adapted our natures so we can live here even as He adapted the fish to the water and the birds to the air. So, He made the earth to be our home and our garden, our workshop and our bed.

But, as we know, the conditions of the earth which God made specifically for mankind were not those we know today. It is the same body geographically—but in its creation it was the Eden of perfect love, where God walked with men in peace and beauty. In the beauty of His living presence God created the heaven and the earth, and the downshining of God upon the earth made the very fields and meadows and arbors and grassy places glorious and heavenly.

Then came the fall of man.

No one should ever be able to argue and persuade us that the fall of man from his glory and perfection was not real. Many already challenge our right to believe that man is a fallen creature—but that is exactly what he is.

The fall of man set in motion a great moral shock. It was a shock felt in the heart of God and in all of earth's circumference and certainly in the whole nature of man—body and soul and mind and spirit.

It is not too much to say that this disaster that we describe as the fall of man was of a magnitude never known before in all of the vast creation of God. It was of greater magnitude than the fall of angels whom the Bible says kept not their first estate but left their proper habitation and because of this were hurled down into everlasting darkness and judgment.

This is the magnitude of man's fall and man's sin—man lost his God-given franchise to this earth, and thus can remain here only for a brief time!

Bernard of Cluny wrote of man: "Brief life is here thy portion"—but that was not God's plan and desire for man in the beginning. God adapted man to the earth and the earth to man when He said, "Increase and multiply and replenish the earth, and subdue it . . . it shall be thine . . . thou shalt eat of every tree of the garden, and the herbs of the field shall be thine for food."

Then man sinned and lost his franchise and it was necessary for the Creator to say: "You can now stay only for a little while." And during that little while that he is staying here, he suffers the loss of Eden with its paradise of peace and love, while the earth itself suffers pollution. Sickness and disease must be reckoned with, toil and sorrow, and mortality and death itself.

Someone is likely to challenge the listing of both mortality and death as though the two are identical.

Actually, mortality is the sentence of death. Death is the carrying out of the sentence of mortality. They are not the same. Death is the final act— man's mortality lies in his knowledge that he can never escape!

In history there is the account of a famous political prisoner standing before his judge. Asked if he had anything to say before sentence was pronounced, the man said "No." The judge intoned, "I therefore pronounce that on a certain day you shall be hanged by the neck until death. I sentence you to die." It was then that the prisoner spoke: "Your honor, nature has sentenced you to die, as well." In dignity, he turned and walked away to his cell.

For mankind, the earth has become the symbol of death and mortality, of the loss of Eden with all of its joys and the loss of paradise of peace and the presence of God. That is why the earth does not have a good reputation with believing Christians. The more mature we become in spiritual life and in dedication to Christ, the less we desire the things of this earth. It has become plain to us that this earth, with its darkness and shadows, with its empty promises and disappointments, with its lies and deceptions, its pains and sorrows and griefs that cry out in the night, is a symbol of everything that is unlike God.

In the very face of this truth, the Christian still knows for certain that God has not forgotten him. Man who was made in the image of God has not been forsaken—God promised a plan to restore that which had been made in His image.

Those angels that rebelled and did not keep their first estate have no redeemer, for they were not made in the image and likeness of God. Those strange, weird creatures we call demons were not made in His image. They have no redeemer. Lucifer, the son of the morning, who said, "I will be like God," has no redemption and salvation from his fall, for he was not created in God's image.

Only that creature whom he called "man" did God make in His own image and likeness. So, when man failed and sinned and fell, God said, "I will go down now."

God came down to visit us in the form of a man, for in Jesus Christ we have the incarnation, "God manifest in the flesh." God Himself came down to this earthly island of man's grief and assumed our loss and took upon Himself our demerits, and in so doing, redeemed us back unto Himself. Jesus Christ, the King of glory, the everlasting Son of the Father, in His victory over sin and death opened the kingdom of heaven to all believers!

That is what the Bible teaches. That is what the Christian church believes. It is the essence of the doctrines of the Christian church relating to atonement and salvation.

Beyond His death and resurrection and ascension, the present work of Jesus Christ is twofold. It is to be an advocate above—a risen Saviour with high priestly office at the throne of God; and the ministry of preparing a place for His people in the house of His Father and our Father, as well.

Now, it must be said that sin necessitates a separation of body and soul. While it is proper to say that man is made for the earth, it is actually necessary to say that man's body is made for the earth. It was his body that was taken from the dust of the ground, for man became a living soul when God breathed into his nostrils the breath of life. The image of God was not in the body of the man, but in the spirit that made him man. The body is simply the instrument through which the soul manifests itself down here—that is all.

It is out of this context, however, that we need the caution that the worth and value of our human body should not be played down.

God has seen fit to give us this amazingly delicate and adaptable and beautiful instrument—the human body. If there had been no sin, there would never have been even the remotest shadow of doubt concerning the beauty, the dignity and usefulness of the body.

We should not think it is humility to berate and cry down this body which God has given us. It serves us well, but it has no power in itself. It has no will of its own. The body cannot express affection or emotion. The human body has no thought processes. Our human thought processes lie within the soul, in the human mind, in the human spirit. But God has ordained that it is through the instrument of the body that our ability to think shines forth and expresses itself.

The apostle Paul gave us plain teaching in this regard when he said: "Let not sin therefore reign in your mortal body, that ye should obey it in the lusts thereof. Neither yield ye your members as instruments of unrighteousness unto sin: but yield yourselves unto God, as those that are alive from the dead, and your members as instruments of righteousness unto God . . . . But God be thanked, that ye were the servants of sin, but ye have obeyed from the heart that form of doctrine which was delivered you. Being then made free from sin, ye became the servants of righteousness. I speak after the manner of men because of the infirmity of your flesh: for as ye have yielded your members servants to uncleanness and to iniquity unto iniquity; even so now yield your members servants to righteousness unto holiness."

It is important that we realize the human body is simply an instrument, because there are those who have taught that Christ could not be God in the flesh because the body is evil and God would not thus come in contact with evil.

The false premise there is the belief that the human body is evil. There is no evil within inert matter. There is nothing evil in matter itself. Evil lies in the spirit. Evils of the heart, of the mind, of the soul, of the spirit—these have to do with man's sin, and the only reason the human body does evil is because the human spirit uses it to do evil.

For example, a gun lying in a drawer is a harmless thing and of itself has no power to injure or harm. When an angry man takes the gun in his hand he becomes the lord of that instrument. The instrument is said to inflict pain and death, but that is not really true. The motive and intent and the direction to harm is in the will and the emotion of the man and he uses the gun as an instrument.

Men have been known to use their hands to choke others to death in the high pitch of human anger and jealousy and lust. The hands kill—but yet the hands do not really kill. Take the direction of that distorted spirit away from these hands and they will lie inert until they rot.

No, sin does not lie in the human body. There is nothing in the human body that is bad. Sin lies in the will of the man and when the man wills to sin, he uses his body as a harmless, helpless instrument to do his evil purposes.

The fact that the body cannot act apart from the spirit of man is good truth and we cite it here as prelude to the fact that there are many mansions in our Father's house in heaven, in the New Jerusalem, in the city four-square.

I think Christians ought to know and understand God's reasoning and philosophy behind His eternal provision for His children. I am not happy with the attitude of some Christians who are little more than parrots concerning the truths of God.

Some people think it is spiritual just to accept all of the dogmas without any real thought or comprehension—"Yes, I believe it. The Bible says it and I believe it."

We are supposed to be mature and growing Christians, able to give an answer with comprehension concerning our faith. We are supposed to be more than parrots.

The parrot in the pet shop can be taught to quote John 3:16 or portions of the Apostles' Creed if you give him tid-bits as a reward. If all we want is to have someone feed truth into us without knowing or understanding why it is like it is, then we are simply Christian parrots saying "I believe! I believe!"

111

I think we Christians should spend a lot more time thinking about the meaning and implications of our faith, and if we ask God Almighty to help us, we will know why He has dealt with us as He has and why the future holds bright promise for God's children.

So, the scriptures do support our belief that while the body cannot act apart from the spirit, it is possible for the spirit to act apart from the body.

Do you remember what the Apostle wrote in First Peter 3:18? Peter said that "Christ also hath once suffered for sins, the just for the unjust, that he might bring us to God, being put to death in the flesh, but quickened by the Spirit: By which also he went and preached unto the spirits in prison; which sometime were disobedient, when once the longsuffering of God waited in the days of Noah."

Now, that tells us very plainly that Christ Jesus was actively doing something specific and intelligent and creative while His body was resting in Joseph's new tomb. The body could not move, it could do nothing apart from His spirit; but while the body was still in the tomb of Joseph, His spirit was busy and active about His Father's business, preaching to the spirits in prison, which aforetime were disobedient in the days of Noah.

"But, that was Jesus the Christ," you may say. "What about others?"

Let me refer you to the sixth chapter of Revelation, beginning at verse nine:

"When he had opened the fifth seal, I saw under the altar the souls of them that were slain for the word of God, and for the testimony which they held: and they cried with a loud voice, saying, How long, O Lord, holy and true, dost thou not judge and avenge our blood on them that dwell on the earth? And white robes were given unto every one of them, . . . that they should rest yet for a little season, until their fellowservants also and their brethren, that should be killed as they were, should be fulfilled."

We notice that here were some souls, tucked up safely under the altar of God, and they were the souls of the men and women who had been slain. What was slain? The bodies, not the souls. Jesus told His disciples: "Fear not them which kill the body, rather fear him which is able to destroy soul and body in hell."

It is interesting and profitable for us to note what these souls were doing. We find them intelligent, we find they had memory, we find they prayed, we find that they have a sense of justice. Further, we note their knowledge that God is holy and true, that men dwell on the earth and they know that God is a judge who avenges Himself and those whose blood had been shed. All of these things were true of the souls of those whose bodies had been slain.

So, it is fully possible for your spirit to act without your body, but it is not possible for your body to act without your spirit. Further, I would suggest that you do not try to demonstrate the actions of your spirit without your body while in this life. God does not suggest it in this life.

The spiritists, so-called mediums, tappers, peepers and glass-ball gazers try to loose the spirit and talk about it soaring off and freeing man here below. No, no, not that! Ghosts and wizards and spooks—all of that activity is under the stern interdiction of the God Almighty. God expects us to stay inside these bodies now, serving Him until that day when the Lord releases us and our spirits can soar away.

Why can't we take our bodies along in that day? I say it is because of sin. Man's sin has separated us in terms of our spirits and bodies.

At this point in our thinking, the question must occur: "If our bodies are separated at death, why have a heaven at all?" Some have actually taken the position at this point that there is no such thing as heaven—that the earth is to be man's heaven, and that man will receive immortality and the earth will be his sphere of operation.

That may be an interesting thought from the human point of view, but that is not what the Bible teaches!

The Bible has a definite answer for us. It tells us that God made us in His image in giving us His breath, making us living souls. Then, in that indescribable calamity, that moral disaster of the fall, all men lost the blessings of that first estate and have felt the sad results of that fall ever since in spirit, soul, mind and body.

The Bible answer includes God sending His Son to redeem us and to make us whole again. Some people seem to think that Jesus came only to reclaim us or restore us so that we could regain the original image of Adam. Let me remind you that Jesus Christ did infinitely more in His death and resurrection than just undoing the damage of the fall. He came to raise us into the image of Jesus Christ, not merely to the image of the first Adam. The first man Adam was a living soul, the second man Adam was a life-giving Spirit. The first man Adam was made of the earth earthy, but the second man is the Lord from heaven!

Redemption in Christ, then, is not to pay back dollar-for-dollar or to straighten man out and restore him into Adamic grace. The purpose and work of redemption in Christ Jesus is to raise man as much above the level of Adam as Christ Himself is above the level of Adam. We are to gaze upon Christ, not Adam, and in so doing are being transformed by the Spirit of God into Christ's image.

So, we can say that earth may have been good enough for that creature who was created from the dust and clay, but it is not good enough for the living soul who is redeemed by royal blood! Earth was fit and proper to be the eternal dwelling place for that creature who was made by God's hand, but it is not appropriate nor sufficient to be the eternal dwelling place of that redeemed being who is begotten of the Holy Ghost. Every born-again Christian has been lifted up—lifted up from the level of the fallen Adamic race to the heavenly plane of the unfallen and victorious Christ. He belongs up there!

But, in the meantime, sin separates body and soul. That is why the Lord Jesus Christ, as He was about to leave the earth after His resurrection, told His disciples: "In my Father's house are many mansions ... I go to prepare a place for you. And if I go and prepare a place for you, I will come again, and receive you unto myself; that where I am, there ye may be also."

It is an amazing thing that Jesus Christ claimed that He never left the bosom of the Father. He said the Son of Man, who is in the bosom of the Father, hath declared it. While Jesus was upon earth, walking as a man among men, by the mystery of the ever-present God and the indivisible substance of the Deity, He could remain in the bosom of the Father, and He did.

So, you and I are to be elevated and promoted. Let us not forget that it was the Lord God Almighty who made man and blew into him the breath of life so that he became a living soul. That was man—and then in redemption God raised him infinitely above that level, so that now we hear the Lord and Saviour promising, "I have gone to prepare a place for you." In the time of our departure, the body that He gave us will disintegrate and drop away like a cocoon, for the spirit of the man soars away to the presence of God. The body must await that great day of resurrection at the last trump, for Paul says, "The dead shall be raised incorruptible, and we shall all be changed."

With the promises of God so distinct and beautiful, it is unbecoming that a Christian should make such a fearful thing of death. The fact that we Christians do display a neurosis about dying indicates that we are not where we ought to be spiritually. If we had actually reached a place of such spiritual commitment that the wonders of heaven were so close that we longed for the illuminating Presence of our Lord, we would not go into such a fearful and frantic performance every time we find something wrong with our physical frame.

I do not think that a genuine, committed Christian ever ought to be afraid to die. We do not have to be because Jesus promised that He would prepare a proper place for all of those who shall be born again, raised up out of the agony and stress of this world through the blood of the everlasting covenant into that bright and gracious world above.

Notice that Jesus said, "In my Father's house are many mansions." If it is His Father's house, it is also our Father's house because the Lord Jesus is our elder brother. Jesus also said, "I go to my Father and your Father—my God and your God." If the Father's house is the house of Jesus, it is also the house of all of His other sons and daughters.

Yes, we Christians are much better off than we really know—and there are a great many things here below that we can get along without and not be too shaken about it if we are honestly committed to the promises concerning the Father's house and its many dwelling places. It is one of the sad commentaries on our times that Christians can actually be foolish enough to get their affections so centered upon the things of this earth that they forget how quickly their little time in this body and upon this earth will flee away.

I am sure that our Lord is looking for heavenly-minded Christians. His Word encourages us to trust Him with such a singleness of purpose that He is able to deliver us from the fear of death and the uncertainties of tomorrow. I believe He is up there preparing me a mansion—"He is fixing up a mansion which shall forever stand; for my stay shall not be transient in that happy, happy land!"

Read again what John said about his vision of the future to come.

"I saw a new heaven and a new earth: for the first heaven and the first earth were passed away; and there was no more sea. And I John saw the holy city, the new Jerusalem, coming down from God out of heaven, prepared as a bride adorned for her husband."

Brethren, I say that it is just too bad that we have relegated this passage to be read mostly at funeral services. The man who was reporting this was not on his way to a funeral—he was on his way to the New Jerusalem!

He continued: "And I heard a great voice out of heaven saying, Behold, the tabernacle of God is with men, and he will dwell with them, and they shall be his people, and God himself shall be with them, and be their God. And God shall wipe away all tears from their eyes; and there shall be no more death, neither sorrow, nor crying, neither shall there be any more pain: for the former things are passed away."

John then describes that great and beautiful city having the glory of God, with her light like unto a stone that was most precious, even like as jasper, clear as crystal.

"And I saw no temple therein: for the Lord God Almighty and the Lamb are the temple of it. And the city had no need of the sun, neither of the moon, to shine in it: for the glory of God did lighten it, and the Lamb is the light thereof."

Ah, the people of God ought to be the happiest people in all the wide world! People should be coming to us constantly and asking the source of our joy and delight—redeemed by the blood of the Lamb, our yesterdays behind us, our sin under the blood forever and a day, to be remembered against us no more forever. God is our Father, Christ is our

117

Brother, the Holy Ghost our Advocate and Comforter. Our Brother has gone to the Father's house to prepare a place for us, leaving with us the promise that He will come again!

Don't send Moses, Lord, don't send Moses! He broke the tables of stone.

Don't send Elijah for me, Lord! I am afraid of Elijah—he called down fire from heaven.

Don't send Paul, Lord! He is so learned that I feel like a little boy when I read his epistles.

O Lord Jesus, come yourself! I am not afraid of Thee. You took the little children as lambs to your fold. You forgave the woman taken in adultery. You healed the timid woman who reached out in the crowd to touch You. We are not afraid of You!

Even so, come, Lord Jesus!

Come quickly!

Chapter Nine

Will You Allow God to Reproduce
Christ's Likeness in You?

*"I am crucified with Christ: nevertheless I live;
yet not I, but Christ liveth in me: and the life
which I now live in the flesh I live by the faith
of the Son of God, who loved me, and gave himself for me." Galatians 2:20*

There seems to be a great throng of professing
Christians in our churches today whose total and
amazing testimony sounds about like this: "I am
thankful for God's plan in sending Christ to the cross
to save me from hell."

I am convinced that it is a cheap, low-grade and
misleading kind of Christianity that impels people
to rise and state: "Because of sin I was deeply in
debt—and God sent His Son, who came and paid
all my debts."

Of course believing Christian men and women are
saved from the judgment of hell and it is a reality
that Christ our Redeemer has paid the whole slate
of debt and sin that was against us.

But what does God say about His purposes in
allowing Jesus to go to the cross and to the grave?
What does God say about the meaning of death and
resurrection for the Christian believer?

Surely we know the Bible well enough to be able

to answer that: God's highest purpose in the redemption of sinful humanity was based in His hope that we would allow Him to reproduce the likeness of Jesus Christ in our once-sinful lives!

This is the reason why we should be concerned with this text—this testimony of the apostle Paul in which he shares his own personal theology with the Galatian Christians who had become known for their backslidings. It is a beautiful miniature, shining forth as an unusual and sparkling gem, an entire commentary on the deeper Christian life and experience. We are not trying to take it out of its context by dealing with it alone; we are simply acknowledging the fact that the context is too broad to be dealt with in any one message.

It is the King James version of the Bible which quotes Paul: "I am crucified with Christ." Nearly every other version quotes Paul as speaking in a different tense: "I have been crucified with Christ," and that really is the meaning of it: "I have been crucified with Christ."

This verse is quoted sometimes by people who have simply memorized it and they would not be able to tell you what Paul was really trying to communicate. This is not a portion of scripture which can be skipped through lightly. You cannot skim through and pass over this verse as many seem to be able to do with the Lord's prayer and the twenty-third Psalm.

This is a verse with such depth of meaning and spiritual potential for the Christian believer that we are obligated to seek its full meaning—so it can become practical and workable and liveable in all of our lives in this present world.

It is plain in this text that Paul was forthright and frank in the matter of his own personal involvement in seeking and finding God's highest desires and provision for Christian experience and victory. He was not bashful about the implications of his own personality becoming involved with the claims of Jesus Christ.

Not only does he plainly testify, "I have been crucified," but within the immediate vicinity of these verses, he uses the words *I, myself* and *me* a total of 14 times.

There certainly is, in the Bible, a good case for humility in the human personality, but it can be overdone.

We have had a dear missionary veteran among us from time to time. He is learned and cultured—and overly modest. With a great wealth of missionary exploits and material to tell, he has always refused to use any first person reference to himself.

When asked to tell about something that happened in his pioneer missionary life, he said: "One remembers when one was in China and one saw . . ." That seems to be carrying the idea of modesty a bit too far, so I said to him, in a joking way, that if he had been writing the Twenty-third Psalm, it would likely read: "The Lord is one's shepherd, one shall not want; he maketh one to lie down in green pastures. He leadeth one . . ."

I believe Paul knew that there is a legitimate time and place for the use of the word *I*. In spiritual matters, some people seem to want to maintain a kind of anonymity, if possible. As far as they are concerned, someone else should take the first step. This often comes up in the manner of our praying, as well. Some Christians are so general and vague and uninvolved in their requests that God Himself is unable to answer. I refer to the man who will bow his head and pray: "Lord, bless the missionaries and all for whom we should pray. Amen."

It is as though Paul says to us here: "I am not ashamed to use myself as an example. I have been crucified with Christ. I am willing to be pin-pointed."

Only Christianity recognizes why the person who is without God and without any spiritual perception gets in such deep trouble with his own ego. When he says *I*, he is talking about the sum of his own individual being, and if he does not really know who he is or what he is doing here, he is beseiged in his personality with all kinds of questions and problems and uncertainties.

Most of the shallow psychology religions of the day try to deal with the problem of the ego by jockeying it around from one position to another, but Christianity deals with the problem of *I* by disposing of it with finality.

The Bible teaches that every unregenerated human being will continue to wrestle with the problems of his own natural ego and selfishness. His human nature dates back to Adam. But the Bible also teaches with joy and blessing that every individual may be born again, thus becoming a "new man" in Christ.

When Paul speaks in this text, "I have been crucified," he is saying that "my natural self has been crucified." That is why he can go on to say, "Yet I live"—for he has become another and a new person —"I live in Christ and Christ lives in me."

It is this first *I*, the natural me, which stands confronted with the just anger of God. God cannot acknowledge and accept me as a natural and selfish man—I am unregenerate and an alien, the complete essence of everything that is anti-God!

I know there are men and women who dismiss the idea of anything being anti-God or anti-Christ. They are not willing to pay any heed to the teachings of scripture relative to prophecy and eschatology.

Nevertheless, it is a biblical fact that whatever does not go through the process of crucifixion and transmutation, passing over into the new creation, is anti-Christ. Jesus said that all of that which is not with Christ is against Christ—those who are not on His side are against Him. We do not quite know what to do with those words of Christ, so we try to evade or work them over to a smooth, new version, but Jesus said, "If you do not gather with me, you scatter abroad."

There is a great hue and cry throughout the world today on behalf of tolerance and much of it comes from a rising spirit of godlessness in the nations. The communist nations, themselves the most intolerant, are preaching and calling for tolerance in order to break down all of the borders of religion and embarrass the American people with our social and racial problems.

This is the situation of the people of God: the most intolerant book in all the wide world is the Bible, the inspired Word of God, and the most intolerant teacher that ever addressed himself to an audience was the Lord Jesus Christ Himself.

On the other hand, Jesus Christ demonstrated the vast difference between being charitable and being tolerant. Jesus Christ was so charitable that in His great heart He took in all the people in the world and was willing to die even for those who hated Him.

But even with that kind of love and charity crowning His being, Jesus was so intolerant that He taught: "If you are not on my side, you are against me. If you do not believe that I am he, you shall die in your sins." He did not leave any middle ground to accommodate the neutral who preach tolerance. There is no "twilight zone" in the teachings of Jesus—no place in between.

Charity is one thing but tolerance is quite another matter.

Tolerance easily becomes a matter of cowardice if spiritual principles are involved, if the teachings of God's Word are ignored and forgotten.

Suppose we take the position of compromise that many want us to take: "Everyone come, and be saved if you want to. But if you do not want to be saved, maybe there is some other way that we can find for you. We want you to believe in the Lord Jesus Christ if you will, but if you do not want to, there may be a possibility that God will find some other way for you because there are those who say that there are many ways to God."

That would not be a spirit of tolerance on our part—it would be downright cowardice. We would be guilty with so many others of a spirit of compromise that so easily becomes an anti-God attitude.

True Christianity deals with the human problem of the self life, with the basic matter of "me, myself and I." The Spirit of God deals with it by an intolerant and final destruction, saying, "This selfish *I* cannot live if God is to be glorified in this human life."

God Himself deals with this aspect of human nature—the sum of all our proud life—and pronounces a stern condemnation upon it, flatly and frankly disapproving of it, fully and completely rejecting it.

And what does God say about it?

"I am God alone, and I will have nothing to do with man's selfish ego, in which I find the essence of rebellion and disobedience and unbelief. Man's nature in its pride of self and egotism is anti-God —and sinful, indeed!"

It is in this matter of how to deal with man's proud and perverse and sinful human nature that we discover two positions within the framework of Christianity.

One position is that which leans heavily upon the practice of psychology and psychiatry. There are so-called Christian leaders who insist that Jesus came into the world to bring about an adjustment of our ego, our selfishness, our pride, our perversity. They declare that we may become completely adjusted to life and to one another by dealing with the complexes and the twisted concepts that we have gotten into because our mothers scolded us when we were babies! So, there are thousands of referrals as the clergymen shift our problems from the church to the psychiatric couch.

On the other hand, thank God, the Bible plainly

says that Jesus Christ came to bring an end of *self* —not to educate it or tolerate it or polish it! No one can ever say that Jesus Christ came to tell us how to cultivate our natural ego and pride. Jesus never taught that we could learn to get along with the big, proud *I* in our lives by giving it a love for Bach and Beethoven and Da Vinci.

Paul outlined the full spiritual remedy: "I am crucified with Christ . . . and the life which I now live in the flesh I live by the faith of the Son of God, who loved me, and gave himself for me."

This is a decision and an attitude of faith and commitment called for in the life of every believing Christian.

When we see that Jesus Christ came into the world to deal effectively and finally with our life of self and egotism and pride, we must take a stand.

With God's help, we say to that big *I* in our nature: "This is as far as you go—you are deposed. You are no longer to be in control!" In true repentance and in self-repudiation, we may turn our backs on the old self life. We may refuse to go along with it any longer. We have the right and the power to desert its ranks and cross over to spiritual victory and blessing on Emmanuel's side, walking joyfully under the banner of the cross of Jesus Christ from that hour on.

This is what it means to deal with and finally dispose of the "old man," the old life of self, which is still causing problems in so many Christian lives. We take a place of actual identification with Jesus Christ in His crucifixion, burial, and resurrection.

In the Christian life, that is what baptism is supposed to mean, but sad to say, baptism is nothing but a quick dip to the average person because that one does not know what baptism represents. He does not know that baptism genuinely ought to be an outward and visible testimony of a spiritual and inward transformation that has taken place; a symbol declaring that the old selfish and perverse human nature is repudiated in humility, and put away, crucified, declared dead!

That is what baptism should mean to the believer —death and burial with Christ, then raised with Him in the power of His resurrection! It can happen apart from water baptism of any mode. but that is what water baptism should indicate. It should set forth that identification with the death and resurrection of Jesus Christ just as a wedding ring witnesses and sets forth the fact that you are married.

Now, it is impossible to bring together and synchronize these two positions concerning the old life and nature of self. I do not believe that we are ever obliged to dovetail these two positions. Either the Lord Jesus Christ came to bring an end of self and reveal a new life in spiritual victory, or He came to patch and repair the old self—He certainly did not come to do both!

I expect someone to say, "We are interested in spiritual victory and blessing in our group, but our approach doesn't agree with yours at all!"

In answer I can only say that on the basis of the Word of God, true identification with Jesus Christ in His death, burial and resurrection will lead men and women to Christ-likeness. God has never promised to work out His image in us in a variety of ways according to the inclinations of our own group. Forming the likeness to Jesus Christ in human lives and personalities is something that He does alike in all groups and all conferences and all fellowships around the world regardless of what they may be called.

There really is no way to patch up and repair the old life of self. The whole burden of New Testament theology insists that the old human self is ruined completely. It has no basic goodness, it holds to false values and its wisdom is questionable, to say the least. It is the new self in Christ Jesus—the new man in Christ—which alone must live. Onward from the point of this commitment, we must reckon ourselves indeed to have died unto sin, to be alive unto God in Christ Jesus.

But the natural self, the natural "I, myself and me," is continually taking inventory, seeking and hoping to find some human help in trying to forget and escape the guilty past, something that will make it more acceptable in God's sight, something that will enable it to develop to the fullest the potential of its nature.

Part of man's natural frustration is the inner feeling and realization that he is never measuring up and achieving to the full potential given him in creation. Actually, I believe God has created each one of us with a master blueprint representing His highest desires for the use of our many capacities in this life.

With God's blueprint stretching forth in all directions, what usually happens to the human life and personality? Well, we may see a utilitarian little house or shack there in the middle of it, and after a few years of hard work, an addition of some kind, but the outreach of our human personality which we picture in this way never stretches out to the limits of the blueprint.

The human nature in its striving and its groping has never been able to finally roll up the blueprint, put it away on the shelf, and say, "Thank God, my earthly existence is everything God desired it to be! The last wall has been raised, that final arch is complete, the roof is without a flaw—it is a habitation that can be considered to be perfect!"

The potential and the abilities of man's mighty nature are almost limitless—but we have to add, not quite! I am always stirred in my being to consider all that created man can do, the great powers and ability to think, the powers of imagination and creativity. Yet, if men and women do not find a way to properly use all of those powers and talents and gifts in bringing praise and honor and glory to God the Creator and the Redeemer, they are still not what they ought to be.

I believe there is a subconscious desire deep within every human being to realize and utilize his full potential—the desire to live a full and complete life, which often means the hope of escaping the past and the ability to face the future in confidence.

But what do men and women actually find when they look into their own hearts in this quest? They find nothing that measures up to their dreams and hopes. They find that they possess nothing of eternal value. They find that they know nothing with any certainty. They find that they can do nothing which is acceptable in the sight of a holy God.

Human beings continue to lean on a variety of crutches to support the ego, to nourish the pride, to cover the obvious defects in human existence. Many have believed that continuing education would provide that missing link between personality and potential. Many have turned to the pursuits of philosophies; others to cultural achievements. Ancestry and environment and status occupy many more.

But the ability to brag about human ancestors, to point with pride to the nation of our descent or the cultural privileges we have known—these do not transform and change and regenerate the human nature. Regardless of our racial strains, regardless of our cultural and educational advantages, we are all alike as human beings. In my own nature, I am nothing. Of myself, I know nothing. In God's sight, without His help and His enabling, I have nothing and I can do nothing.

But the inventory of the new man in Christ Jesus is so different! If he has found the meaning of commitment, the giving up of self to be identified with Jesus Christ in His crucifixion and death, he discovers in an entirely new measure the very presence of Christ Himself!

This new person has made room for the presence of Christ, so there is a difference in the persona inventory. It is no longer the old do-nothing, know-nothing, be-nothing, have-nothing person! That old assertive self died when the crucified and risen Saviour was given His rightful place of command and control in the personality. The old inventory cried out: "How can I be what I ought to be?" but the inventory of the new man is couched in faith and joy in his recognition that "Christ liveth in me!"

Paul expressed it to the Colossians in this way: "Christ in you, the hope of glory!" and then proceeded to assure them that "You are complete in Him!"

Paul wrote to the Ephesians to remind them that the essence of faith and hope in Christ is the assurance of being "accepted in the Beloved."

To the Corinthian believers, Paul promised full spiritual deliverance and stability in the knowledge that Jesus Christ "is made unto us wisdom, righteousness, sanctification and redemption."

Our great need, then, is simply Jesus Christ. He is what we need. He has what we need. He knows what we need to know. He has the ability to do in us what we cannot do—working in us that which is well-pleasing in God's sight.

This is a difficult point in spiritual doctrine and life for many people.

"What about my ambition? I have always been ambitious so it is a part of my being. Doesn't it matter?"

"I am used to doing my own thing in my own way—and I am still doing it in the church. Do I have to yield that?"

"I have always been able to put my best foot forward to get recognition and publicity. I am used to seeing my name in the paper. What do I get from crucifixion with Christ?"

Brothers and sisters, you get Christ and glory and fruitfulness and future and the world to come, whereof we speak, and the spirits of just men made perfect; you get Jesus, the mediator of a new covenant, and the blood of the everlasting covenant; an innumerable company of angels and the church of the firstborn and the New Jerusalem, the city of the living God!

And before you get all that, you have the privilege and the prospect of loving and joyful service for Christ and for mankind on this earth.

This is a gracious plan and provision for men and women in the kindness and wisdom of God. He loves you too well and too much to let you continue to strut and boast and cultivate your egotism and feed your *I*. He just cannot have that kind of selfish assertion in His children, so Jesus Christ works in us to complete Himself and make Himself anew in us.

So, you see, that is really why Jesus Christ came into this world to tabernacle with us, to die for us. God is never going to be done with us in shaping us and fashioning us as dear children of God until the day that we will see Him face to face, and His name shall be in our foreheads. In that day, we shall genuinely be like Him and we shall see Him as He is.

Truly, in that gracious day, our rejoicing will not be in the personal knowledge that He saved us from hell, but in the joyful knowledge that He was able to renew us, bringing the old self to an end, and creating within us the new man and the new self in which can be reproduced the beauty of the Son of God.

In the light of that provision, I think it is true that no Christian is where he ought to be spiritually until that beauty of the Lord Jesus Christ is being reproduced in daily Christian life.

I admit that there is necessarily a question of

degree in this kind of transformation of life and character.

Certainly there has never been a time in our human existence when we could look into our own being, and say: "Well, thank God, I see it is finished now. The Lord has signed the portrait. I see Jesus in myself!"

Nobody will say that—nobody!

Even though a person has become like Christ, he will not know it. He will be charitable and full of love and peace and grace and mercy and kindness and goodness and faithfulness—but he will not really know it because humility and meekness are also a part of the transformation of true godliness.

Even though he is plainly God's man and Christ's witness, he will be pressing on, asking folks to pray for him, reading his Bible with tears, and saying, "Oh, God, I want to be like Thy Son!"

God knows that dear child is coming into the likeness of His Son, and the angels know it, and the observing people around him know it, too. But he is so intent upon the will and desires of God for his life and personality that he does not know it, for true humility never looks in on itself. Emerson wrote that the eye that sees only itself is blind and that the eye is not to see with but to see through. If my eye should suddenly become conscious of itself, I would be a blind man.

Now, there is a practical application of the crucified life and its demands from day to day. John the Baptist realized it long ago when he said, "He must increase but I must decrease!"

There must necessarily be less and less of me—and more and more of Christ! That's where you feel the bite and the bitterness of the cross, brother! Judicially and potentially, I was crucified with Christ, and now God wants to make it actual. In actuality, it is not as simple as that. Your decision and commitment do not then allow you to come down from that cross. Peace and power and fruitfulness can only increase according to our willingness to confess moment by moment, "It is no longer I, but Christ that liveth in me."

God is constantly calling for decisions among those in whom there is such great potential for displaying the life of Jesus Christ.

We must decide: "My way, or Christ's?"

Will I insist upon my own righteousness even while God is saying that it must be the righteousness of His Son?

Can I still live for my own honor and praise? No, it must be for Christ's honor and praise to be well-pleasing to God.

"Do I have any choice? Can I have my own plan?"

No, God can only be honored as we make our choices in Christ and live for the outworking of God's plan.

Modern theology refuses to press down very hard at this point, but we still are confronted often with spiritual choices in our hymnology. We often sing: "Oh, to be dead to myself, dear Lord; Oh, to be lost in Thee."

We sing the words, we soon shut the book, and drift away with friends to relax and have a pleasant soda. The principle does not become operative in most Christians. It does not become practical. That is why I keep saying and teaching and hoping that this principle which is objective truth will become subjective experience in Christian lives. For any professing Christian who dares to say, "Knowing the truth is enough for me; I do not want to mix it up with my day-to-day life and experience," Christianity has become nothing but a farce and a delusion!

It may surprise you that Aldous Huxley, often a critic of orthodox and evangelical Christianity, has been quoted as saying: "*My* kingdom *go* is the necessary correlary to *Thy* kingdom *come*."

How many Christians are there who pray every Sunday in church, "Thy kingdom come! Thy will be done!" without ever realizing the spiritual implications of such intercession? What are we praying for? Should we edit that prayer so that it becomes a confrontation: "My kingdom go, Lord; let Thy kingdom come!" Certainly His kingdom can never be realized in my life until my own selfish kingdom is deposed. It is when I resign, when I am no longer king of my domain that Jesus Christ will become king of my life.

Now, brethren, in confession, may I assure you that a Christian clergyman cannot follow any other route to spiritual victory and daily blessing than that which is prescribed so plainly in the Word of God. It is one thing for a minister to choose a powerful text, expound it and preach from it—it is quite something else for the minister to honestly and genuinely live forth the meaning of the Word from day to day. A clergyman is a man—and often he has a proud little kingdom of his own, a kingdom of position and often of pride and sometimes with power. Clergymen must wrestle with the spiritual implications of the crucified life just like everyone else, and to be thoroughgoing men of God and spiritual examples to the flock of God, they must die daily to the allurements of their own little kingdoms of position and prestige.

One of the greatest of the pre-reformation preachers in Germany was Johannes Tollar, certainly an evangelical before Luther's time. The story has been told that a devout layman, a farmer whose name was Nicholas, came down from the countryside, and implored Dr. Tollar to preach a sermon in the great church, dealing with the deeper Christian life based on spiritual union with Jesus Christ.

The following Sunday Dr. Tollar preached that sermon. It had 26 points, telling the people how to put away their sins and their selfishness in order to glorify Jesus Christ in their daily lives. It was a good sermon—actually, I have read it and I can underscore every line of it.

When the service was over and the crowd had dispersed, Nicholas came slowly down the aisle.

He said, "Pastor Tollar, that was a great sermon and I want to thank you for the truth which you presented. But I am troubled and I would like to make a comment, with your permission."

"Of course, and I would like to have your comment," the preacher said.

"Pastor, that was great spiritual truth that you brought to the people today, but I discern that you were preaching it to others as truth without having experienced the implications of deep spiritual principles in your own daily life," Nicholas told him. "You are not living in full identification with the death and resurrection of Jesus Christ. I could tell by the way you preached—I could tell!"

The learned and scholarly Dr. Tollar did not reply. But he was soon on his knees, seeking God in repentance and humiliation. For many weeks he did not take the pulpit to preach—earnestly seeking day after day the illumination of the Spirit of God in order that objective truth might become a deep and renewing and warming spiritual experience within.

After the long period of the dark sufferings in his soul, the day came when John Tollar's own kingdom was brought to an end and was replaced by God's kingdom. The great flood of the Spirit came in on his life and he returned to his parish and to his pulpit to become one of the greatest and most fervent and effective preachers of his generation. God's gracious blessings came—but Tollar first had to die. This is what Paul meant when he said, "I have been crucified with Christ."

This must become living reality for all of us who say we are interested in God's will for our lives. You pray for me and I will surely pray for you—because this is a matter in which we must follow our Lord!

We can quote this text from memory, but that is not enough. I can say that I know what Paul meant, but that is not enough. God promises to make it living reality in our lives the instant that we let our little, selfish kingdom go!

Chapter Ten

Christian, Do You Downgrade Yourself Too Much?

"Looking for that blessed hope, and the glorious appearing of the great God and our Saviour Jesus Christ; Who gave himself for us, that he might redeem us from all iniquity, and purify unto himself a peculiar people, zealous of good works."
Titus 2:13-14

The people of God, Christians who are living between the two mighty events of Christ's incarnation and His promised second coming, are not living in a vacuum!

It is amazing that segments in the Christian church that deny the possibility of the imminent return of the Lord Jesus accuse those who do believe in His soon coming of sitting around, twiddling their thumbs, looking at the sky, and blankly hoping for the best!

Nothing could be further from the truth. We live in the interim between His two appearances, but we do not live in a vacuum. We have much to do and little time in which to get it done!

Stretch your mind and consider some very apparent facts of our day.

Who are the Christians leaving all to staff the missionary posts around the world? Who are the

Christians staying at home and sacrificing in order to support the great evangelical thrust of the Christian gospel everywhere? Those who fervently believe that He is coming.

What kind of churches are busy praying and teaching and giving, preparing their young people for the ministry and for missionary work? Churches that are responding to Christ's appeal to "occupy until I come!"

Well, in this text Titus has given us Christian doctrine that has validity both in the light of the expected return of Jesus Christ as well as in the face of death.

It is in the record of the early Methodists in England, when there was persecution and testing in every direction, that John Wesley was able to say, "Our people die well!"

In more recent years, I have heard a quotation from a denominational bishop who estimated that only about ten per cent of the men and women in the membership of his church body are prepared and spiritually ready to die when their time comes.

I believe you can only die well when you have lived well, from a spiritual point of view. This doctrine of the Christian life and spiritual vitality of the believer as propounded by Titus has full validity in the face of any contingency which awaits us.

Titus quickly identifies Jesus Christ as the Saviour "who gave himself for us," and we can quickly learn the value of any object by the price which people are willing to pay for it. Perhaps I should qualify that—you may not learn the true value, for it is my private opinion that a diamond or other jewelry has no intrinsic value at all.

You may remember the story about the rooster scratching around in the barnyard for kernels of corn. Suddenly he scratched up a beautiful pearl of fabulous price which had been lost years before, but he just pushed it aside and kept on looking for corn.

The pearl had no value for the rooster, although it had a great value for those who had set a price upon it.

There are various kinds of markets in the world, and something which has no value for a disinterested person may be considered of great value by the person desiring it and purchasing it.

It is in this sense, then, that we learn how dear and precious we are to Christ by what He was willing to give for us.

I believe many Christians are tempted to downgrade themselves too much. I am not arguing against true humility and my word to you is this: Think as little of yourself as you want to, but always remember that our Lord Jesus Christ thought very highly of you—enough to give Himself for you in death and sacrifice.

If the devil does come to you and whispers that you are no good, don't argue with him. In fact, you may as well admit it, but then remind the devil: "Regardless of what you say about me, I must tell you how the Lord feels about me. He tells me that I am so valuable to Him that He gave Himself for me on the cross!"

So, the value is set by the price paid—and, in our case, the price paid was our Lord Himself!

The end that the Saviour had in view was that He might redeem us from all iniquity, that is, from the power and consequences of iniquity.

We often sing the words of a hymn by Charles Wesley in which the death of our Lord Jesus is described as "the double cure" for sin. I think many people sing the hymn without realizing what Wesley meant by the double cure.

"Be of sin the double cure, Save me from its wrath and power." The wrath of God against sin and then the power of sin in the human life—these both must be cured. Therefore, when He gave Himself for us, He redeemed us with a double cure, delivering us from the consequences of sin and delivering us from the power which sin exercises in human lives.

Now, Titus, in this great nugget of spiritual truth, reminds us that the redemptive Christ performs a purifying work in the people of God.

You will have to agree with me that one of the deep and outbroken diseases of this present world and society is impurity, and it displays itself in dozens of symptoms. We are prone to look upon certain lewd and indecent physical actions as the impurities which plague human life and society—but the actual lusting and scheming and planning and plotting come from a far deeper source of impurity within the very minds and innermost beings of sinful men and women.

If we were people of clean hands and pure hearts, we would be intent upon doing the things that please God. Impurity is not just a wrong action; impurity is the state of mind and heart and soul which is just the opposite of purity and wholeness.

Sexual misconduct is a symptom of the disease of impurity—but so is hatred. Pride and egotism, resentfulness and churlishness come to the surface out of sinful and impure minds and hearts, just as gluttony and slothfulness and self-indulgence do. All of these and countless others come to the surface as outward symptoms of the deep, inward disease of selfishness and sin.

Because this is a fact in life and experience, it is the spiritual work of Jesus Christ to purify His people by His own blood to rid them of this deep-lying disease. That is why He is called the Great Physician —He is able to heal us of this plague of impurity and iniquity, redeeming us from the consequences of our sins and purifying us from the presence of our sins.

Now, brethren, either this is true and realizable in human life and experience or Christianity is the cheap fraud of the day. Either it is true and a dependable spiritual option or we should fold up the Bible and put it away with other classical pieces of literature which have no particular validity in the face of death.

Thank God that there are millions who dare to stand as if in a great chorus and shout with me, "It is true! He did give Himself to redeem us from all iniquity and He does perform this purifying work in our lives day by day!"

The result of Christ's purifying work is the perfecting of God's very own people, referred to in this passage from the King James version as "a peculiar people."

Many of us know all too well that this word *peculiar* has been often used to cloak religious conduct both strange and irrational. People have been known to do rather weird things and then grin a self-conscious grin and say in half-hearted apology: "Well, we are a peculiar people!"

Anyone with a serious and honest concern for scriptural admonition and instruction could quickly learn that this English word *peculiar* in the language of 1611 describing the redeemed people of God had no connotation of queerness, ridiculousness nor foolishness.

The same word was first used in Exodus 19:5 when God said that Israel "shall be unto me a peculiar treasure above all people." It was God's way of emphasizing that His people would be to Him a treasure above all other treasures. In the etymological sense, it means "shut up to me as my special jewel."

Every loving mother and father has a good idea of what God meant. There are babies in houses up and down every street, as you can tell by the baby clothes hanging on the lines on a summer day.

But in the house where you live, there is one little infant in particular, and he is a peculiar treasure unto you above all others. It does not mean necessarily that he is prettier, but it does mean that he is the treasure above all other treasures and you would not trade him for any other child in the whole world. He is a *peculiar* treasure!

This gives us some idea, at least, of what we are—God's special jewels marked out for Him!

Titus then clearly spelled out one thing that will always characterize the children of God—the fact that they are zealous of good works.

Titus and all of the other writers who had a part in God's revelation through the scriptures agree at this point—our Lord never made provision for any of His followers to be "armchair" Christians. "Ivory tower" Christianity, an abstract kind of believing, composed simply of fine and beautiful thoughts, is not what Jesus taught at all.

The language in this passage is plain: The children of God in Jesus Christ, redeemed by the giving of Himself, purified and made unto Him as special jewels, a peculiar people, are characterized by one thing—their zeal for good works.

Because of the grace of God, we learn, these followers of Jesus Christ are zealous of good works and in their daily experience they live "looking." The Christian should always live in joyous anticipation of the blessed hope and the glorious appearing of the great God and our Saviour Jesus Christ!

Now, there is something in Christian theology that I want to share with you. Some people say they cannot bother with theology because they do not know either Greek or Hebrew. I cannot believe that there is any Christian who is so humble that he would insist that he knows nothing about theology.

Theology is the study of God and we have a very wonderful textbook—actually 66 textbooks rolled into one. We call it the Bible. The point I want to make is this: I have noted in study and in experience that the more vital and important any theological or doctrinal truth may be, the devil will fight it harder and bring greater controversy to bear upon it.

Consider the deity of Jesus, for example.

More and more people are arguing and debating and fighting over this absolutely vital and foundational truth.

The devil is smart enough not to waste his attacks on minor and non-vital aspects of Christian truth and teaching.

The devil will not cause any trouble for a preacher who is scared stiff of his congregation and worried about his job to the extent that he preaches for thirty minutes and the sum of what he says is "Be good and you will feel better!"

You can be as good as you want to and yet go to hell if you have not put your trust in Jesus Christ! The devil is not going to waste his time causing any trouble for the preacher whose only message is "Be good!"

But the believing Christian lives in joyful anticipation of the return of Jesus Christ and that is such an important segment of truth that the devil has always been geared up to fight it and ridicule it. One of his big successes is being able to get people to argue and get mad about the second coming— rather than looking and waiting for it.

Suppose a man has been overseas two or three years, away from his family. Suddenly a cable arrives for the family with the message, "My work completed here; I will be home today."

After some hours he arrives at the front door and finds the members of his family in turmoil. There had been a great argument as to whether he would arrive in the afternoon or evening. There had been arguments about what transportation he would be using. As a result, there were no little noses pushing against the window glass, no one looking to be able to catch the first glimpse of returning Daddy.

You may say, "That is only an illustration."

But what is the situation in the various segments

of the Christian community?

They are fighting with one another and glaring at each other. They are debating whether He is coming and how He is coming and they are busy using what they consider to be proof texts about the fall of Rome and the identification of the anti-Christ.

Brethren, that is the work of the devil—to make Christian people argue about the details of His coming so they will forget the most important thing. How many Christians are so confused and bewildered by the arguments that they have forgotten that the Saviour has purified unto Himself a peculiar people, expecting that we will live soberly, righteously and godly, looking for the glorious appearing of the great God and Saviour.

That is the Epiphany, which is an expression in the Christian church, and it is used in reference to Christ's manifestation in the world.

It is used in two senses in 1 Timothy and 2 Timothy.

First, Paul says in 2 Timothy 1:8-10: ". . . God, who hath saved us, and called us with an holy calling, not according to our works, but according to his own purpose and grace, which was given us in Christ Jesus before the world began, but is now made manifest by the appearing of our Saviour Jesus Christ, who hath abolished death, and hath brought life and immortality to light through the gospel."

In that passage we have the record of His first appearing, the shining forth when He came into the world to abolish death by His death and resurrection.

Then, the apostle in one of those moving and wonderful doxologies, said in 1 Timothy 6:13-16: "I give thee charge in the sight of God, who quickeneth all things, and before Christ Jesus, who before Pontius Pilate witnessed a good confession; that thou keep this commandment without spot, unrebukeable, until the appearing of our Lord Jesus Christ."

Paul speaks of the second appearing, when Christ

"shall shew, who is the blessed and only Potentate, the King of kings, and Lord of lords; Who only hath immortality, dwelling in the light which no man can approach unto; whom no man hath seen, nor can see: to whom be honour and power everlasting. Amen."

When I read something like this given us by the apostle Paul, it makes me think of a skylark or a meadowlark mounting a branch and bursting into an unexpected but brilliantly melodious song. Paul often breaks forth with one of his wonderful and uplifting ascriptions of praise to Jesus Christ in the midst of his epistles, and this is one of those!

Paul reminds Christian believers here that when Jesus Christ appears again, He will show forth, and leave no doubts at all, as to the Person of the King of kings and Lord of lords.

Paul was also careful to comfort those in the early church who feared that they might die before this second appearing of Jesus Christ. Actually, there were believers in the Thessalonian church who were worried on two counts, the first of which was their thought that the Lord had already come and they had been passed by. The second was their thought that they would die before He came and that through death, they would miss out on the joys of His appearing.

So, Paul wrote the two epistles to the Thessalonian church to straighten them out on the truth concerning Christ's second appearing.

"If we believe that Jesus died and rose again, even so them also which sleep in Jesus will God bring with him"—that is, if you die and go to be with the Lord, God will bring you along with Jesus at His appearing—"for this we say unto you by the word of the Lord, that we which are alive and remain unto the coming of the Lord shall not (run ahead of those) which are asleep. For the Lord himself shall descend from heaven with a shout, with the voice of the archangel, and with the trump of God: and the dead in Christ shall rise first: Then we which are alive and remain shall be caught up together with them in the clouds, to meet the Lord in the air: and so shall we ever be with the Lord. Wherefore comfort one another with these words."

You see, Paul's inspired explanation instructs us that those who died before the coming of Jesus will not be at a disadvantage. If anything, they will be in a position of advantage, because before the Lord glorifies the waiting saints throughout the earth, He will raise in glorified bodies the great company of believers who have been parted from us by death throughout the centuries.

Brethren, that is very plainly what the apostle Paul tells us in the instructions originally given to the Thessalonian Christians.

Don't we have the right to think that it is very strange that the majority of the Christian pulpits are completely silent concerning this glorious truth of the imminent return of Jesus Christ? It is paradoxical that there should be this great silence in Christian churches at the very time when the danger of suddenly being swept off the face of the earth is greater than it has ever been.

Russia and the United States, the two great nuclear powers, continue to measure their ability to destroy in terms of *over-kill.* This is a terrible compound word never before used in the history of the English language. The scientists had to express the almost incredible destructive power of the nuclear bombs in our stockpiles—so the word *over-kill* is a new invention of our times.

Both the United States and Russia have made statements about the over-kill power of nuclear stockpiles sufficient to kill every man, woman and child in the world—not once, but 20 times over. That is over-kill!

Isn't it just like that old enemy, Satan, to persuade

the saints in the Body of Christ to engage in bitter arguments about post-tribulation rapture and pre-tribulation rapture; post-millennialism, a-millennialism and pre-millennialism—right at the very hour when over-kill hangs over us like a black, threatening cloud.

Brethren, this is the kind of age and hour when the Lord's people should be so alert to the hope and promise of His coming that they should get up every morning just like a child on Christmas morning—eager and believing that it should be today!

Instead of that kind of expectancy, what do we find throughout His church today? Arguments pro and con about His coming, about the details of the rapture—and some of this to the point of bitterness. Otherwise, we find great segments of Christians who seem to be able to blithely ignore the whole matter of the return of Jesus Christ.

Very few ministers bother to preach from the Book of Revelation any more—and that is true of large areas of evangelicalism and fundamentalism, too! We have been intimidated by the cynicism and sophistication of our day.

There are so many apparent anomalies and contradictions in society and in the ranks of professing Christians that someone will certainly write a book about it.

There is the anomaly of the necessity of getting to know one another better in order to love and understand one another better. Millions are traveling and meeting other millions and getting acquainted, so if the premise is true, we ought all to love each other like one big blessed family.

Instead, we hate each other like the devil. It is true that all over the world the nations are hating each other in startling, record-breaking measure.

I will mention another contradiction that is all too apparent. Our educators and sociologists told us that all we had to do was allow the teaching

146

of sexual education in the schools and all of our vexing sexual problems in society would disappear.

Is it not a strange anomaly that the generation that has been teaching and outlining more about sexual practices than any twenty-five generations combined did in the past is the generation that is the most rotten and perverted in sexual conduct?

And is it not strange, too, that the very generation that might expect to be atomized suddenly by over-kill is the generation that is afraid to talk about the coming of the Lord and unwilling to discuss His gracious promises of deliverance and glorification?

You may not expect me to say it, but I will: what a bunch of weirdies we are! What a strange generation we are!

God has said that He would place a great premium on the holy, spiritual consistency of the Christian saints, but how inconsistent we are when we allow the devil and our own carnality to confuse and mix us up so that we will be diverted from patient waiting for His appearing!

So, we live between two mighty events—that of His incarnation, death and resurrection, and that of His ultimate appearing and the glorification of those He died to save. This is the interim time for the saints—but it is not a vacuum. He has given us much to do and He asks for our faithfulness.

In the meantime, we are zealous of good works, living soberly, righteously, godly in this present world, looking unto Him and His promise. In the midst of our lives, and between the two great mountain peaks of God's acts in the world, we look back and remember, and we look forward and hope! As members of His own loving fellowship, we break the bread and drink the wine. We sing His praise and we pray in His Name, remembering and expecting!

Brethren, that moves me more than anything else

in this world. It is such a blessed privilege that it is more beautiful and satisfying than friendships or paintings or sunsets or any other beauties of nature. Looking back to His grace and love; looking forward to His coming and glory; meanwhile actively working and joyously hoping—until He comes!

Chapter Eleven

Do You Love Your Lord,
Never Having Seen Him?

"...Jesus Christ, whom having not seen, ye love..." 1 Peter 1:8

I think it may be safely said of the human family that it is possible to love someone we have never seen, but that it is totally impossible for us to love one whom we have not "experienced" in some way.

The apostle Peter, who had seen Jesus Christ in the flesh with his own eyes, passed along to every believing Christian the assurance that it is possible for us to love the Saviour and to live a life that will glorify Him even though we have not yet seen Him.

It is as though Peter is urging: "Love Him and work for Him and live for Him. I give you my testimony that it will be worth it all when you look upon His face—for I have seen Him with my own eyes, and I know!"

Once Peter was occupied with the chores of his fishing trade along the shores of Galilee as a quiet Man passed by, a Man with a marvelous magnetism, a glorious wonder about His face. When He flipped His pleasant finger at Peter, the big fisherman jumped up and followed and was in His company for three years.

Peter came to know personally the meaing of bit-

149

ter tears and strong weeping after his denial of the Lord. I am sure he wept often when his thoughts would sweep him along to the memories of the broken body of the Messiah hanging on a cross. But his eyes had also seen Jesus after He was risen from the grave, for the Lord came forth and put His hand on Peter's head and forgave him!

Peter had also seen Him before that in the glory of the transfiguration—the preview of the glory that awaited the Son of Man. Finally, Peter stood with the other disciples as Jesus bade them farewell and ascended into heaven from the Mount of Olives. All of these were incidents in Peter's life which were actual experiences in his relationship with the person of Jesus Christ, his Lord and Master.

So, Peter had seen Jesus in the flesh, and was moved to write to the strangers scattered abroad— the Christians of the dispersion—to remind them that they should love Jesus Christ even though they had not seen Him in the flesh.

The Lord Jesus Himself had set His own stamp of approval and blessing upon all Christians who would believe, never having seen Him in the time of His own flesh. He told Thomas after the resurrection, "Because thou hast seen me, thou hast believed: blessed are they that have not seen, and yet have believed."

I think it is a mistake for Christians to nurture a kind of plaintive and pensive regret that they did not live 2,000 years ago when Christ was upon the earth. We are reminded of this attitude in a children's hymn that most of us have sung at one time or another:

"I think when I read the sweet story of old,
How Jesus was here among men;
How He called little children as lambs to His fold,
I would like to have been with Him then."

I do not go on record as objecting to that song,

but I do not think it has any biblical authority. I truly believe that God has ordained that we may actually know Jesus now, and love Him better never having seen Him, than Peter did when he saw Him!

Now, about this matter of being able to "experience" others.

In our human race, some persons unfortunately are born without the ability to hear and others are born without the great gift of sight.

One who is born without the ability to hear may still know and experience and appreciate relatives and friends through the communication of the eyes.

One who is blind but has the faculty of hearing soon discovers the ability to experience and to come to know those who are around him by hearing their voices and learning all the sweet cadences of affection and love through the ears.

Even those who have had the double handicap of deafness and blindness have come to experience and know and appreciate other human beings—like Helen Keller, for instance, who learned to love people by feeling their faces with her sensitive fingers.

The story has been told that when Helen Keller was a young woman, she was introduced to the great tenor, Caruso. Unable to hear him, of course, she asked for the privilege of putting her fingers on his neck and chest bones while he sang one of his favorite operatic renditions. Her sensitive hands experienced the great range of the vibrations of his voice, and she stood as though transfixed. She could not hear his voice, but she experienced him in a most unusual way through the reading of her fingers.

I am sure it is true that we can love people we have not seen—but that it is impossible to love one whom we have not experienced in any way. It is a total impossibility for me to find any emotional response toward a person who has never come within the circle of my human experience.

For instance, do I love Abraham Lincoln?

Well, Abraham Lincoln is dead. I respect and admire his memory and I honor his great contributions to our nation and society. I believe he was a great man, but I feel no emotional response or personal human affection toward him.

If I had lived in the day of Lincoln and there had been opportunity for some correspondence between us, that opportunity to know and feel his great depth of personality would have certainly given me an emotional sense of affection and attachment. But as it is, I only know about Lincoln. I had no communication with him.

Actually, there have been people who confessed that they had fallen in love with another person through the writing of letters and the use of the mail. It is possible to experience others through the writing of letters—you get the pulse of them through the things they write and your imagination pieces it out and you may well experience love for the person of one whom you have not seen. It has happened.

God has seen fit to give us wonderful and mysterious faculties, and thus we human beings are able to know and experience and love someone we have not seen.

That is why Peter was able to witness to us of Jesus Christ and to tell us that we could and we should love Him, never having laid eyes upon His person in the flesh.

Notice that Peter did not assure us that we could love Jesus Christ without meeting Him in experience, in spirit, in His Word.

I think that one of the most hopeless tasks in the world is that of trying to create some love for Christ our Saviour among those who refuse and deny that there is a need for a definite spiritual experience of Jesus Christ in the human life.

I cannot understand the activities of many churches—their futile exercise of trying to whip up love and concern for Jesus Christ when there is no teaching of the new birth, no teaching of redemption through His blood, no dependence upon spiritual illumination by the Spirit of God!

No one can love the Lord Jesus Christ unless the Spirit of God is given opportunity to reveal Him in the life. No one can say that Jesus is Lord except the Holy Spirit enables him through spiritual life and experience.

Knowing this fact makes me question how any congregation can love and serve and glorify a Saviour whose very saviourhood is denied from the pulpit.

Peter writes that we are dedicated to the glory of the One whom we have not seen, because we love Him. That is the sum of Christianity—to know Him and to love Him!

"This is eternal life, that they might know me," Jesus taught. So, the knowledge of God is eternal life and the knowledge of setting forth the life of God in man is the business of the church.

It is a wonderful facet of love that we always take pleasure and delight in doing those things that are pleasing to the one we love. I find that the believing Christian who really loves his Lord is never irked or irritated in the service he is giving to Jesus Christ. The Lord will give him delight in true service for God—and I say it this way because generally the irksome and boring features of Christian service are some of the things that people and organizations have added on. I refer to things that have no scriptural validity.

It is always pleasant and delightful to set forth the praises of someone you really love. I think I see the illustration of that very often among the grandparents I meet, for they always whip out a wallet or a sheaf of pictures of their beautiful and talented grandchildren—whom they dearly love!

Those who truly love Jesus Christ find it one of the greatest pleasures in life to be able to simply describe how we discovered His great love for us, and how we are trying to return that love and devotion as we follow and serve Him in faith each day.

Now, Peter speaks out of a close relationship to Jesus, and in all of his writings speaks often of Jesus Christ, our Lord. He knew Jesus and had been instructed and taught of the Lord. There is reverence and dignity in his manner whenever he uses the name and titles of the Saviour.

Jesus was His name for Mary was told, "Thou shalt call his name Jesus because he is to be the Saviour of the world." The name Jesus had the same meaning as Joshua, which is "Jehovah saves."

Then, when Jesus went to the Jordan river and was anointed by the Holy Spirit, the title of Anointed One was His, which we express in the English language as Christ. This is His name and title—Jesus the Christ. Jesus, the Anointed One!

When Jesus Christ arose from the dead He took precedence over all creatures, whether in heaven or earth or hell. His exalted position in relation to all beings everywhere gave Him the title Lord, one who has the right and the power and the wisdom and the ability for sovereignty and dominion.

So, Jesus means Saviour. Christ means the Anointed One. Lord means just what it means in English— one who rightfully holds dominion, and, in this case, our Lord Jesus Christ is the One about whom the entire creation turns.

Now, before considering further the place of Jesus Christ in the creation, I want to remind you that the whole Bible and the complete life of the believing church also are wholly dependent upon God's final revelation of Himself in the person of Jesus Christ, His Son.

Our Lord Jesus Christ was that One who was with the Father and who was God and who is God and who was given the divinely-bestowed commission to set forth the mystery and the majesty and the wonder and the glory of the Godhead throughout the universe. It is more than an accident that both the Old and New Testaments comb heaven and earth for figures of speech or simile to set forth the wonder and glory of God.

The Son of God is described by almost every fair and worthy name in the creation. He is called the Sun of Righteousness with healing in His wings. He is called the Star that shone on Jacob. He is described as coming forth with His bride, clear as the moon. His Presence is likened unto the rain coming down upon the earth, bringing beauty and fruitfulness. He is pictured as the great sea and as the towering rock. He is likened to the strong cedars. A figure is used of Him as of a great eagle, going literally over the earth, looking down upon the wonders and beauties of lake and river and rock, of the mountains and the plains.

Brethren, you can be perfectly free to go to your Bible with assurance that you will find Jesus Christ everywhere in its pages. I am convinced that it was God's design that you should find the divine Creator, Redeemer and Lord whenever you search the scriptures, and you do not have to "read" anything into the Word that is not already there.

Where the person of Jesus Christ does not stand out tall and beautiful and commanding, as a pine tree against the sky, you will find Him behind the lattice, but stretching forth His hand. If He does not appear as the sun shining in his strength, He may be discerned in the reviving by the promised gentle rains falling from the heavens above.

I do not mind telling you that I have always found Jesus Christ beckoning to me throughout the scriptures. Do not be disturbed by those who say that Old Testament portions cannot be claimed by the Christian church. God has given us the Bible as a unit, and Jesus referred in His teachings to many Old Testament portions which foretold His person and His ministries.

For illustration, I would say that it would be very difficult for a man to live and function in a physical body that existed only from the waist up. He would be without some of the vital organs necessary for the sustenance of life.

Similarly, the Bible contains two parts of one organic revelation and it is divided so that the Old Testament is the Bible from the waist down and the New Testament is the Bible from the waist up. This may give an understanding to my expression that if we have one organic Bible and we cut it in two, we actually bleed it to death and we can, in effect, kill it by cutting it.

Let us read the Bible as the Word of God and never apologize for finding Jesus Christ throughout its pages, for Jesus Christ is what the Bible is all about!

As for the men who seem to be able to preach the Bible without finding Jesus Christ as the necessary way and truth and life, I can only comment that they are more blind than I ever thought it possible for anyone to be. Jesus Christ the Lord is the revelation from the Father—and His being has made God's written record for man both a necessity and a reality.

Now, in our day, the Christian church seems to have a variety of concerns, but in reality it has only one reason for being—and that is to show forth the life and mercy and grace of Jesus Christ. Study the relationship of the Body of Christ to Jesus Christ, its Head, and you soon realize that the life and witness and proclamation of the church is all about Jesus Christ.

You will understand that when I speak of the Christian church I am not speaking of any particular denomination. Christ's church is the church of the firstborn, purchased with His blood. Christ's church includes all twice-born believers who have been inducted into the kingdom of God by the operation of the Holy Spirit.

There is an example of what the church is all about in Acts 13. The believers had met together. They ministered unto the Lord and prayed. That is the chief concern and ministry of the Christian church, and it cancels out any question about the problem of "which denomination?"

Wherever you find the Lord Jesus Christ you will find the church. Our Lord Jesus and the company of His people—in that fellowship you find His church.

Years ago they described the teaching prowess of a certain well-known educator in this way: Put that accomplished teacher-communicator on one end of a log and a boy on the other—and instantly you had a college!

It is even more true that when Jesus Christ by His Spirit meets with two of His believing people, you have a church! You have it without any upkeep and without any overhead and without any elections. But Jesus Christ must be central and His Presence must be known among His people.

Some Christian groups seem to think that doctrine comes first. Doctrine is necessary to the understanding of Christ—but it will be a rather sad Christian group if it has only doctrinal emphasis and fails to recognize first of all the Presence of Jesus Christ. A church pleasing to Jesus Christ must be dedicated to honoring Him who shows forth the wonder and the glory of the Godhead.

Those who are engaged merely in ecclesiastical motions have missed the point—Jesus Christ Himself wants to be known and honored in the midst of His people, and this is what our life and fellowship is all about. Peter says it will be true above all in the midst of the church that we will honor and love Him, although we have not yet seen Him! In the Christian church, then, our objectives and our activities should only be those which scripturally point to the Lamb of God who takes away the sins of the world and which minister to the eternal welfare of men and women.

Now, let us consider the Person of Jesus Christ and His mandate from the Father in the creation of all things.

In a more relaxed generation, when people did not have to hustle and scurry to keep out of the way of automobile traffic, men would often go out and lie down under the stars, gaze up, and say: "What is man that Thou art mindful of him?" Now, it is hard to see through the smoke and the smog.

Modern man does occasionally halt long enough to think and wonder about the creation of the universe. With the use of one word in this passage, the word *whom*, referring to Jesus Christ, Peter gives the only possible answer—the creation is about *whom* —"Jesus Christ, *whom* having not seen, ye love."

The believing Christian who sees in the creation of all things the setting forth of the wonder and glory of Jesus Christ as Lord and Sovereign will have no more unholy days. He will no longer be inclined to divide existence between secular interests and holy interests. There is a divine sanctification of everything in his life when the believer fully realizes that God has made His creation as a garment to show forth the Lord Jesus Christ. I do not believe that any scientist or educator or anyone else can ever know or fathom the deep mysteries of creation without admitting that there is One *whom*—One who holds all things together in the vast universe, the One in whom all things cohere, as Paul told the Colossians.

Brethren, creation is the setting forth of Jesus Christ as Lord and Sovereign, for Jesus Christ is the purpose of God in creation! Let me urge you to go back and read again the first chapter of Ezekiel in which the man of God said, "I saw heaven opened, and I saw visions of God."

Ezekiel had a remarkable vision in which there were whirlwinds, great clouds, an unusual fire and brightness, and out of which came four living creatures, and the four had the face of a man, the face of a lion, the face of an ox and the face of an eagle.

Now, these living creatures coming out of the mysterious fire, it seems to me, stand for a heavenly and visible representation of the creation, and our Lord Jesus Christ, whom we have not yet seen, is the One that creation is all about.

Those strange creatures out of the fire show forth, in some measure, what our Lord Jesus Christ is like. The prophet saw the fourfold representation of the faces of a man, a lion, an ox and an eagle.

Years ago it was called to my attention that this fourfold division of the character of Jesus corresponds in a remarkable way to the presentation of His ministries recorded in the four Gospels.

This is not new to us by any means, but it is of great significance to students of the Word of God and to all who love our Lord Jesus Christ in truth.

Luke in his record clearly sets forth the emphasis upon the man, Jesus. Matthew sets Him forth as a lion and Mark, as an ox. John's record refers to His heavenly qualities, with the representation of the high-flying eagle.

Jesus was indeed a man and Luke's record seems suited particularly for the Greek culture which had long sought for perfection in manhood.

Matthew's record is intent upon its appeal to the Jewish heart and mind, giving emphasis to the messianic and kingly fulfillment of Jewish hopes in Jesus Christ, and thus the figure of the Lion of Judah.

Mark gives a brief, straight-from-the-shoulder record of Jesus, the man of action and power, a mighty worker. The representation in figure is that of the strength and faithfulness of the ox and the appeal, no doubt, was to the Roman mind and mentality of the day.

Coming to John's Gospel, we note a different emphasis. Luke had traced the genealogy back to Adam. Matthew had traced the ancestors of Jesus back to Abraham. But John goes back to the beginning of all things and appeals to all men and the whole world to consider the necessity for Jesus, the Divine Son of God, to become flesh and dwell among us.

John, in his record, insists that Jesus antedates all biography and all chronology, and he goes back to the beginning to set forth the wonder and the mystery and the glory of Jesus Christ. Let me tell you one of my fancies—something that I cannot actually prove.

I believe that there is a time coming in the plan of God when it will be plainly seen that all of the laws of nature and all of the beings that are in nature —beasts on the earth and fish that swim in the waters and birds that fly in the air, even tiny hoppers and creeping things that lisp their pitifully little note on the night breezes—are all necessary in setting forth even a little of the wonder of Jesus Christ!

You will recall that Jesus sent disciples to bring a little donkey for His use with the words, "Say that the Lord hath need of him." Even the sad-faced, comical, long-eared donkey was necessary to set forth the glory of the Messiah-Saviour on that day when the cries of "Hosannah" came from the admiring multitudes.

Now, I did not intend to say this, but I might as well make the application. I do not infer that there is any relation between the little beast and us, but I want to emphasize that many men and women have lost all sight of the fact that they are important to God. We are all important to God in setting forth the glory of the Lord Jesus Christ.

In a good sense, I want you to think more of

yourself. My appeal is that you should love Christ and then love yourself for Christ's sake, because you are important. It is not an accident of fate that God created you and redeemed you—if you are a Christian. Your Saviour and Lord does have need of you to show forth His glory and praise.

I thank God that the kingdom of God is not divided into areas for big, important people and areas for little, unimportant people. Every one is just as needful in God's sight as any other!

So, I conclude here with this idea: there are two levels on which Christians are living.

It has been revealed that animals have one level while angels live on a completely different level, and we human beings are a cross between angels and beast. We have bodies like the animals and we have souls like the angels above.

God has made us a little lower than the angels, but He has made us a little higher than the animals.

We have a body that came from the earth. But in that precious human body, the like of which our Lord yielded to a cross, we also have a spirit like unto that of the angels above. When God said we were made a little lower than the angels, He did not mean that He made our spiritual part lower than the angels—He did not! He made man's spiritual being higher than the angels, for that was made in the very image of God!

So, it is with these two levels of our human being that we look at Jesus. These human and physical eyes have never seen Him. These eyes that gaze out like the deer gazes out of the thicket—these eyes have not seen Him.

But we do love Him, do we not? Yes—and the reason is that there is another level, another part of us! There is the invisible, the eternal, inward and spiritual being, which has its own sight and its own vision, and with those eyes we have seen Him, known Him and loved Him.

Brethren, Peter encourages every Christian believer to know and serve and love Jesus Christ now, our understanding being enlightened through this inner spiritual sight He has given us! We live to show forth the honor of our God in Jesus Christ, until that gracious day of the Lord when we shall see Him face to face!

Chapter Twelve

Will There Be Any Lazy Folks in Heaven?

*". . . and shewed me that great city, the holy Je-
rusalem, descending out of heaven from God, having
the glory of God . . ." Revelation 21:10-11*

Are you among those who hold the mistaken idea
that there will be nothing to challenge you in the
life to come? Are you among those who have read
the account of the New Jerusalem, the City of God,
and have wondered if it will be just a haven for
the lazy and an endless gathering of bored and listless
beings?

Let me refer you to the biblical doctrine of the
image of God in man. I say this to you, sir, that
apart from God Himself, the nearest thing to God
is a human soul. And I promise you that in that
Great Day you will not be without something to do,
for God Himself is the great worker. He is the Creator
—He is creative. All that He does is creative.

God did not create the heaven and the earth and
all of the universe and then put a period after it,
and write, "It is done—finale!" He is always creating.
He has made us in His image. God is the great worker
without limit, and we are the little workers with limit,
or up to our limits, which we haven't found yet.
But our creative powers will be in use.

Actually, one of the supreme glories of man is

his many-sidedness. He can be and do and engage in a variety of interests and activities. He is not fatally formed to be only one thing. A rock is formed to be a rock and it will be a rock until the heavens melt with fervent heat and the earth passes away. A star is made to shine and a star it ever will be. The mountain that pushes up into the sky has been a mountain since the last geological upheaval pushed it up there. Through all the years it has worn the garment of force on its back but it has always been a mountain—never anything else.

But man can be both cause and effect—he can be servant or master. He can be doer and thinker. He can be poet and philosopher. He can be like the angels to walk with God or like the beasts to walk the earth. Man is a many-faceted diamond to catch and reflect back the glory of the only God.

It is this versatility in the nature of man which has enabled him to enjoy both solitude and togetherness. If a human being is normal, he will need and enjoy both of these extremes.

Jesus said, "Enter into thy closet"—there is solitude.

The Apostle said, "Forsake not the assembling of yourselves together." There is society. These words, of course, were spoken to Christian believers, and it is true that every believing child of God is supposed to be able to enjoy, understand and appreciate both solitude and fellowship with others.

Every normal person must have time to be alone. He must have time and inclination to become acquainted with himself. He must become oriented to the universe in which he lives. He must have the blessing of quietness to send out his thoughts like flocks of obedient birds exploring the wonders of the universe. He must get acquainted with God and himself in the solitude of his own chamber.

But remember that there must always be a reaction for every action. As the moon must always wane after it waxes and the tide must always go out after it comes in, so mankind must have society as well as solitude.

After a time of loneliness and heart-searching and communion with the living God through His Spirit, a person must again seek the face of his fellowmen. God has meant it to be so. God has meant that we should be together in fellowship.

The fact is that God has made us for each other, and it is His will and desire that Christian believers should understand and appreciate one another.

Why, then, we ask, do we have such problems in our togetherness?

You cannot talk for five minutes about mankind without coming to the ugly, hissing word we call *sin*. It is sin, the disease of the human stream, that ruined everything. It is sin that has made us greedy, sin that has made us hate. Sin makes us lust for power, sin creates jealousy and envy and covetousness.

Anything that comes close to being peace in our society will be destroyed by the ravages of sin, and men without God and His grace and His will cannot know or attain to the gracious blessings of true peace.

But in the final state of humanity, in the final state of perfection minus all of the diseases of the mind and of the being, we will dwell in perfect enjoyment of each other's company and that will be the New Jerusalem, the holy city, that descends out of heaven from God.

It will be in that blessed society that we will truly appreciate one another and we will be recognized truly for what we are in Christ. In this present earthly order, it seems the one who gets attention and notice and appreciation is the noisy one or the aggressive one. Many worthy and splendid persons never have the opportunity to enrich the lives and friendship of others because they are quiet, self-effacing persons who will not push themselves to the front. Some others are handicapped by features that may not be considered attractive and others do not have a "winsome" personality. When will we humans learn that we lose the richness of many a rewarding personality because we are not more discerning and wiser?

But in that final consummation, when the City of God descends, we shall be able truly to appreciate each other. If it were not for the deadening and corroding effects of sin, the human soul would catch and reflect the light of God as diamonds catch and reflect the light of the sun, and we would know each other for we would see in each other something of the nature and beauty of God. God is infinite and without limit and through Him we could come to know one another without ever feeling "I am weary of him and bored with him."

We have assurance in the Word of God that in that day when the limitations of the flesh are removed and the negative qualities in our personalities are gone and the minor notes are all taken out of the symphony of personality, we will thank God for one another. We will know God better through one another as we find that we are simply prisms and lenses through which God shines. God shines in many ways throughout His universe, but I do believe that He shines best of all in the lives of men and women He created and then redeemed.

It is only sin that has cracked the lenses and distorted the image. It is only sin that has marred the vision and spoiled the picture, so that when we look at each other we do not see the true depth of potential.

When our Lord looked at us, He saw not only what we were—He was faithful in seeing what we could become! He took away the curse of being and gave us the glorious blessing of becoming. Scoffers say a man can only be what he is, but Jesus Christ said, "No, he is not what he is—but what he can become."

It is the Lord Jesus Christ who gives us the power to "become." John the Apostle sensed this in his words: "It doth not yet appear what we shall be, but we know that, when he shall appear, we shall be like him; for we shall see him as he is." It is the ability to become—to grow, to change, to develop, to move out to the edges of the perfection of human personality—that is the glory of the Christian life!

Therefore, in that day when the holy city descends, there will no longer be the blight of jealousy. No personality in that day will want to ensnare or enslave another. There will be no one with the spirit of war or force to march on another's domain, or make others subject to his greed. We will not suspect one another, there will be no arrests and there will be no courts in which to file a grudging complaint. Violence and murders will be gone and in that society all will fare graciously as one—there will be no slums and no ghettos and there will be no private compounds of the rich marked "No Trespassing."

Many wary humans have said, "The prospect is too good to be true!" But it is written, "I heard a great voice out of heaven saying, Behold, the tabernacle of God is with men, and he will dwell with them and they shall be his people. And God himself shall be with them, and they shall be his people, and God himself shall be with them, and be their God. And God shall wipe away all tears from their eyes; and there shall be no more death, neither sorrow, nor crying, neither shall there be any more pain: for the former things are passed away."

Anyone who has love and concern for the human race will say a quiet but fervent "Amen" to this prospect for the future with God and man dwelling together and with the former things—tears, sorrow, pain and death—having passed away.

We give credit to men in all ages of human history who have dreamed and longed for a perfect human society. They wanted to make the world a better place in which to live, but all have had to settle for a dream. All of their dreams and all of their utopian ideas have been spoiled and brought to naught by human forces of pride and prejudice, of selfishness and cynicism.

This world system in which we live can never be made perfect by a social regeneration based on man's own hopes and dreams, foibles and failures. We notice that the man who was in the Spirit on the Lord's day did not refer to social regeneration. He clearly and plainly said that this perfect, future world comes down out of heaven from God. Man's hopeless condition cannot be perfected by some slow process of social regeneration—it must be brought about through the miraculous process of individual regeneration.

Actually, there is really no such thing as "society." It is a word that reaches out and rakes in a whole world of ideas, but in truth, I am society, you are society, and the man next door and the boy that sells papers and the milkman and the mayor of the city and the president and the office boy that does the chores—that is society. It is the individual, actually, so when we try to put them together and call it society, we are building a false concept. We are likely to think of society as an organism, which it is not! Society is a name given to a great number of individual organisms.

It was for that reason that Jesus Christ rebuked completely any idea of the regeneration of human society when He came into this world. He said to a man, "You must be born again." He said, "Where two or three are gathered together in my name, there am I in the midst." He spoke of an individual and exclaimed, "One soul is of more value than all the world." Study the New Testament and you will find Jesus continually placed His emphasis upon the value and worth of the individual.

An individualist Himself, Jesus still plainly taught

that there would ultimately be a society of the blessed, an assembly of the saints, a happy gathering of the children of God. There would be a New Jerusalem with the spirits of just men made perfect. He promised many mansions in the Father's house where these individuals—regenerated—could come together and form that holy society.

It is impossible to talk to people about blessedness and holiness and heaven without talking about God's provision of spiritual transformation. Everyone knows there are worldwide forces in our day which emphasize nationalism to the point that the individual is completely forgotten—but the only regeneration known in the entire world is individual regeneration. Many church groups seem to have joined forces with the political and social reformers in the dream that the effective way to bring about a perfect society is to reform and redeem society itself—rather than the redemption of the individual human natures which compose society, so-called.

What does the Bible say? It says there will not be one soul, not one member of that heavenly population, that will not have experienced the mystical and mysterious and spiritual regeneration of the new birth in some way, somewhere, during the brief earthly existence. It must be said of him, as Paul said of the new man in Christ, "Old things have passed away; all things have become new."

It is more than coincidence, then, that we find the same thing said about the New Jerusalem: "Old things have passed away; lo, I make all things new!"

How is it that the Holy Ghost said the same thing about the New Jerusalem that He had said about the converted man? Because the New Jerusalem will be the city of the converted man! This New Jerusalem will be filled with those who can say while they are on earth: "Old things have passed away, and all things have become new!" And then they will be able also to say: "He makes all things new, and the former things have passed away!"

God Himself will have a gracious plan for everyone in that great and eternal and holy city—and it will be a city that will satisfy all of man's nature.

I find that many men and women are troubled by the thought that they are too small and inconsequential in the scheme of things. But that is not our real trouble—we are actually too big and too complex, for God made us in His image and we are too big to be satisfied with what the world offers us!

Augustine put it in classical language when he said, "O God, Thou hast made us for Thyself, and our hearts are dissatisfied until they find their rest in Thee." That expression has been echoed and reechoed and written into our hymns, because it is true! Man is bored, because he is too big to be happy with that which sin is giving him. God has made him too great, his potential is too mighty. People do not actually commit suicide because they are too little and insignificant, but because they are big in a little world. God made man to be able to enjoy all of the vast expanses of His heaven and they have been forced through sin to be satisfied with paying their taxes and mowing the lawn and fixing the car and keeping the kids out of jail and paying their debts—yes, and getting older every day! They are sick of it, actually sick of it! Their bodies are breaking down and their tabernacle is too small for the spirit that dwells within.

That is the reason why humans are always trying to explore some new place. That explains the interest in trying to visit the moon. That explains why we want to be able to travel faster than sound. It explains, at least in part, why Charles Lindbergh jumped in an old egg-beater and was the first man to fly alone over the ocean to Paris. It explains why Admiral Byrd went down to the Antarctic and Admundsen explored the North Pole region. It is the reason for men always trying to do the impossible. It explains why we explore the secrets of the universe and come up with the atomic bomb—men are too big for the little world that sin has given them!

But the society that God is promising from above, that great City of God, will truly satisfy man's full nature. The day will be a long golden day without a cloud and without a sundown. Travel where you will in all those wide regions above and you will not find a wrinkle on anyone's face nor a gray hair on anyone's head. You will never hear anyone mutter, "I am discontented." You will never hear a voice raised in criticism. You will never meet a peevish man and you will never see an unkind face. You will never hear a growl from any throat, never a scream of fear or pain. You will never see a tear running down anyone's cheek.

Someone will break in here and say, "Just a minute, Mr. Tozer! That is the old-fashioned idea of heaven, where we are kind of glorified butterflies waving our wings gently in the zephyrs that flow down from the celestial mountains. What about a challenge? What about something to work for? How will the redeemed be occupied?"

Well, I can set you right there, because God promised that in the New Jerusalem He has provided all that is good and blessed and useful and has ruled out and barred only those things that offend.

When God put Adam and Eve in the garden, He did not put them there to sit and look at each other and to hold hands. He said they were to take care of the garden. You remember that—they were given something to do. Some people believe that work is a result of the curse, but that's not true. The idea is abroad that the man who works is a boob, and that work is only for fools—but God made us to work.

You know, the anthropologists say that when God made man with his four fingers and his thumb opposite those four fingers so that he could hold and use every kind of tool and instrument, He guaranteed that man would conquer the world. God made you and me like that, you see. So, sometime when you have a little time alone, look at that hand of yours, that amazing hand of yours!

The plain truth is that in all the machinery and all the gadgets and all the instruments around your house put together there is nothing that can remotely compare with the intricacy, beauty of performance and versatility of that right hand of yours. And God did not give you that hand to hang on to some chandelier in the New Jerusalem—God means that you are to go to work up there.

But it will be a tireless work—it will not be a work of boredom. It will be happy, joyous work. It will be work without fatigue. I do not know what God will have us doing. Maybe He will have you doing something that you can do.

"Our Lord was a worker," says one of our hymns, and our Lord is always looking for workers. So we are all going to be workers, and you need not imagine for a second that you will have nothing to do in heaven.

But along with work, heaven is also a place for you to rest.

You say, "How can you make these two statements agree?"

Well, you will work and you will not be tired. Jesus now works but without tiring. He rests always while He works. So the saints of God will work.

What was that which Kipling said?

"When earth's last picture is painted, and the tubes are twisted and dried; the brightest colors have faded and the youngest critic has died; we shall rest and they that need it shall lie down for an aeon or two; and the Master of all good workmen shall put us to work anew."

Kipling goes on to say, "We'll sit in a golden chair

and splash on a ten-league canvas with brushes of angel hair."

I do not know whether angels have hair—Kipling thought so. He thought it was a nice thing to do—to use a ten-league canvas instead of a miniature and sit there and work.

I think in that sense Kipling was right—heaven is not going to be a haven for lazy bums. Heaven is going to be a place where men released from tensions and inhibitions, released from prohibitions from the outside, released from sin, and made in the image of God can go to work like the young gods they are. For He said, "Ye are gods"—He didn't mean you are God, but "You are little images of mine, born to do the kind of work I do, creative work."

So, the New Jerusalem will be fresh opportunity for all of the imaginative and the industrious and the busy—who, like God, must find expression.

Ah, the beauty of it all—how can I go on? The beauty of it—not the done-up beauty of a woman's face, not the beauty of a carefully-padded form, not the beauty of the primrose that smiles in the sunshine, but the great, rich, strong beauty of eternity in God. Ah, that city of gold, with all its beauty!

Way back there in the beginning, God made man to live with Him. Sin came and God divorced man like an unfaithful wife from His presence. But through the miracle of redemption, through the cross of Jesus Christ, man is reborn back to his ancient place and raised yet above that.

Now, why was there no mention here of a temple, a church, a synagogue? Why was there no meeting place for worshipers?

Because all of that new City of God was a temple. God Himself was the temple. Like a great expanse of beautiful arches, the Father, Son and Holy Ghost surrounded and settled down and mingled with all of that carefree, busy, joyous throng. There they do not have to wait for an hour in which to pray— all hours are prayer hours there.

You won't have to wait to go to a special place to pray there—all of it is a temple and God and the Lamb are the temples thereof. There's no need for an artificial light to brighten the night, for the Lamb is the light thereof.

We must seriously consider whether we are headed in that direction. Every one of us must seriously consider whether we have—by the blood of the Lamb and the word of our testimony—overcome and escaped from the thralldom of sin, or whether we are still bound by it, cursed with the curse, and about to be destroyed in the destruction.

This is the gracious reality of our look to the future: We are by faith the children of God, given a place in that great society of the ransomed and promised an eternal inheritance in that Great City because our names are written in the Lamb's Book of Life!